"AUTHORITATIVE AND HIGHLY READABLE . . . offers invaluable insight."

—Douglas Frantz, *Los Angeles Times*

"PROVIDES GREAT INSIGHT into how S&L's and their regulators operated . . . brings many of the key players to life."

—*San Jose Mercury News*

"A DISQUIETING TALE OF CORPORATE GREED AND GOVERNMENT NEGLECT."

—*Dallas Times Herald*

"A vivid picture of the evolution of the thrift problem . . . should stimulate focus on the development of solutions to the massive problems facing the financial service industry in the U.S."

—Thomas A. Cooper,
CEO & President, Goldome

"Places the crisis-triggering deregulation within a larger context of economic mismanagement that included years of bloated federal budgets and overexpansion."

—*Publishers Weekly*

MICHAEL A. ROBINSON was nominated for a Pulitzer Prize for his coverage of the 1984 Democratic National Convention and has received UPI and Associated Press journalism awards. Most recently he served as bureau chief of *American Banker* in San Francisco, where he currently makes his home.

OVERDRAWN

The Bailout of American Savings

MICHAEL A. ROBINSON

A PLUME BOOK

PLUME
Published by the Penguin Group
Penguin Books USA Inc., 375 Hudson Street, New York, New York 10014, U.S.A.
Penguin Books Ltd, 27 Wrights Lane, London W8 5TZ, England
Penguin Books Australia Ltd, Ringwood, Victoria, Australia
Penguin Books Canada Ltd, 10 Alcorn Avenue, Toronto, Canada M4V 3B2
Penguin Books (N.Z.) Ltd, 182-190 Wairau Road, Auckland 10, New Zealand

Penguin Books Ltd, Registered Offices: Harmondsworth, Middlesex, England

Published by Plume, an imprint of New American Library, a division of Penguin Books USA Inc. Previously published in a Dutton edition.

First Plume Printing, November, 1991
10 9 8 7 6 5 4 3 2 1

LIBRARY OF CONGRESS CATALOGING-IN-PUBLICATION DATA
Robinson, Michael A.
Overdrawn : the collapse of Financial Corporation of America /Michael A. Robinson.
p. cm.
Includes bibliographical references.
ISBN 0-525-24903-6
1. Financial Corporation of America. 2. Savings and loan associations—California—Corrupt practices.
HG2626.S76R63 1990
332.3'2'09794—dc20 90-36825
CIP

Printed in the United States of America

For my dad,
for teaching me to write,
and for my mom,
for teaching me to laugh

Acknowledgments

This is a bizarre and at times unbelievable story, but one that is nonetheless true. Unfortunately, for the U.S. taxpayers it is not over yet. By the summer of 1990 estimates of the cost of the S&L bailout were reaching to the stratosphere—perhaps as much as $500 billion.

As of mid-1990, the failure of American Savings was still the largest single S&L bailout, using the only available accurate yardstick, official U.S. government estimates. It may also prove to be one of the more controversial and certainly one of the most profitable corporate acquisitions of all time.

This book could not have been completed without the help of several key individuals. At the top of the list is Bill Popejoy, who spent two full days being interviewed by the author. Other interviews followed. We spent at least 20 hours talking in person and by telephone. Rather than rely on his excellent memory, Popejoy provided access to many of his former associates, whose recollections, diaries and memorandums proved crucial.

Catherine Keeler spent mind-numbing hours transcribing the taped interviews, and her intelligence and insight were invaluable tools in my research. Tracy Fisher put her MBA and experience as an analyst for a respected S&L to use by reading the manuscript for accuracy about the U.S. financial system. Doug Frantz and Gary Hector, both authors and top-notch reporters, served as important sounding boards and as sources of inspiration. So did Mia Navarro of *The New York Times*. I thank her for her consideration. Peter Scott provided comfortable and well-equipped office space; Cheri Loustalet helped with the legal research; and Camille Hudson provided expert advice on computer systems.

Finally, I might never have written this book without the emotional support of my agent, Denise Marcil, who told me 18 months before we sold the manuscript, even before the project began, that we would work on a book together someday. My editors at New American Library, Arnold Dolin and John Paine, did a brilliant job with the manuscript and tried (often in vain) to keep me from red-lining the metaphor meter. See what I mean?

Contents

OVERDRAWN

Prologue: Hurry Home

A hard rain pelted the windshield of his rented subcompact as Ed Gray drove down a slick French highway on a secret mission.

He had to get back to Washington in a hurry. Every minute mattered. Paul Volcker would be waiting at the Federal Reserve. The two men had to contain the threat of severe damage from a financial storm gathering in California.

It was 5:00 A.M. on this Tuesday, August 21, 1984; Gray was groggy from lack of sleep and needed a cigarette as he drove the little car along the Loire River in the storm. He was worried, for he realized all too clearly what would happen if reporters discovered that Gray, the chairman of the Federal Home Loan Bank Board, the top regulatory body for the savings and loan (S&L) industry, had been summoned back to the Federal Reserve from his European vacation.

The journalists would then understand the full extent of a harrowing crisis: the imminent collapse of the Financial Corporation of America (FCA), one of the nation's largest financial institutions. Additional publicity would surely escalate the problem, perhaps to the point that the entire U.S. banking system would be in jeopardy.

Having just completed a two-week trip to London and Paris trying to peddle bonds to European banks, he had driven to his father-in-law's house in the small village of Chateauneuf-sur-Sarthe the previous evening. He had no sooner arrived than he received a conference call from anxious thrift regulators in Washington and San Francisco monitoring the unfolding catastrophe.

Throughout his trip, Gray had kept tabs on Financial Corporation of America and its subsidiary, American Savings and Loan Association of Stockton, California, the nation's largest thrift, with more than $30 billion in assets. For the past few weeks, the S&L had experienced a run of withdrawals that had now turned into a tidal wave. Depositors were removing hundreds of millions of dollars each day.

Ironically, Gray was partly responsible for the mess. A year earlier, he had approved a daring merger that had more than doubled American's size. Since then, his staff had been unable to prevent American from growing by nearly $1 billion a month, a rate that if maintained would make the company larger than General Motors by the end of the decade.

Gray was convinced that the collapse of American would bankrupt the Federal Savings and Loan Insurance Corporation, the industry's woefully inadequate insurance fund. Panic would then spread to other S&Ls and possibly to commercial banks as well.

He had been expecting trouble for months. American was by far the largest thrift in the country, but it was not the only one with severe problems. The whole industry was headed for disaster.

It was a gross oversimplification, but in a word, the trouble was *deregulation.* At first, Gray had enthusiastically endorsed the unprecedented new powers Congress and the state legislatures had bestowed on S&Ls. Now, however, he harbored grave doubts.

Once known for their conservative business practices, S&Ls now gambled federally insured funds on a wide array of risky investments. Unless these investments were curbed, the industry might decline to the point that a taxpayer bailout would be needed to rescue hundreds of S&Ls, a solution Gray strongly opposed.

Clearly, he would have to rein in the S&Ls and the new breed of entrepreneurs who were plundering the system. But his agency was understaffed; his examiners were poorly paid and were not trained to spot all the pitfalls these sophisticated new investments entailed. As a result, the examiners often failed to detect wrongdoing at S&Ls before it was too late.

Although he had been in office for more than a year, Gray was still searching for ways to curb what he saw as the industry's excessive and imprudent growth. But he might never get the chance to protect the system against these abuses unless he could prevent the collapse of American.

During his entire trip, Gray had stayed in constant contact with his chief of staff, Shannon Fairbanks, a tough and energetic Washington insider. Fairbanks in turn had been talking with Preston Martin, vice chairman of the Federal Reserve and the central bank's liaison with the thrift industry. It was Martin who had told Fairbanks he wanted Gray to get home from France as fast as he could to deal with the situation at FCA. That meant taking an ultraexpensive trip on the Concorde.*

Gray reached the airport in Nantes with plenty of time to catch his seven-o'clock flight to Orly Airport in Paris. As he checked in, he flipped through his complicated itinerary. In Paris, he would grab a ride to De Gaulle Airport where he would fly to Kennedy Airport in New York and then race over to La Guardia for the shuttle to Washington.

Gray started on his whirlwind trip with his mind made up. He was going to get rid of Charlie Knapp, FCA's shrewd, aggressive chairman. For the good of the nation's financial system, Knapp had to go. The man was a menace.

As Ed Gray boarded the Concorde, Jim Cirona was settling into his hotel room in Beverly Hills. It was still Monday night on the West Coast. If all went well, tomorrow he would attend FCA's board-of-directors meeting and deliver some stunning news.

Sitting in on the board meeting was an unusual procedure for a thrift regulator, even for the head of the Federal Home Loan Bank in San Francisco, which regulated S&Ls in the West. But these were extreme circumstances, to say the least.

Like Gray, Cirona had kept a close watch on American Savings for the past few months. Now that the run threatened American's survival, the company needed to borrow heavily from Cirona's regional bank. Billions were at stake.

---

*Fearing the political repercussions of a $4,000 plane ride, Gray had refused to leave France on the Concorde until Martin drafted an official request for the trip on Federal Reserve stationery. He had recently been probed by the FBI after being falsely accused of using money to renovate his office so he could live there. Additional embarrassments would follow.

Of course, if the San Francisco regulators had been more diligent, American might never have been pushed to the edge of insolvency. These regional examiners were supposed to ensure the safety and soundness of the system by auditing an S&L's books to prevent imprudent business practices. Not only had Cirona's staff failed to spot many of American's unsound loans, but Cirona's top deputy had argued in favor of American's merger.

Now Cirona was extremely concerned about the company's high level of bad loans. He did not want to jeopardize the safety of his own bank by lending to a thrift that in all likelihood was already beyond repair.

Earlier that summer, Cirona and his staff had started meeting secretly with ranking members of the Federal Reserve Bank of San Francisco, trying to line up additional money for American. Some staff members had taken a conference room at a local hotel under an assumed name to avoid detection by the media, which were giving extensive coverage to the company's travails. At the incognito conference, Cirona's crew met with some of Knapp's top executives and were shocked to learn how poorly prepared they were for the enormous task confronting them.

Well, the run certainly had to be stopped, but so did Charlie Knapp. If everything went smoothly, Jim Cirona would go to FCA's board meeting tomorrow and demand Charlie Knapp's head.

In Los Angeles, the directors of FCA were on red alert. For the last several days, the directors had been in one meeting after another; some at the company's headquarters on the borderline of Beverly Hills, others in a string of telephone conference calls.

Foster Fluetsch, chairman of FCA's American Savings unit, had flown to Los Angeles from Stockton in a company jet to make the board meeting. He had known Knapp for years. The two men were friends, even though Knapp would sometimes suggest that the beefy Fluetsch and his chunky wife should lose a little weight. But that was Charlie Knapp. He was not always a subtle man. You couldn't take those things too seriously.

Now Knapp was in trouble. There was no getting around that. Fluetsch could sympathize with him. For the last several months, Fluetsch had felt he was in over his head. Things were happening so fast, he just couldn't keep up. The company was too big. The growth had gotten out of hand.

Those were matters of philosophy though. Right now, the paramount issue was surviving the run that was paralyzing the company. The regulators were obviously out to get Knapp, and there were already rumors of his imminent departure.

Knapp was being accused of running a company that grew too aggressively, foolishly bet its assets on erratic interest rates, had booked hundreds of millions in bad loans, and had reported profits when the S&L had actually lost money.

American had once been one of the industry's healthiest members, concentrating on safe single-family home loans. But under Knapp and Fluetsch, the company had continued lending during the recession when other S&Ls were retrenching because so many borrowers were likely to go out of business. The company made vast sums of money available to real-estate developers who were willing to pay astronomical mortgage rates. And for a while, the strategy worked as FCA grew and reported record earnings.

Some of those loans were now going sour. Sure, the company would have to tighten up its procedures, but Fluetsch was confident that once the run subsided, American could work its way out of its problems. Many of the bad loans could be recovered, and others could be sold for huge profits.

Fluetsch thought the regulators just couldn't seem to understand that interest rates would go down in the next few months and that American's investments would pay off. In a few months, Charlie Knapp would be a hero.

Book One

Waste Not, Want Not

Chapter 1

A Philanthropic Miser

Dapper Mark Taper was suspicious of paper, for the hard-bitten multimillionaire had little faith in these newfangled stock swaps. An autocratic ruler whose colorful career spanned six decades and two continents, Taper had a strong craving for cash. Why would a miser want anything less?

For weeks, Taper had been meeting secretly with a powerful business rival, Robert Dockson, attempting to negotiate the largest merger in the S&L industry's history, creating a $20 billion behemoth that would be nearly 20 percent bigger than its next-largest competitor.

Ernie Leff, Taper's attorney, wondered if an agreement could be reached. The talks had broken down once before and had remained stalled for a month. As Leff saw it, the two principals in the transaction were brilliant, hard-driving executives whose business philosophies were reflected in the companies they ran.

Dockson, the 65-year-old former dean of the University of Southern California School of Business, liked expensive suits, took sumptuous lunches in his company's executive dining room, and sometimes flew to his appointments by helicopter.

His company, California Federal Savings and Loan Association, the nation's fourth-largest thrift, was an unbridled proponent of the new powers won under deregulation of financial services. For one, Cal Fed had been among the first thrifts to use federally assisted mergers to expand into new states. Then, through an arrangement with Merrill, Lynch, Pierce, Fenner & Smith, the noted brokerage house, the company had become one of the most successful marketers of the popular tax-advantaged "all savers certificates." Cal Fed had also started to push into other new products, including stock brokerage and trust services.

By contrast, Mark Taper paid strict attention to two principles: make good loans, and hold the line on costs. Although generous when donating to the arts or wooing one of the celebrities he dated, in business he was notoriously cheap. If there were a hall of fame for corporate misers, Mark Taper would be one of its first inductees.

One of the richest men in the Los Angeles area, Taper not only brought his lunch to work each day in a brown paper bag but frequently folded up the bag, took it home, and used it the next day. His Beverly Hills office was decorated with cheap green carpet and low-budget furniture. His senior executives once found themselves being lectured at a management meeting about excessive use of number-two pencils.

Stories of his parsimony were legion. For instance, he decreed that all the scraps of paper left from the paper cutter should be stapled together and used as writing tablets. Employees called them Taper Tablets. He once decided it would be cheaper to buy sugar cubes for the employee coffee room. But when he found that sugar consumption increased, he had the cubes ground into granules. When a piece of carpeting in front of his desk wore out, he replaced it with a section cut out from under the sofa. In his branches, Taper favored orange carpeting and drapes because that color faded the least in direct sunlight and therefore lasted longer. Employees called the branches two-story Taco Bells. Some Taper associates said the old man would have roses cut from his garden and wrapped in colored paper, so that they looked as though they had come from a florist, and then give the flowers to a date. Through a family intermediary, Taper inquired if he would be remunerated for providing an interview for a book on American Savings. If no payment was forthcoming, the family member inquired, could a donation to charity be made instead?

In the 1960s, Ernie Leff had given the short bald Taper the nickname "Uncle Mark" for Taper's tendency to lecture subordinates by saying, "Children, children, children. When will you ever learn?" The nickname stuck.

He certainly had his eccentricities, but Mark Taper ran his company with a firm hand and was both feared and admired as a result. First Charter Financial Corp., whose subsidiary, American Savings and Loan, was then the industry's third-largest member, had a fortress balance sheet. Under the new federal rules, S&Ls were required to maintain a net-worth ratio of only 3 percent, but American Savings had more than double that figure. American Savings also had 102 branches around the state, one of the largest S&L networks in California, the focal point for an industry that had skyrocketed by catering to one of the world's greatest housing booms.

Taper also had a well-deserved reputation as a tough negotiator. When bargaining over a loan with a real-estate developer, Taper would strike a deal, then tell the developer the loan had to be approved by the company's loan committee. He neglected to mention that he was the committee for all large loans. Taper would then go back and ask for a larger fee to write the loan and an interest rate half a percentage point higher. He usually got both.

These days, however, the 81-year-old Taper was doing little of that. He had made up his mind long ago to sell the company and had quietly shopped it around for years. Now he had a new sense of urgency, for not even Mark Taper could get through the S&L crisis unscathed. American Savings had lost $55.7 million in 1981 and would likely lose more than that for 1982. The high interest rates that crippled or destroyed hundreds of other thrifts ate away at his personal net worth, and Taper had come too far to let his fortune slip away.

Sydney Mark Taper was born on Christmas Day 1901 in a small town just outside Warsaw. Two years later, the family moved to London where several uncles already lived. Even as a youngster, Taper stood out for his intelligence and his business acumen. When World War I broke out, Taper was a student at St. Anne's, and soon afterward, the school lost all its male teachers to the war effort. The headmaster then called Taper to his office and said he was going to make a teacher out of him. Taper started teaching the first two grades.

The deprivation that lasted throughout the war left an indelible mark on Taper. He learned to despise waste and began to save string and paper, highly valued items in a nation fighting for survival. Taper also started to display his business talents and innate sense of salesmanship by buying candy in bulk and selling it retail to classmates.

Although extremely bright, he ended his formal schooling at age 14 when he started to work for his father, a manufacturer of military uniforms. When Benjamin Taper was seriously injured two years later in a zeppelin raid over London, Mark Taper took over his father's plant.

At age 19, Taper struck out on his own, acquiring a retail shoe store on the outskirts of London in High Barnett, Hertfordshire. By 1925, he owned five thriving stores in the London area. The next year, at 25, Taper sold the business and with the resulting profit, no longer needed to work.

Less than two years later, he was bored. Reflecting on the direction he wanted to take, he decided the most exciting part of the shoe business had been the planning and the real estate. So he went back to school and studied surveying and appraising. In 1929, Taper bought an 80-year-old real-estate business from two retiring partners.

By 1933, Taper claimed to have the largest real-estate agent's office in the area and had begun building several hundred homes as Great Britain attempted to cope with a housing shortage by subsidizing construction. Real-estate development seemed to come naturally to Taper. In 1934 and 1935, he built two streets of houses in southeast London. He named one Millmark Road, after his wife's nickname, Milly. Taper called the other one Barrydale after his only son, Barry.

By 1937, Taper had become one of London's most successful builders and subdividers, and was involved with two savings-and-loan associations, called building-and-loans in England. He decided to retire again to devote more time to his family.

Taper said he sought the "secret paradise" that was "free from pressure and care." But war was coming to Europe as Nazi Germany began invading its neighbors. Fear began to spread throughout London's Jewish community. Taper and his wife brought hundreds of Catholic and Jewish children out of Nazi Germany and found them homes in England and America. In the spring of 1939, Taper took his family to the safe and prosperous shores of America, determined to go to California for the sunshine and favorable climate.

That summer, Taper arrived in Los Angeles and headed south to Long Beach. The family settled into the Huntington Beach Hotel, spending $80 a month on a penthouse. Word spread that

Mark Taper was a man of means and an expert on real estate. Taper began to receive offers to buy big tracts of land at favorable prices. Los Angeles had become a key production center for defense contractors, and the federal government made housing for defense workers a major priority. Once again, Mark Taper came out of retirement.

The influx of war workers made Taper a wealthy man. On June 18, 1942, Taper completed construction of a home in the North Long Beach–Lakewood area, and twenty-five years later, the *Los Angeles Times* would mark the beginning of southern California's building boom with the house that Mark Taper built at 620 Harding Street.*

Between 1942 and 1955, Taper and his partners built some 35,000 homes in southern and northern California, selling some tract homes for as little as $3,000. Those in Norwalk, typical of his range, sold for $6,500 with only $85 down. Each home came with carpeting, a refrigerator, a stove, and a Waste King garbage disposal. As Taper said, all you needed to move in was $85 and a sleeping bag.

The federal government had made housing a highly lucrative field. During the war, the economy operated at full throttle. Consumers had little outlet for their pent-up demand because the government curtailed production of civilian goods. Savings soared, as did the purchase of war bonds. From 1940 to 1945, deposits at savings banks and S&L associations rose some 50 percent, from roughly $16 billion to about $24 billion.

With the government's emphasis on military construction, mortgage lending became dormant during the war. As the end of the war approached, S&Ls were flush with cash and war bonds, and sought more profitable investments, particularly home loans.

Meantime, the U.S. government found a way to help servicemen and their families make a smooth adjustment to civilian life. In 1944, Congress passed the Servicemen's Readjustment Act, more popularly known as the G.I. Bill of Rights. This legislation would have a dramatic impact on both S&Ls and home builders like Taper because it gave veterans easier access

---

*In that same period, Los Angeles County had grown from 2.9 million to 7 million residents.

to mortgage money. Under the act, the government guaranteed it would repay part of the loan under certain conditions, greatly reducing the risk to lenders. They in turn could grant mortgages with smaller down payments, generally charging veterans half a percentage point less than the going rate of 4.5 percent. VA loans represented 35 percent of all mortgages granted by S&Ls in 1946 and would continue to play a major role in the mortgage market.

With car sales also on the rise, suburbs sprang up across the American landscape, seemingly overnight. And the population was expanding at a breakneck pace, growing at an annual rate of 2.5 million.

Drawing on his experience in England, Taper saw big opportunities in construction finance, particularly with an S&L. In 1950, he purchased a bank and a thrift. He later sold the bank but kept the S&L because at the time, thrifts paid no federal income taxes. Nor did S&Ls have to distribute dividends to their stockholders, giving Taper, the majority shareholder, two ways to avoid the tax collector.

Taper founded First Charter Financial as a holding company in 1955. That same year, he purchased American Savings of Redondo Beach and began to build the enterprise through a series of mergers and acquisitions.

The postwar boom was extremely kind to southern California thrifts. Indeed, as California's economic boom continued, the industry grew enormously. From 1939 to 1949, assets at S&L associations grew by about 330 percent, from $275 million to $1.2 billion. By 1959, the twenty-year growth topped 3,000 percent, with total assets of about $9 billion. Total assets for the California industry reached $100 billion in 1979. In 1989, nine of the nation's ten largest S&Ls had their headquarters in California, and these institutions rivaled even the largest commercial banks in power and market penetration. California thrifts had $395.4 billion in assets in 1988, representing almost 30 percent of the industry's nationwide total.

As much as Taper overshadowed his rivals, there was one competitor Taper could not dominate—Howard F. Ahmanson, a man who would remind the business press that he had been called a genius since boyhood. *Fortune* magazine called him Emperor Ahmanson. Starting as an 18-year-old college sophomore, Ahmanson took an investment portfolio worth $20,000 and built it into the largest S&L empire in the land, Home Savings of America.

Taper and Ahmanson even competed in philanthropy and in monuments to their accomplishments. In 1962, Taper donated $1 million to the Music Center for the Performing Arts in Los Angeles. Three years later, Ahmanson's charitable foundation donated another $1 million. Taper and Ahmanson shared the billing when the $43 million three-building complex opened in April 1967 with the Mark Taper Forum and the Ahmanson Theater.

Even after Ahmanson's death from a heart attack in 1968, Home Savings remained a tough challenge for Mark Taper, who merged his two savings units into one American Savings that December. But by that time, Home Savings had pulled clearly ahead with $2.75 billion in assets, compared with American's $2.25 billion.

Although he never caught up with Ahmanson, Taper left his own legacy in the S&L industry. His company was highly profitable because of low costs and a tight focus on conservative home lending. But by the early 1980s, Taper was being left behind. His competitors were harnessing the new financial tools available under deregulation and technological breakthroughs. Some S&L executives had their own company jets or flew to meetings in helicopters. The headquarters of some S&Ls had become opulent corporate palaces, complete with expensive art, high-tech furniture, and meals prepared by the finest chefs. But not at American Savings. Mark Taper still clung to the old ways that had allowed a Polish immigrant and high school dropout to become fabulously rich.

On October 26, 1982, Mark Taper and Robert Dockson prepared to sign a letter of intent to merge their two companies.

Under the proposed merger, Dockson's Cal Fed would convert to stock ownership (from a mutual association owned by the depositors) with current account holders getting first crack at new First Charter stock. The combined institutions would become a wholly owned subsidiary of First Charter and would be named First Federal of America. This type of transaction, a conversion from a mutual company to stock ownership simultaneous with a merger, had been legal only a few months and would be the first of its kind.

Although technically First Charter was the acquiring firm, Dockson would serve as chairman and chief executive officer, while Taper became chairman of the executive committee. Since he would remain the largest single shareholder, Taper could exert great control. To Leff, this presented an almost insurmountable obstacle. How would Dockson remain at the forefront of the unfolding revolution in financial services with cautious Mark Taper constantly looking over his shoulder?

Also, in striking the deal, Taper had agreed to a stock swap when Leff knew full well that what Taper really wanted was to cash out of the company free and clear. This desire for money rather than stock was more than a minor wrinkle in a major deal.

Taper told the media that he did not intend to sell his shares in the new firm once the merger was completed, but behind the scenes, the two sides spent the next few weeks looking for ways to dilute Taper's power while giving him more cash. They failed to find a solution.

On December 6, six weeks after the two sides had signed the letter of intent, the merger formally collapsed. And when it did, it was like sending smoke signals throughout the S&L market: If you want to buy American Savings, the crown jewel of a battered industry, come up with cash.

Chapter 2

Cash McCall Wants It All

Charlie Knapp had style. He had charm. He had salesmanship. When he spoke, he spread enthusiasm through a room, a room filled with bright, suspicious minds. He possessed such spellbinding talent, he could sell a case of whiskey to a gathering of Moslem fundamentalists. Maybe two cases.

Knapp had grand visions of his own greatness. He would tell his friends that he was going to build one of the largest financial institutions in the country, maybe as big as Bank of America. Who knew where it would all end? Today America—tomorrow the world.

Very shortly, he was going to make that dream a reality. For some time now, he had coveted American Savings and that thick stack of capital Mark Taper had accumulated.

Conservative in dress, arrogant in attitude, risky in the pursuit of pleasure, and brilliant in business, Knapp often ridiculed his competitors. He said they were struggling through the recession like dying dinosaurs waiting for the Ice Age to end. Except perhaps in his own mind, Knapp had been a virtual nobody in the corporate world just six years before when he was the head of a struggling financial holding company that owned a small thrift in Stockton, California, a tranquil farming community eighty-two miles east of San Francisco and nearly four hundred miles north of FCA's Los Angeles headquarters. Stockton was a far cry from Charlie Knapp's world, the world of Learjets, balloon races, and beautiful women.

In eight years, Knapp's FCA had doubled in size nearly four times. When Knapp made a bid to buy American Savings in early 1982, Mark Taper told Knapp that FCA was too small to consummate the deal. A guppy couldn't swallow a whale. Now, a year later, the Cal Fed deal had just fallen through, and Mark

Taper was more anxious to do business with this young upstart. So when Knapp phoned to suggest that FCA merge with First Charter, Mark Taper took the suggestion very seriously indeed.

Charlie Knapp was a senior in college when he found a role model for success and an outline for life. Both were in a book. But this was not one of the great classics of literature, like *War and Peace* or *For Whom the Bell Tolls*. No, Knapp was inspired by Cameron Hawley's 1955 novel *Cash McCall* about a blood-and-guts business tycoon who had the strength of conviction and self-confidence to be a lone hungry wolf. Cash McCall, the novel's main character, made his fortune as a buccaneer who stood apart from the crowd. An argument for free enterprise and the profit motive, the novel almost served as a schematic diagram for budding entrepreneurs.

Long before Carl Icahn and other corporate raiders had become famous, the hero of this novel found a struggling company saddled with weak management and took it over, building a successful enterprise in the process. "I'm what you might call a dealer in second-hand companies," Cash McCall said. He spoke his mind and flaunted his wealth. He bought a B-26 bomber, spent a small fortune refurbishing it, and then used it as a private plane to fly around the country, buying and selling companies, primarily those mismanaged by founders who had long since run out of steam.

Charlie Knapp seemed to have followed the novel like a script. In his rise to the top, he bought six vintage airplanes, including a 1936 Bucker Jungmeister and a 1944 P-41 Mustang. He also became a champion balloon racer. Knapp liked being in charge and strove to be the master of his own universe. He took control of a financial-services firm from an ailing chairman who had sought Knapp's help in turning the company around. He then built FCA into a flashy operation whose top managers drove expensive cars and flew around the country in a fleet of Learjets.

Charlie Knapp was born in Honolulu on October 14, 1934. He was orphaned at an early age and lived with foster parents, who raised him as a Mormon. After attending the University of Hawaii for two years, Knapp transferred to the University of

Utah in Salt Lake City, graduating with a bachelor's degree in economics in 1955. He served two years in the army and spent one year at Hastings School of Law in San Francisco.

In the late 1950s, he joined the San Francisco securities firm of Schwabacher-Frey, starting in the back office and working his way up to broker. He joined Shearson Hammill & Co. in 1964 and ran the West Coast corporate-finance operations before leaving the firm in 1969.

Knapp loved being an investment banker because he was independent and could second-guess a company's senior management. Nevertheless, he left the securities business altogether in 1971 when he became president of Shappell Industries, a large home builder in Los Angeles. In this, his first attempt at managing a company, he learned a lot about the construction business and a valuable lesson about himself. Charlie Knapp didn't like being second-in-command; he needed to be the chief executive. He left Shappell in 1972 and formed Trafalgar Associates, a small investment company.

Shortly thereafter, he got an important call from an old business acquaintance, Charles S. Offer, the chairman and chief executive officer of Budget Industries, which he had founded in 1937 as Budget Finance Plan in a Hollywood storefront with an initial investment of $12,500. By the beginning of World War II, Offer had five offices in the Los Angeles area. Budget Finance specialized in small loans to consumers for home appliances, vacations, bill consolidation, and used cars, a fertile field virtually untouched by banks and S&Ls. After the war, business boomed, and Offer opened offices around the country. He started insurance subsidiaries and a company that financed receivables for corporations, and envisioned developing a "department store" for financial products.

In 1965, he acquired majority control of State Savings and Loan in Stockton, in the heart of California's San Joaquin Valley, and later acquired control of Century Bank, just outside Los Angeles in Century City. He now had a full-service financial company. But by 1972, Offer was in trouble, facing a revolt by dissident shareholders who wanted a seat on the board of directors. In addition, Budget had gone over budget on a mammoth real-estate project in the resort community of Padre Island, Texas. The project was supposed to be finished for $50 million.

About two years into development, the price tag had risen to $250 million and was still only 25 percent complete.

Offer had already started searching for a president when he heard that Knapp had left Shappell. He needed someone who understood both finance and construction. He had met Knapp years earlier and considered him bright and capable. But Knapp said he didn't want to be president unless he could be chief executive officer, and Offer wouldn't agree to that. He wasn't about to yield control. Knapp became a consultant and director, and was supposed to help look for a president as he worked on fixing the problems at Padre Island. As it turned out, his bailout plan involved a series of questionable loans that amounted to little more than loan-sharking and ultimately helped sink the whole company.

Two years later, Offer, then 63, suffered a massive heart attack that required a triple-bypass operation. A few months later, he called Knapp and said the consultant ought to take over the company. Knapp agreed to buy out Offer's controlling interest over the next five years and became chairman and chief executive officer. He quickly began restructuring Budget Industries, making State Savings, the small S&L, its focal point. Like his fictional hero, Cash McCall, Charlie Knapp had big plans for his company.

Knapp quickly developed a reputation as an innovator. Although it had a scant $666 million in assets in 1977, State Savings became the first S&L in the nation to offer Visa credit cards and had some 6,000 accounts by the end of the year. Because the name Budget Industries no longer fit the aggressive new outlook, the company sponsored an employee contest to come up with a new name for the corporation. From five hundred entries emerged the name Financial Corporation of America.

Growth came quickly. Knapp hired account executives who earned a commission for selling deposits. State used the money to build its base of real-estate loans, assiduously searching for the kind of high-interest deals some of his competitors were content to pass up because of their dubious value. With State Savings accounting for the bulk of FCA's operations, assets nearly doubled by the end of 1979.

In 1980, when the rest of the industry cut back during the

severe recession, State Savings was quickly writing loans to home buyers and builders, particularly big developers. It then sold many of those loans to investors. Total loans at State Savings jumped 63 percent that year as FCA's assets climbed to $1.8 billion. FCA doubled in size by the end of 1981 during the toughest period for the S&L industry since World War II. The company nearly doubled in size again in 1982, to $6.6 billion. The growth in profits was nothing short of amazing. Between 1976 and 1982, profits increased more than tenfold, to $36.7 million. In 1982 alone, when most of the big S&L operators registered large losses, FCA's profits more than doubled, and the company earned an eye-popping 33 percent return on equity.

This earnings record made his competitors not only envious but suspicious. How could they be losing their shirts while he jetted his way to riches? Sure, Charlie Knapp was smart, but they weren't exactly idiots either. Maybe, just maybe, everything wasn't aboveboard at FCA.

When Knapp broached the subject of a merger with Mark Taper, the aging financier said he wanted to contact his attorney. He hung up and placed a call to Ernie Leff, who said he would get there as soon as he could.

As he drove from his Beverly Hills office to First Charter's headquarters, Leff thought this might be just another false alarm. It had been his experience over the years that far more deals were dreamed of than came together. Leff had never met Knapp, but he knew of his reputation as a maverick, and he was well aware of the enormous and alarming growth at State Savings. Through his contacts in the industry and the government, he knew the regulators were displeased with Knapp and his S&L. He also had his doubts about whether FCA, a holding company with $6.6 billion in assets, could digest First Charter, which was 40 percent bigger, with $9.4 billion in assets.

Leff also couldn't help but wonder why Uncle Mark had called him to help with the biggest deal of Taper's life, not once but twice in the last five months. Leff had kept up his friendship with Taper, and his firm had done some work for First Charter over the years. The two men lived only a mile apart in Beverly Hills. But Taper had a clever attorney on his board of directors,

R. Bradbury Clark, a partner with the Los Angeles firm of Omelveny & Meyers, which did corporate work for First Charter. Leff was a good attorney, but he was by no means an expert on legal matters involving the Securities and Exchange Commission, which would have to approve the deal. So why not use Clark?

After Leff arrived at Taper's spartan ninth-floor office about half an hour later, the two men discussed how seriously to take the proposal and whether FCA would have the funds for a merger. Then they returned the call to Knapp, who laid out his proposal to acquire First Charter right then, over the phone. Knapp knew what he wanted and seemed to understand what Taper needed as well. He proposed to cash out Taper and his family interest, and to swap FCA securities for First Charter stock to obtain the remainder of the company.

The two chairmen were on the same wavelength. For his part, Taper not only didn't want to hold any FCA stock but also wanted no role in the new company. If Cal Fed had been a bit too modern for Taper, FCA's State Savings was like a spaceship from another planet. State Savings used pushy salespeople to raise large deposits and then wrote and purchased loans from other banks and thrifts so quickly, it could take your breath away. For his part, Knapp had big plans for FCA. He needed American Savings and its $634 million in capital to keep growing, and he didn't want an old-fashioned guy like Mark Taper reading his mail.

Charlie Knapp, a master of telemarketing, took just ten minutes on the phone to pitch a deal worth several hundred million dollars.

"Sounds very interesting," Taper told Knapp. "We'll get back to you."

The old man turned to his lawyer for advice. Leff, who remained skeptical, asked Taper if he really wanted to sell since he had seemed halfhearted during the Cal Fed talks.

Leff went through the reasons for selling. "You know as well as I do that you're getting on in years," Leff said. "There's no one in the family who can take over the company for you. This seems like a better offer than the Cal Fed deal. You'll be cashed out. You won't have to take any FCA stock. It seems pretty clear that it's the kind of deal you've been looking for."

"But I wonder if they can really afford it? It's a lot of money for a company that size."

"That's the question. They certainly don't have much capital. They've been growing awfully fast. But let's face it, they're the only ones in the business reporting a profit these days."

"I want to sell," Taper said. "But I want to make sure he can really do it."

Over the next few days, Taper and Leff conferred with Knapp and his key aides several times to examine key points of the proposal and determine whether FCA could afford the merger. Finally, Knapp provided some numbers based on what his company's accountants, Arthur Anderson & Co., said FCA could afford, according to Leff. Taper liked what he saw.

On January 11, Taper decided he would sign an agreement in principle to sell the company he had run for more than thirty years. He had Leff come to his two-story brick home at the corner of Alpine Drive and Sunset Boulevard, a house that had once belonged to movie star Wallace Beery, who had died thirty years before. The two men met in Taper's spacious den, sitting in musty overstuffed chairs that Leff jokingly said must have been there since Beery died.

For the next three hours, Taper and Leff went over the agreement, line by line. After every nuance had been checked and cleared by his attorney, Taper signed the document, and Leff called an anxious Charlie Knapp to tell him they had a deal.

Under the agreement, FCA would pay $27 a share for the 11 million shares, representing 35 percent of First Charter, controlled by the Taper group. The rest of the shareholders would get securities valued at $23 a share. The total deal was worth $734 million and would make American Savings, the surviving thrift, about the same size as Home Savings of America, the nation's largest thrift.

Leff had just nailed down the largest deal of his life in a matter of days. Several obstacles still lay ahead, primarily an examination by the federal regulators, but the arrangement fell together like clockwork. Maybe it had been a little too easy.

Knapp was ecstatic. Now he was really on his way to the big time. For the past few years, he had heard plenty of criticism from his competitors about the way he operated. They said he took too many chances. They said he couldn't possibly sustain his rate of growth. They said he had problems in his loan portfolio. But it was Charlie Knapp who had soared past them all. It was Charlie Knapp, the orphan from Honolulu, who had just pulled off the largest thrift merger ever, casting his shadow over all the living and the dead of the S&L industry.

It would be difficult to imagine two companies with more radically different philosophies. Whereas Mark Taper ran American savings with a firm hand, at State Savings, Charlie Knapp chose to delegate. Compared with the frugal Taper, Knapp threw caution and money to the wind.

Like his fictional hero, Knapp believed that in order to succeed in business, you had to be willing to share the wealth. Employees and management owned about 40 percent of the firm's stock, Knapp owning 6.68 percent.

Knapp's deposit salesmen were richly rewarded for their initiative. Manning money desks scattered throughout the country, some two hundred salespeople cranked up the deposit-gathering machine each day, concentrating on certificates of deposit (CDs) of $100,000 or more, most of which were not insured by the federal government. These deposits were easy to obtain because large investors like pension funds and government agencies needed to earn interest on their funds. Many were willing to avoid breaking up large sums of money into accounts of $100,000 that would have been insured as long as they received a competitive rate of return and FCA seemed healthy.

Under Knapp, FCA paid its salesmen an eighth of 1 percent on every CD sold. The commission came on top of an annual base of more than $30,000.

Some salesmen made a killing. In 1981, George Terzakis, a 45-year-old former butcher, earned $117,500, and as the company's top salesman, he was awarded a Porsche 928. The next year, FCA's top nine salesmen earned more than $200,000 as the company added $2.2 billion in deposits.

"People work for pride and greed and no other reason," Knapp told the *Wall Street Journal* in an April 1981 article. "You satisfy those two things and they will meet impossible goals."

The jumbo deposits gave FCA enormous economies of scale. But they were costly and left the company vulnerable to sudden withdrawals. In such instances, FCA would have to pay a premium of two percentage points or more to keep the money coming in the door. By 1982, more than 90 percent of FCA's deposits were in short-term large CDs, called "hot money" in the industry because depositors would switch institutions in a blinding flash if trouble seemed imminent. Retail deposits are considered much more stable, in part because these customers have to go to the branch to withdraw the money and these accounts typically are fully insured by the government.

Not only was hot money a volatile and expensive source of funds, but it underscored a serious flaw in FCA's operations. The rest of the industry was submerged in red ink in the recession of the early 1980s because it borrowed short and loaned long. That was a disastrous business plan when interest rates were rising because the cost of funds would go higher than the yield on mortgages.

But Knapp figured he could outsmart the industry. The scope of financial services had changed radically, he explained. The small saver was gone. Financial institutions had no choice but to turn to institutional depositors. Retail deposits were small potatoes. If you wanted to thrive in the new environment, you had to do business with the big boys.

Knapp correctly predicted the changing economics rupturing the industry. High interest, expensive labor, and sky-high real-estate prices made brick-and-mortar branches a poor investment. Developing a retail delivery system was painstakingly slow. Why bother? The mutual funds sold through advertisements in newspapers and the yellow pages. Others in the industry who shared Knapp's desire for fast growth latched on to brokered funds, large chunks of money that were raised by professional brokers who funneled cash to an institution, charging a small percentage fee as a cut of the action. With his adroit sales force, Knapp went them one better. Brokers charged too much and couldn't care less about the company. It was better to hire your own salespeople. All they needed was a telephone and a pep talk. But the big question facing the company was what to do with all that hot money.

Despite the credit squeeze gripping the rest of the country, Knapp decided he would continue booking loans, especially big loans to real-estate developers. He could sell a lot of them at a profit in the secondary market, a national market for mortgages. In the secondary market, a bank or S&L buys or sells an existing loan or securities backed by mortgages. Knapp believed that the high interest rates of the early 1980s were a historical aberration and that the price of money would fall to more ordinary levels.

Once rates declined, FCA's loans would increase in value. The company's loan portfolio carried an average yield of more than 14 percent. In addition, loans to developers were written at a premium over the bank prime rate, and some carried interest rates as high as 24 percent, an astounding $24 million on a $100-million mortgage. On top of that, the developers paid huge fees to get the money. Loans with interest rates of 15 percent or more would be valuable commodities once mortgage rates fell below 10 percent because they could be sold at a substantial premium. Charlie Knapp was betting his assets on the belief that fickle interest rates would do what he predicted.

Occasionally, Knapp's strategy drew favorable reviews from the business press. The *New York Times*, in a story headlined "Thrift Unit Thrives as Maverick," observed that Knapp intended to sell his Century Bank subsidiary and concentrate on State Savings. The paper noted that State Savings would be developed along "untraditional" but profitable lines.

"We won't function out of the Harvard Business School textbook," Knapp told the *Times*. "Harvard caused the last two recessions."

Forbes magazine found value in FCA stock. The magazine pointed out that S&L stocks had been hammered in the market but suggested that FCA might be underpriced, given its robust profits. *Forbes* revealed that FCA's stock had risen from 88 cents a share (adjusted for splits) in 1974 to just over $17 a share around March 1981.

When it came to lending, Knapp put in a phenomenal performance. FCA's ability to originate and purchase loans was unmatched in the industry. In 1981, State's access to the wholesale market for assets helped it put $1.8 billion in net new loans on the balance sheet and an additional $2.4 billion in 1982.

The feverish lending activity made other S&L executives extremely skeptical of the underlying health of State Savings.

These competitors, often quoted in the press anonymously, said there was no way to book that many new loans without getting stuck with a lot of bad paper. And any good thrift operator would tell you that if the default rate on your loans went much higher than the industry average of less than 2 percent, you could be dead before you knew what hit you. Any developer willing to pay five points or more in loan-origination fees and interest rates approaching 20 percent had a bankrupt project on his hands before the ink had dried on the closing documents.

Knapp said there was no reason to worry. A thrift growing as quickly as State Savings was bound to have some loan problems. In fact, his loss ratio was climbing to one much higher than the industry average, but he said FCA could handle the losses as it expanded. Besides, the company had an aggressive program for getting bad loans and foreclosed real estate off its books. (Later, the program of dumping bad loans would reveal that the company filed highly inaccurate financial statements.)

FCA also did a booming business in selling commitments to make loans to developers and to buy loans from other companies. Fees ranged from 2 percent to 4 percent of the commitment amount. From 1980 to 1982, more than 25 percent of the company's revenue came from sources other than interest on loans, much of it in fees. In fact, FCA told investors that the industry's traditional practice of measuring profitability by return on assets was "outdated and not relevant" for a company with so much fee income.

Buying loans from other companies left State Savings vulnerable in another way. Other companies could write loans that did not meet their own standards and then sell them to State Savings. With so much growth in the loan portfolio, State Savings was susceptible to poor underwriting standards and sloppy appraisals. The huge volume and quick growth made it difficult to keep track of all the key loan documents. State's loan personnel and computers couldn't handle the action. Sooner or later, FCA's problems with loan documentation were bound to catch up.

When the pressures of running a hard-charging, high-profile company got to be too much, Knapp had a quick remedy. He would jump in one of his antique planes and go stunt-flying, defying death as he pulled off difficult and dangerous maneuvers. In a sense, he was writing his name in the skies above Los Angeles as he pushed the envelope of adventure to its outer limits.

Even in his personal life, Charlie Knapp had a lot of panache. Not only was he a titan of industry who lived in a lovely clifftop home in elegant Bel Air, but he had a highly intelligent wife who was a beautiful and glamorous blonde. Brooke Knapp, an honors graduate and former stockbroker whom he married in 1968, was also one of the world's top aviators.

Though her husband was an ace pilot, Brooke Knapp had suffered a fear of flying just a few years before. She liked to make a list of her fears and attack them one by one. So she learned to fly. Then she became a professional pilot. Brooke Knapp later formed her own charter aircraft company, flying executives and celebrities to out-of-the-way locations. Two FCA officials were her business partners, and much of the income at Jet Airways depended on flights made for the S&L, a very cozy arrangement that would bring scrutiny and criticism from the federal government.

Friends said a sense of competition invaded the Knapps' relationship. Brooke was also a great golfer and tennis player, and was fluent in French. She was a student of karate as well. One day, Knapp walked into the house with Foster Fluetsch, State's president, who had a full beard, large frame, and fun-loving attitude. Brooke reached out, grabbed Charlie, and flipped him on the floor. All in good fun of course.

Despite his own accomplishments, Knapp was sometimes overshadowed by his wife. He could win dangerous races in helium-filled balloons, but that was nothing compared with Brooke's success in early 1983. Brooke Knapp set a new world speed record for business-class jets. Piloting an eight-passenger Navajo equipped with a wood-paneled bar and named the *American Dream*, Brooke Knapp flew around the world in 50 hours, 22 minutes, 42 seconds, knocking 15 hours off the old record. She liked the high-flying lifestyle. "Let's face it," she told *People* magazine, "flying is sexy. It's romance beyond your wildest dreams."

All in all, Cash McCall would have been proud and maybe

even a little envious of Charlie Knapp's world—except that Cash McCall never broke the rules.

Despite Knapp's bold comments about FCA's bright future, the company was actually in a state of rapid decline, going downhill so quickly that the government should have been considering liquidating it. What the stockholders of Knapp's FCA and Taper's First Charter did not know was that State Savings had already gotten into serious trouble with the federal regulators who were supervising the institution and would play an important role in approving the merger.

As the two companies prepared to merge, examination reports showed that FCA's State Savings had a variety of severe deficiencies, and federal regulators considered some of the thrift's business practices "hazardous."

The FCA subsidiary was a state-chartered federally insured thrift that was subject to examination by both the state and federal governments, and accordingly on January 15, 1982, examiners from the federal Bank Board and the California Department of Savings and Loan began their task.

An examination of a savings institution, like that of a bank, is supposed to be a thorough review of the company's operating results, lending practices, level of bad loans, reserves to cover loan losses, competency of management, and adequacy of record keeping. In 1982, the federal Bank Board used a rating system under which each institution was graded in several key categories and also received a composite rating.

Under that system, thrifts received overall ratings on a scale of 1 to 4, a 1 being the best, a 4 the worst. An S&L with a 4 rating had "major and serious problems which management appears to be unable or unwilling to correct," according to the government's manual on examination and supervision in effect until October 1984. "In these cases, the problems may not be soluble, but the situation is of such large dimensions and so critical that drastic corrective action appears necessary. This may require reorganization, liquidation, or other action." Some of the individual problems would be considered "hazardous" to the company's health, the manual said.

On May 10, 1982, a team of state and federal examiners met

with Knapp's top managers from State Savings to discuss the results of the latest examination. State Savings received the federal government's lowest rating.

The examiners told company officials that the government was worried about the company's continued fast growth and its high level of jumbo CDs. The company was also informed that it had major deficiencies in the underwriting of loans, a significant flaw because *underwriting* refers to the policies and procedures by which a lender makes profitable loans. Unprofitable loans kill financial institutions.

Those were not the only problems. The examiners raised serious questions about the way State conducted business with people affiliated with the company. The exact transactions were not disclosed, but the relationship with Jet Airways serves as a good example. Jet Airways leased three aircraft in 1982 from limited partnerships owned by officers of State Savings. The partnerships were called Blazing Saddles, in reference to the Mel Brooks comedy. A number after the name was used to designate the various partnerships. J. Foster Fluetsch, president of State Savings, owned 30.8 percent, and John J. Borer, FCA's general counsel, owned 21.2 percent of Jet Airways. Neither official received remuneration from Jet Airways except for dividends that accrued to them.

FCA paid Jet Airways $2.9 million in 1982, and clearly some of the money must have gone to some FCA officials either as dividends or lease payments. It was a cozy relationship similar to having a company's annual convention and directors' meetings catered by the chairman's wife, who in turn bought her supplies from the corporation's top officers.

The regulators also expressed concern over how State Savings accounted for all the loan fees it had booked and the association's decline in net worth (the amount by which assets exceed liabilities). State's managers indicated they were aware of the problems and had taken corrective action in most areas. (This seems highly unlikely.)

In reality, the situation at State Savings had been getting worse for some time. In February 1981, State had received a composite rating of 3. A 3 rating was certainly nothing to brag about since such a low rating indicates that the S&L has one or more serious problems, including asset weakness, violations of thrift laws or regulations, weak or dangerous operating practices, or failure to pursue sound administrative policies. "Such associations require close supervisory attention and constant pressure for correction," the supervisory manual said.

As FCA reported record earnings and Charlie Knapp criticized his competitors and bragged to the media, the underlying health of his S&L was quickly deteriorating. Indeed, three weeks after meeting with the company's management and discussing the 4 rating, the state and federal regulators met privately to discuss the situation at State Savings. Among other things, the examiners discussed the possibility of issuing a cease-and-desist order against State Savings.

A cease-and-desist order is a serious occurrence at an S&L. Short of placing the company in receivership or replacing management through a conservatorship, it is the harshest action the Bank Board can take. The order is designed to stop unsafe and unsound business practices and is undertaken when the Bank Board lacks confidence that management can or will take action on its own. Once issued, a cease-and-desist order that is violated can be enforced in federal court.

Two weeks later, Knapp met with state and federal regulators. The spellbinding speaker must have made a convincing pitch that the company could correct the problems since no cease-and-desist order was issued. Instead, three weeks later, on July 9, State Savings received a supervisory letter attached to the official examination report. The letter addressed a number of issues, including State's operating philosophy and practices, loan-underwriting policies, and substandard assets. At a follow-up meeting on July 29, a supervisory agent for the Bank Board suggested that it might be a good time for State to sell its high-yielding loans, which presumably were some of the riskier assets on its books.

State and federal thrift regulators weren't the only ones concerned with the health of State Savings. Shortly after becoming vice chairman of the Federal Reserve in 1982, Preston Martin called the San Francisco Federal Reserve Bank and told high-level officials there that he wanted to be kept informed of FCA's activities.

Martin had just joined the Fed from Sears Savings where he

had heard stories of FCA executives attending industry conferences and telling their colleagues at other companies that they were looking to buy loans in bulk. Martin thought that a company that aggressive must be getting a substantial number of bad loans. Although he did not intervene to stop the merger of FCA and First Charter, Martin would later conduct a personal crusade to keep Charlie Knapp from producing what the Fed vice chairman thought were highly questionable financial statements.

Technically, the thrift industry and the Bank Board are independent of the central bank, but Martin was worried that FCA could crash at any time and that the Fed would be called into action as the nation's "lender of last resort." He thought FCA's mushrooming growth, coupled with what looked like the booking of garbage loans, left the Fed vulnerable. Martin told the San Francisco Federal Reserve Bank to give him regular reports that delved into FCA's cash flows, deposits, growth rates, and other indicators of FCA's underlying strength.

Meanwhile, State Savings continued to receive critical reports from the Bank Board. On October 15, 1982, another joint examination began. Two months later, the Bank Board's district accountant in San Francisco told State's outside auditors, Arthur Anderson, to expand the scope of company audits pertaining to real estate owned by the S&L, property generally obtained through foreclosure. The district accountant wanted Arthur Anderson to look at independent appraisals and examine State's practice of giving favorable loan rates to customers who bought FCA's foreclosed property.

On February 7, 1983, three weeks after FCA agreed to merge with First Charter, the Bank Board's district appraiser in San Francisco told State Savings he had selected twenty properties that would receive test appraisals to determine if the company had appropriate reserves for its loan losses.

Six weeks later, on March 23, the report regarding the examination begun the previous October was sent to State Savings. Once again, the report uncovered a variety of problems. And once again, State Savings received a composite rating of 4.

All in all, with its high-octane growth, low-quality loans, and hazardous business practices, State Savings did not appear ready to double in size and become the nation's largest thrift, especially if the authorities in Washington were wise to the sinister economic forces taking shape and had any sense of history.

Chapter 3

The American Spirit

In many ways, the death of hundreds of American S&Ls in the 1980s, in what became the financial equivalent of the Vietnam War, began with the industry's birth, for trouble emerged the minute Comly Rich got his home loan, the nation's first S&L mortgage.

A civic-minded man of modest means, Rich embodied the American spirit. He struggled to provide a better life for his burgeoning family and like many of his contemporaries in this proud new nation, dreamed of owning his own home.

The son of a storekeeper, Rich was born in 1795 in Oxford Township, a part of Philadelphia. His father died while he was a teenager, and Rich became an apprentice for a comb maker in nearby Frankford. Sketchy historical records show that he was a member of the Frankford town watch and also served as the lamplighter, going through the village igniting street lamps so that local residents could find their way in the dark.

Like other men of his day, Comly Rich faced the prospect of working his whole life and never owning his home. Banks at that time did not make long-term loans that could be repaid on easy monthly terms. Most workmen rented a home or room from the owner of the mill or factory where they worked.

January 3, 1831, marked the beginning of a new era. On that date, the Oxford Provident Building Association was formed to help workers afford homes. The nation's first S&L proclaimed that anyone could become a member by agreeing to pay a $5 initiation fee and monthly dues of $3. Members received dividends and could borrow money to buy a home, repaying in convenient monthly sums plus a small interest charge.

The concept of a savings institution came from England where the first building and loan opened for business in Birmingham in 1781, five years after Adam Smith wrote his *Wealth of Nations*, which proved that the real value of a nation's economy wasn't its store of gold and silver but its production of goods and services. In this he was certainly correct. Home building would eventually prove to be a vital part of the American economy.

Comly Rich, Oxford Provident's first borrower, became the first person to receive a mortgage from an S&L on April 11, 1831, when he borrowed $375 for a tiny frame house. Later that year, he obtained an additional $125 to refurbish it. Two stories tall with a white picket fence in front, the house still stands at 4276 Orchard Street in Philadelphia.

Ironically, Comly Rich also became the industry's first deadbeat. Poor Rich fell behind in his mortgage payments and had to be bailed out by a family member. Since the first S&L in this country experienced trouble with the very first mortgage, it was logical to assume that other problems would follow. If customers defaulted on their loans, someone would have to come to the rescue, or disaster would result. This important lesson, like other warning signs that would emerge, was largely ignored.

In fact, despite this inauspicious start, the idea of a cooperative institution dedicated to home building took hold. At first the growth was gradual. Five years after the founding of Oxford Provident, the Brooklyn Building and Mutual Loan Association was born in New York. In 1843, an S&L opened in South Carolina, the first in the South. By 1887, every state on the eastern seaboard had at least one savings institution.

S&Ls began as self-liquidating associations. Each member contributed a specified sum each month for home construction, and often the associations did not charge interest on mortgages. The members borrowed the money in turn until each one had built a home. A drawing was used to ration the supply of funds. Once each member bought or built a home and repaid the mortgage, the association dissolved.

This practice, while helpful to individual members, kept the supply of mortgage money relatively fixed. As the demand for housing grew and savers wanted to earn money on their deposits, another system developed. Associations began to ration the supply of funds by charging interest.

S&Ls continued to flourish until the panic of 1893. In the

depression that followed, hundreds of savings associations failed, especially national thrifts whose controversial and corrupt activities included loans on risky projects at high interest rates—the very practices that contributed to the great S&L bailout ninety-six years later.

Nevertheless, the federal government took no action after the panic, leaving thrift regulation to the states. All Congress did in response was grant a tax exemption for S&Ls in 1894. The tax-exempt status of S&Ls helped spur the industry's enormous growth. In 1900, the country had 5,356 thrifts, compared with 12,427 banks. By 1925, when the number of thrifts reached its peak, some 12,403 S&Ls were operating, compared with 28,442 commercial banks.

The heady times of the Jazz Age ended abruptly with the stock market crash on October 29, 1929, and as the Great Depression gripped the nation, banks dropped dead in droves. In 1930, some 600 banks folded as the economy contracted and depositors removed their money. Between 1930 and 1933, 9,000 banks folded. Two days after his inauguration in 1933, Franklin Delano Roosevelt declared a bank "holiday": depositors could not withdraw their money.

Thrifts did not escape the onslaught. From 1930 to 1933, some 500 thrifts failed, representing a 15 percent reduction in the size of the industry. With their accounts frozen, some S&L customers took a loss on their accounts by selling their passbooks in the black market. About 1,200 more thrifts folded by 1939, but that was still a much smaller percentage of failures than the industry suffered in the 1980s.

Congress reacted to the crisis by passing the first of several major reforms that had a dramatic and lasting impact.

On July 16, 1932, after seven months of debate, Congress passed the Federal Home Loan Bank Act, which established the industry's regulatory structure. The act created the Federal Home Loan Bank Board, then a five-member commission, and authorized eight to twelve district banks. Later that year, the Bank Board created twelve district banks to serve member institutions in a variety of ways, particularly by making loans to member institutions and regulating member associations. The district banks are owned by member thrifts, which collect dividends on their investments.

The idea was to rescue the savings and home-financing industries by making credit available to S&Ls. But the 1932 act also established a hybrid regulatory system in which regulators had divided loyalties. The Bank Board and the district banks were supposed to supervise and regulate S&Ls and at the same time serve as industry boosters. This inherent conflict gave rise to an often cozy relationship between the regulators and industry executives, many of whom worked for the government before turning to the industry for a better-paying job.

FDR had been in office only four months when Congress passed the Home Owners' Loan Act of 1933. Under the act, the Bank Board administered a government corporation that saved nearly 1 million American homes from foreclosure. The 1933 act also gave the Bank Board the power to charter federal S&Ls. Federal institutions were required to be mutual associations, owned by member-depositors rather than stockholders, and were supposed to make mortgage loans secured by real estate located within fifty miles of the thrift.

The next year, Congress created the Federal Savings and Loan Insurance Corporation (FSLIC), which protected deposits of $5,000 against loss. Modeled after the Federal Deposit Insurance Corporation (FDIC), which had been established the year before for the commercial-banking sector, the FSLIC was not designed to save any particular institution from failure but to protect the system against a general run.

Some observers would later say that the thrift industry's structure was fundamentally, perhaps fatally, flawed from the outset because it left S&Ls vulnerable to swings in interest rates. The problem was simple. Thrifts borrowed short-term from depositors (in passbook savings accounts) and loaned long-term (in mortgage loans) to home buyers. As long as interest rates remained stable, the system worked. But when interest rates rose, the costs of deposits would rise more quickly than the yield on loans. If interest rates went too high, disaster would result; S&Ls would pay more for deposits than they could earn on loans.

In the optimism of post–World War II America, however, the industry zoomed ahead during a period of stable interest rates and steady economic expansion. From 1950 to 1960, the number of accounts at insured institutions nearly tripled, from 10 million to 28 million. Total assets grew to $70 billion.

The industry remained healthy in the first half of the 1960s, but the costs of the Vietnam War and Lyndon Johnson's Great Society took their toll. As inflation rose, so did interest rates. In 1966, a process known as *disintermediation* resulted: savers removed their money from thrifts (and banks) in search of higher yields. Thrifts had to raise interest rates on savings accounts to keep their customers.

As the economy seesawed in the 1970s, so did the fortunes of S&Ls. With Arthur Burns as chairman, the Federal Reserve pumped up the money supply in 1972 as Richard Nixon was running for reelection. Inflation roared, increasing from 3.3 percent in 1972 to 11 percent in 1974. Nixon's successor, Gerald Ford, tried to stop the wage-price spiral, in part by donning a lapel button: Whip Inflation Now.

Over the next five years, thrifts gradually won new powers designed to make them more competitive in the higher-interest-rate environment. But by 1980, the economy was in a shambles, and so was the S&L industry. Interest rates rose to historic levels, with the bellwether prime rate, the rate the most creditworthy companies pay, eventually reaching 21 percent.

Congress clumsily reacted to the chaos in 1980 by passing the ill-conceived Depository Institutions Deregulation and Monetary Control Act. The 1980 act increased the ceiling on insured accounts at banks and S&Ls from $40,000 to $100,000 while allowing greater risks with deposits. The legislation also required that all interest-rate controls be phased out by 1986; as interest rates were shooting up, thrifts now had to keep pace, ensuring they would lose money as a result. Besides ushering in enormous losses in the process, the act also removed the quarter-point advantage that thrifts had over commercial banks on savings accounts, a differential that had ensured a steady supply of funds for the housing market.

That same year, the Bank Board compounded congressional mistakes by lowering the industry's safety standards, decreasing the minimum net worth of a savings association (the amount by which assets exceed liabilities) from 5 percent to 4 percent. Net worth includes such items as cash and equity in the company, often referred to as capital, and is supposed to serve as a buffer against loss. The higher the level of capital, the more solid the company.

The lower net-worth requirement meant that thrifts needed a smaller capital base to comply with federal regulations and could increase the total amount of loans they made with a smaller buffer against losses. S&Ls suddenly got riskier. But Congress, the Bank Board, and state legislatures would soon give S&Ls more new tools with which to damage themselves and the American public.

On April 16, 1981, two days after Richard T. Pratt had been sworn in as the new Bank Board chairman, he declared that the primary thrust of his administration would be to expand the powers of S&Ls and reduce the regulations facing them. He called for short-term restrictions on money-market funds, which were killing the thrifts, by imposing the kind of reserve requirement that banks and thrifts had to observe and by limiting check-writing privileges. Paraphrasing Winston Churchill, Pratt said, "I have not been appointed chairman to preside over the demise of this industry. We are going on to bigger and better things."

Dick Pratt, a noted professor of finance and longtime industry insider who had been selected by presidential adviser Ed Gray, proved to be a strong administrator. Before his first month in office had passed, the Bank Board had authorized federally chartered thrifts to make, purchase, and participate in adjustable-rate mortgages (later referred to as ARMs). ARMs became enormously popular with S&Ls because they allowed the institutions to raise mortgage payments from consumers to adjust for increases in interest rates. Because many ARMs had lower ("teaser") introductory rates, they made it easier for home buyers to qualify for mortgages.

The Bank Board under Pratt adopted several other changes intended to buy time until the economy rebounded. Stoking the fires of financial destruction, the net-worth requirement was further reduced, from 4 percent to 3 percent, making it easier for thrifts to avoid disciplinary action by the regulators. The move greatly aggravated an already dangerous level of risk developing at S&Ls. With this one change in regulations, S&Ls were leveraged at 33 to 1: for $1 in capital, a company could support $33 in liabilities.

In reality, the leverage turned out to be closer to 150 to 1 because the Bank Board also allowed an institution to average in its net worth over five years. On paper, a company with $30 million in deposits would appear to have $1 million in capital. But with five-year averaging, the company could get by with a capital base of only $250,000. In other words, for the cost of a starter home in the San Francisco Bay Area, an S&L executive could buy an entire subdivision.

The Bank Board under Pratt also gave thrifts the right to amortize losses on the sale of assets such as loans whose value had declined in a high-interest environment. This had the effect of understating losses.

Pratt also pushed for new legislation that would be beneficial to thrifts. In October 1981, he offered a restructuring bill to give thrifts broad new powers, some of which were identical to those of commercial banks. Among other things, the Pratt bill called for allowing federal associations to offer demand deposits to any customer, including corporations, and to make corporate, commercial, and agricultural loans.

Senator Jake Garn sponsored the Pratt bill. President Reagan signed the legislation into law on October 15, 1982. By then it was known as the Garn–St. Germain Depository Institutions Act after its two principal sponsors, Garn and Fernand St. Germain, chairman of the House Banking Committee.

This bill was the most important piece of thrift legislation since the Great Depression. It made it easier for thrifts to convert from mutual to stock ownership and granted broad new lending powers to thrifts that had previously been reserved for commercial banks. S&Ls were allowed to offer individual and corporate checking accounts and to invest in other thrifts' savings accounts.

The act was so sweeping that several states, worried that state-chartered institutions would convert to the federal system, adopted even more liberal laws. California allowed thrifts to invest insured funds in virtually any enterprise.

Ronald Reagan gave Garn–St. Germain enthusiastic support. A month after its passage, the president spoke at the annual convention of the U.S. League, an S&L trade association and a powerful lobby in Washington.

Before more than 4,000 league delegates, the president

declared, "When one thinks of people who live by virtues and traditions that make America great—faith in God, love of family and freedom, service to community and country—the leaders of your industry come to mind."

The president said Garn–St. Germain could be the "Emancipation Proclamation for America's savings institutions." Said the president, "The sun is shining on thrifts again."

The Reagan-era reforms were supposed to guarantee the survival of S&Ls by making them more competitive. But the plan backfired. The new laws and regulations guaranteed that unhealthy thrifts would stay in business far longer than was safe, allowing them to continue to put federally insured funds at risk and substantially increasing the cost of the inevitable cleanup.

But as the nation's leaders would soon discover, the attempt to save the S&L industry had become a financial quagmire as deep as the Vietnam War. The number of troops sent in to fight fraud, excessive risk, and poor management would double, but still the war was unwinnable.

The enemy often moved stealthily. Booby traps were everywhere. The cumbersome rules and regulations gave each company its own demilitarized zone. Perhaps if the conflict had made dramatic television footage, the public would have required tougher action sooner. Instead, institutions across the country died in one ambush after another. Industry leaders finally pulled out their white flags and declared surrender in August 1989 with the passage of an enormous federal bailout.

By then, it had become the most expensive financial conflict in the history of the United States. The body count: a $159 billion federal bailout, much of it from the taxpayers, and more than 1,000 companies killed or merged out of existence. Additional casualties are expected.

S&Ls would jump into real-estate development, windmill farms, and junk bonds. S&L managers would defraud the public of untold billions, with some of the money lining not only their pockets but also funding political campaigns, favors it was hoped would reap rewards in the future if the regulators ever caught on to the game.

Within weeks of the president's "emancipation proclamation" address, Charlie Knapp's FCA, the granddaddy of them all and the architect of disaster, was in the headlines once again. For the next several years, American Savings would be one of the most widely reported financial companies in the country and would come to symbolize not only the ills of the S&L industry but the failure of the Reagan-era reforms.

Chapter 4

A Merger Made in Heaven

Ernie Leff, the veteran negotiator, had learned to trust his instincts, and all the warning signs told him to prepare for a tough fight at First Charter.

The offer from Charlie Knapp's FCA had deeply divided the directors of Taper's First Charter, and the board now formed two warring camps. Leff worried that the board's outside directors could muster enough votes to kill the merger. Even if they lost, the dissidents could embarrass the company if word of the opposition got out.

Leff counted the votes. All three directors in the Taper group—Taper, his daughter Janice Ann Lazaroff, and C. S. Diffen, a longtime Taper associate who had retired as First Charter's vice chairman a year ago—would vote in favor of the deal. Diffen had served on the board since 1956, just one year after the holding company was formed, longer than any director except Taper.

In fact, Taper owned only 24,234 shares in FCA stock, worth a paltry $654,318, less than 3,000 more shares than Diffen. But through trusts and a charitable foundation, Taper controlled a total of 10.4 million shares worth $276.7 million.* Besides their personal loyalty to Taper, Diffen and Lazaroff had strong incentives to vote their pocketbooks. Lazaroff owned 337,986 shares worth $9.12 million, and Diffen's 21,599 shares were worth $583,173.

Despite important concessions granted by FCA after the origi-

*The breakdown was 4,519,833 shares through three trusts established for his children in his first wife's will; another trust established in his own name in 1969, 5.7 million shares; the Mark Taper Foundation, which donated money throughout southern California and generated lots of goodwill for the otherwise tightfisted financier, another 101,647 shares worth $2.74 million.

nal offer, the outside directors still strongly opposed the transaction. They included R. Bradbury Clark, Taper's corporate attorney; R. V. Hansberger, chairman and chief executive officer of Futura Industries, Inc.; and Thomas L. Kempner, an investment banker who was chairman and chief executive officer of Loeb Partners, a New York brokerage house.

Phil Brinkerhoff, Taper's politically astute new president, was the swing vote. Of course, if Brinkerhoff sided with the outside directors, Taper probably would fire him on the spot, but the merger would be off, at least until Taper could find a new and presumably more sympathetic director. Leff figured Brinkerhoff probably would side with management in a showdown, but then again, if he approved the merger, he would no longer be head of a large S&L. Brinkerhoff had moved to California from Washington, D.C., just a few months before to become American's president.

As the matter came to a full debate at the directors' meeting on March 7, 1983, the soft-spoken Brinkerhoff kept mostly to himself. He had already let Taper know that the board probably would disapprove of a merger in which the company founder received a cash price higher than what the public stockholders received in securities. It was bad enough that he would get cashed out free and clear, while they got stuck with FCA paper.

Brinkerhoff hadn't been the only one upset with the two-tiered price. Other directors and investors demanded parity. Ralph Stone, a gruff S&L executive from Santa Rosa in northern California and an old friend, told Taper he would oppose the deal unless the other shareholders got the same price as Uncle Mark. Some stockholders tried to block the merger by filing suit in Los Angeles County Superior Court. Shortly after the merger was announced, the court received eight separate suits by First Charter shareholders who claimed their litigation represented a larger class of shareholders.

Finally, faced with shareholder unrest and resentment from some directors, Taper had no choice but to get a better offer. Knapp's board of directors agreed to sweeten the deal on February 7. Under the improved terms, the public shareholders would receive at least $27 a share in FCA securities and could receive more, based on FCA's stock price at the closing of the merger.

Even after the sweetener, though, the dissident directors still opposed merging with FCA. As the board meeting dragged on, Clark especially argued against the transaction, saying he was concerned about the health of FCA and State Savings.

The recalcitrant directors angered and frustrated old man Taper. They had been with him a long time and were now turning against him, just when he most needed their support. He wanted out of the company, and Charlie Knapp was throwing a lot of money around. Clark's resistance was particularly awkward; his law firm represented First Charter and had earned $141,647.45 in fees since January 1, 1981.

But Taper was determined. At Leff's suggestion, he distributed to each director a copy of a written resolution authorizing the merger, which would then go to the shareholders for approval. Then he called for a vote. Clark, Hansberger, and Kempner turned the deal down. Taper, his daughter, and Diffen voted yes. Brinkerhoff was the middleman. The decisive moment had arrived. To Leff's relief, Brinkerhoff joined the Taper group, creating the 4–3 split Taper had expected. Later, Brinkerhoff explained that he believed the shareholders should have the right to decide if they wanted the merger, adding that the transaction would receive extensive examination by the Securities and Exchange Commission (SEC) and the Bank Board, which presumably had a clear picture of State Savings' true operating condition.

Even though his client had just won, Leff weighed the impact of the board's action. Because First Charter was a publicly held company, the shareholders would find out about the narrow vote. The whole deal hinged on a price of at least $27 a share. First Boston had written a fairness opinion in favor of the transaction with that price in mind. The close vote would warn shareholders that their representatives on the board of directors lacked faith in the deal. That in turn could affect the price of FCA's stock, which had been increasing on news of the takeover.

Fortunately for Taper, the outside directors decided to be magnanimous in defeat. Hansberger moved that the vote be counted as unanimous, according to Leff. The motion carried. Thus, the company did not disclose that three outside directors—a lawyer, an investment banker, and a seasoned CEO—

had done their damndest to kill the merger and keep American Savings from Charlie Knapp.

Brad Clark's worst fears about FCA came true just seven weeks later. On April 29, Knapp announced that FCA had asked the New York Stock Exchange to suspend trading in the company's stock, indicating that negative news was imminent.

Knapp's statement to the media and investors said FCA was cooperating with an inquiry by the SEC, which questioned the way State Savings accounted for the disposal of foreclosed real estate and delinquent loans.

Knapp noted that FCA had provided the information in dispute to the SEC. Established by the Securities Exchange Act of 1934, the watchdog federal agency is supposed to insure full disclosure of facts relating to issues of new securities. The SEC has the power to question the accounting methods employed by a company whose stock is publicly traded and can force a corporation to restate its earnings. Toward the end of his two-page press release, Knapp said the company had used the correct accounting procedures but that the SEC might force the company to restate its 1982 earnings. Knapp also said the company was experiencing "an extremely strong earnings trend" for 1983.

News of the SEC inquiry couldn't have come at a worse time. FCA's application to merge with First Charter was winding its way through the Bank Board's bureaucracy, and the company was preparing to mail its proxy statement to shareholders of both companies, asking their support. Trading in FCA stock remained suspended through May 2 when the company announced the restatement of its 1982 earnings in compliance with the SEC directive.

FCA had originally reported that it earned a record $36.7 million for 1982, but because of the SEC's action, the earnings were shaved back by $9.5 million to $27.2 million, a hit of 26 percent.

At issue was FCA's highly aggressive and extremely questionable program for getting bad loans and foreclosed real estate off the books of State Savings. State was peddling delinquent loans and foreclosed property to real-estate syndicators and other investors at discount prices and providing cut-rate loans to clinch the sales. For instance, State loaned the down payment to the buyers with "ancillary loans," secured by mortgages on other properties.

The company lowered the normal origination fees and agreed to significant deferrals of interest and principal payments on the loans, which carried substantially lower interest rates than borrowers were charged for regular real-estate loans. To cleanse the balance sheet of bad assets, State Savings was cutting a lot of corners.

Following the SEC's inquiry, FCA agreed to account for these transactions as though they were not really sales. This had the damaging effect of calling into question the quality of the company's loans. Included in its assets were $176 million in foreclosed property and an additional $251 million in delinquent loans and unpaid interest, a total of $427 million, representing 6.5 percent of total assets. In other words, for every $100 in assets, $6.50 was foreclosed property or bad loans just in this program for sale to real-estate syndicators. Having a high ratio of bad assets was hardly a game plan for prosperity.

SEC officials weren't the first to question the quality of State's loans. Allan B. Bortel, an analyst with Shearson/American Express, had said State's portfolio had problems. That incurred the wrath of Charlie Knapp, who wrote to the analyst on March 15: Knapp accused Bortel of being irresponsible and lacking integrity, adding that the analyst was a disgrace to all that Shearson stood for and a disgrace to the respected profession of stock analysis. He went on to say that he told FCA's senior management not to discuss the company's affairs with Shearson researchers and had asked First Charter executives to break off their contact as well. Knapp's letter was followed by a threatening letter from FCA's lawyer.

The earnings restatement brought on by the SEC in April troubled First Charter's directors as well as Ernie Leff, who thought the difficulty with the SEC could derail the deal. At the very least, the restatement could make it more difficult to get the Bank Board to approve the merger and could cause First Charter's board to pause for a second look.

Many other obstacles already stood in the way. On March 31, the shareholder lawsuits had been consolidated and amended, naming as defendants First Charter, FCA, Mark Taper, Charlie Knapp, and the directors of First Charter. The amended complaint alleged that FCA had followed aggressive lending, accounting, and business practices and that the company's shares were appropriate only for aggressive investors.

In addition, it said, the market price of FCA common stock was artificially inflated, while First Charter's was artificially depressed and undervalued. The suits further alleged that the price First Charter shareholders were to receive was far below the value of the company's assets and that the stockholders could get a much better price if only Mark Taper would run the company properly.

Besides court action, First Charter also faced the unpleasant prospect of a public hearing before the California Department of Corporations. California law at that time suggested that if one class of shareholders received cash while another got securities in a merger, the Corporations Department would have to study the transaction to make sure it was fair. An open hearing could have created a public forum for opponents.

The superintendent of banks and the state insurance commissioner had the power to rule on the fairness of these kinds of mergers in their industries, but the S&L commissioner did not. The two companies did the only logical thing and found a sympathetic state legislator to get the law changed so that the S&L commissioner soon had the same power as his fellow regulators. Larry Taggart, the California S&L commissioner, who later went into business with Knapp, found the deal fair.

The twist that nearly stopped the whole show came from an unlikely source: Mark Taper himself. As the price of FCA stock rose, the price First Charter's public shareholders would receive also increased, finally rising to more than $30 a share. Taper had called Knapp several times to renegotiate the price because the shareholders were getting more money. One of those calls occurred very shortly after Knapp heard that his son Alex had died in a car crash. Knapp accused Taper of being insensitive, trying to turn a personal tragedy to his advantage, and said he wanted nothing further to do with First Charter's chairman. But within a few days, Knapp calmed down, put his personal feelings aside, and proceeded with the merger.

Approval by the Bank Board remained the final hurdle. Guiding the merger application through the Bank Board took a lot of time, more than Leff had expected. He had heard that some thrift executives, particularly those in southern California who opposed the deal, were lobbying the regulators to thwart Knapp. Ed Gray, the Bank Board's new chairman, was a southern California alumnus with a long list of contacts. Time was working against the deal. The two companies had agreed to an automatic kill date of September 15. After that, either side could walk away or demand new terms. As the months dragged on, Leff began to think the bureaucrats in Washington just might let the merger suffer a slow death.

At six feet and 240 pounds, Jack Pullen was a formidable presence. Added to this was his willingness to confront anyone who failed to follow the rules. An S&L executive was wise not to run afoul of Jack Pullen.

In his day, Pullen was one of the most demanding regulators in the Bank Board system. With nearly twenty-five years of experience in the industry, he was a hard man to fool. He had started with the Federal Home Loan Bank of San Francisco back in 1957 and stayed until 1979 when he left to try his hand at managing thrifts. When Pullen came back to the Bank in early 1982, he carried a lot of respect.

But Pullen's day was rapidly becoming archaic as Congress and the Bank Board gave the industry new powers that made examining and supervising S&Ls increasingly more complicated. Not only was it more difficult to keep pace with the changing nature of thrifts, but the Bank Board didn't have the authority to hire new examiners at a time when states like California were rapidly chartering new institutions.

Like other examiners of his era, when S&Ls concentrated on passbook accounts and single-family home loans, Pullen was primarily trained to make sure that thrifts adhered to the thick body of strict regulations that governed their operations. But deregulation demanded a new outlook from examiners. Now they had to review a company's operations to ensure that thrifts weren't using their new powers to take unnecessary risks with federally insured funds. The early days of deregulation proved a difficult transition period for Pullen and hundreds of other Bank Board examiners.

As the supervisory agent for the Federal Home Loan Bank in San Francisco, Jack Pullen got the job of studying the proposed merger between First Charter and FCA. James M. Cirona, the Home Loan Bank's president, had come on the job June 1. Cirona discussed the matter with Pullen but left the decision largely to his top supervisor.

On June 9, Pullen recommended that the merger of American Savings and State Savings be approved if the test appraisals and the examination under way at State did not yield any significant supervisory concerns. Three weeks later, on June 30, the district appraiser's review at State Savings revealed a projected loss of $11.8 million—not an alarming amount for a company of that size but enough to put the squeeze on profits. The appraiser said that with the revamping of State's appraisal staff and management's oral and written statements that operations would improve, fewer losses would occur in the future.

Pullen had been working with Wallace Associates, a Salt Lake consulting group hired by the Bank Board under Pratt, and with the regulatory staff in Washington. Both groups gave the merger their support.

On July 11, Pullen submitted a revised recommendation to the Bank Board in Washington that the merger be approved as long as certain constraints were placed on the combined institutions. Despite State's poor supervisory record, Pullen said the merger would have many beneficial effects and would reduce the agency's concerns about State's operations.

In the view of Pullen and other federal regulators involved in the merger, State Savings had serious deficiencies, while American Savings had good management and a strong balance sheet. Pullen went on to say that the merger would give State access to American's personnel and important financial controls, reduce the thrift's proportion of problem assets, dilute the importance of large uninsured CDs, and reduce the company's interest-rate risk.

However, Pullen wanted some restrictions placed on FCA that would safeguard the Bank Board and protect FSLIC (the federal S&L insurance fund) against State's aggressive actions. Among other things, he wanted the new American Savings to submit a highly detailed business plan and to provide the supervisory agent with periodic reports on the company's compliance with its plans. Pullen also wanted reports detailing cash-flow projections and the length to maturity of the company's assets and liabilities, which provides a measure of vulnerability to swings in interest rates.

Just three weeks after Pullen's recommendation, an examination of State that had begun on May 16 was completed. On August 3, State once again received the government's lowest composite rating, 4. Despite the repeated poor ratings, FCA would receive some exciting news from Washington the next day, some very exciting news indeed.

Ed Gray had been chairman of the Bank Board, succeeding Dick Pratt, for just ninety-five days, and already his tenure as the chief S&L regulator was about to be clouded in controversy. He was on the verge of making a decision that would come to haunt the thrift industry for the next five years.

Although he had put in his time as a senior executive at a large S&L, he had never actually run a company, let alone a sprawling federal agency charged with supervising more than three thousand companies nationwide. Aides would come to complain about his poor administrative skills and his crowded travel schedule.

A paunchy man who chain-smoked and wore horn-rimmed glasses, Gray followed an unusual route in his journey to Washington. A native of Modesto, California, Gray had been a radio reporter for station KMJ in Fresno in the late 1950s. In the early 1960s, he was United Press International's bureau chief in Madrid. In the mid-1960s, he crossed over from journalism to public relations, becoming a publicist for Pacific Telephone. Gray saw Ronald Reagan in action during the former actor's 1966 campaign for governor of California and worked as press secretary for the committee planning the inauguration.

Gray became Reagan's assistant press secretary in 1967 and was elevated to press secretary in 1972, two years before Reagan left the governor's mansion in Sacramento. He learned the S&L business at San Diego Federal Savings and Loan Association, where he worked from 1973 until 1981. He worked with San Diego Federal's Gordon R. Luce, who was considered one of the best marketing men in the business. Shortly after Reagan became president, Gray went to Washington to work on the White House transition team and then returned to San Diego.

The California property-tax revolt of the late 1970s swept Gray in its path, and he served two years as chairman of the San Diego Taxpayers Association. The experience left him with the belief that taxpayer funds should not be used to pay for a bailout of the thrift industry. Although he had personally lobbied Congress for the passage of Garn–St. Germain, Gray would soon begin warning that taxpayers might have to pick up the tab for the industry's follies.

One of his closest allies in the Reagan administration was Ed Meese, the attorney general later forced out of office by scandal. Meese and Gray had known each other since they both worked for Reagan in Sacramento. Meese and Gray's old thrift, Great American, had a comfortable business arrangement as well. Great American loaned Meese $120,000 for a home in California in the late 1970s according to the book *Inside Job*, which cited testimony given at Meese's confirmation hearings. Meese turned to Great American for a subsequent loan of $132,000, which helped him purchase a home in Virginia in 1981. Combined payments on both homes totaled $51,000 a year, leaving Meese strapped for cash since he made only about $70,000 a year as attorney general. But he did not have to worry about foreclosure. In fact, he skipped making the mortgage payments for fifteen months. During that period, Great American granted an additional loan of $21,000, secured by a fourth deed of trust on Meese's California home.

Gray wasn't the only Great American official to get a nice slot in the Reagan administration, again according to *Inside Job*. Gordon Luce, the thrift's president, landed a spot as a delegate to the United Nations. Meese said the appointments were not related to the loans from Great American and the patience the company had shown with his extremely delinquent payments, delays that would have cost most customers their homes.

Despite Gray's skimpy credentials for heading the thrift regulatory agency and his seeming preoccupation with the thrill of travel, the new Bank Board chairman showed good instincts. He questioned the wisdom of allowing a sound and respected company like American Savings to fall into the hands of a fast-moving, smooth-talking operator like Charlie Knapp.

But Gray said he didn't think he could follow his gut feeling. He had received Pullen's report and a recommendation from key staff members that he approve the merger. In addition, he had a copy of the report by Wallace Associates, the Salt Lake consulting group.

Gray thought these recommendations and reports made a combination of State and American sound like a merger made in heaven. American had more than a hundred branches in California, strong management, tight financial controls, and a dependence on retail customers for deposits. State Savings depended almost exclusively on large uninsured deposits for its source of funds, had grown by several billion dollars so far this year, and lacked key controls in its operations. In language similar to Pullen's, the Wallace report said a combination of the two companies would result in a stronger institution with a large branch network, a better balance of retail and wholesale funds, and improved management.

What seems to have received scant attention was the issue of capital. Knapp's payment of cash to the Taper interests was taking that much capital out of the system. In turn, Knapp, the brilliant financier, was essentially replacing that money with an accounting entry known as goodwill, something that was not allowed in the more conservative banking industry.

At a Bank Board meeting on August 4, one day after State received a dismal composite rating of 4 for the third time in the last fourteen months, Ed Gray considered the recommendations he had received. His fellow board members—Don Hovde, who had joined the board just seven weeks before, and Jamie Jackson, the veteran of the group—wanted to see the merger go through. As the board members debated the transaction, Hovde in particular seemed to favor it.

Gray remained skeptical. He had never met Charlie Knapp, but he had heard rumors about FCA's maverick business practices. Still, Gray believed he had no legal justification for blocking the deal. If the Bank Board rejected the merger application and was taken to court, he could hardly cite "gut instinct" as his guiding force.

Thus, despite the State examination reports, which seemed to contradict the reasons favoring the merger, Gray and his colleagues decided to approve the merger, thus creating the largest S&L in the country. Because of State's continued growth, the combined institution would have some $20 billion in assets.

The Bank Board did, however, tack on some conditions designed to safeguard the system by slowing FCA's growth. Some of the restrictions were similar to those proposed by Pullen. They included a requirement that State Savings maintain net worth of 4 percent, one percentage point higher than the rest of the industry: For every $100 million in deposits, FCA would have to have $4 million in capital, $1 million more than other S&Ls. With all these constraints, Gray thought the federal insurance fund would be protected from Charlie Knapp's risky ventures.

The next day, Ernie Leff went to FCA's headquarters with Mark Taper to sign all the legal documents that would conclude the merger. Once the papers were signed, the participants milled about, waiting for the delivery of the checks. A deal now worth more than $915 million would conclude in less than two hours.

Just then the telephone rang. It was for Ernie Leff. Brad Clark talked fast. He sounded anxious. "You've got to stop the closing," Clark said.

"It's a little late for that now, Brad. Why would you want to stop it?"

"State Savings and FCA are not healthy. There's a lot of problems there. State Savings has got a lot of bad loans. We can't let this thing go through."

"I don't think we have much choice."

"I'd like to call a meeting of the board," Clark continued. "I am prepared to come down right now and hold the meeting."

Leff knew of a California law that allowed the board of directors of a public corporation to prevent a merger already approved by the shareholders. Although Clark hadn't cited the statute, Leff presumed he had the law in mind. But he wasn't about to accept Clark's view of the transaction, especially now that it had cleared the Bank Board. Clark wanted to stop the party just as the champagne corks were about to pop.

"I don't know how I could stop it now," he said. "The papers have already been signed. We're just waiting for the checks to come down."

"It's a mistake," Brad Clark said. "This deal is a mistake. Are you sure you can't stop it?"

"It's too late for that now, Brad."

Leff hung up the phone and went back to the closing ceremony. Charlie Knapp brought champagne to celebrate the deal. Taper received his check and handed it to a Bank of America representative who had been standing by, so that Taper's money could begin earning interest immediately.

After he got his check, Taper shook hands with Leff and simply said, "Thank you." And with that, Sydney Mark Taper, the legend of the S&L industry, a man respected by his competitors and feared by his subordinates, turned his back on American Savings. It was Charlie Knapp's company now. He could run it as he saw fit.

The ink had hardly dried on the merger papers when FCA's management ran into trouble with the Bank Board again. Just one week after the merger's approval, the Bank's Board legal division recommended a tough and rigorous examination of old State's operations. State had ceased to exist, since after last week's merger, the surviving thrift was now called American Savings.

Technically referred to as a 407(m)(2) investigation, this special inquiry, if approved by the Bank Board, gave the staff members the power to subpoena witnesses and take testimony under oath, the strongest investigative powers at the agency's disposal. Such a recommendation from the Bank Board's office of the general counsel indicated that the agency's lawyers had serious concerns about how the company conducted its affairs. It seems clear that the recommendation from the legal division was winding its way through the bureaucracy even as Ed Gray and the other Bank Board members were preparing to give the merger their approval.

To justify the investigation, the Bank Board's lawyers listed their apprehension about the thrift's ongoing business transactions with people who were affiliated with the company. They also wanted to look into allegations that important company records had been falsified, to see how State had disposed of problem loans and real estate, and to delve into the SEC investigation that forced the company to write down $9.5 million in 1982. The lawyers also wanted to examine old State's complicated and controversial "buy-sell" program, in which State would refuse to loan money to one developer and instead buy the property he wanted to develop, only to sell it quickly at an enormous profit to a second developer and then write a much larger loan.

On September 7, officials of the San Francisco Federal Home Loan Bank recommended in a memo to Washington that the Bank Board's legal staff cancel the special investigation saying some aspects of the company needed further scrutiny, but this could be handled through the normal examination process. So the special investigation never began. Once again, Charlie Knapp's S&L stayed one step ahead of the regulators.

Chapter 5

The Enemy in Our Midst

Jonathan Gray shook his head in disbelief. The long document before him detailed extensive problems at FCA. He had followed the company for years and had heard rumors about bad loans on FCA's books. But anecdotal information fell far short of solid evidence, and as one of Wall Street's top securities analysts, Gray liked to base his investment decisions on a rigorous examination of the facts.

When Gray first became acquainted with FCA, he saw it as a bold and exciting company with a tremendous profit potential, despite its heavy speculation on interest rates. Based on his research, his firm, Sanford C. Bernstein & Co., had recommended FCA stock, and Gray had purchased some for his own investment portfolio.

Now, however, as he read FCA's proxy statement and prospectus in May 1983, Gray had grave doubts about the quality of that investment. The proxy material, submitted as part of FCA's merger, revealed that the SEC thought FCA had some $425 million in bad loans. That troubled Gray. He didn't want to get bogged down in the dispute between the SEC and the company over accounting treatment. But if FCA reported record earnings when it in fact had substantial loan losses, he'd better find out exactly what was going on.

If FCA had $425 million in bad loans as the SEC alleged, the company was almost certain to suffer a substantial decline in profits. That would lower the earnings-per-share of FCA stock, which would in turn drive down the stock price, meaning that investors like Gray and Bernstein's customers could lose money on FCA stock. There was always the possibility that additional bad loans might be disclosed, which would further retard earnings.

With such a substantial sum in question, Gray wasn't content to ask Knapp and his management team a few questions over the phone. He had too many nagging doubts, and over the years he had learned to trust his instincts. Indeed, he had the skepticism and persistence of an investigative reporter. For the past several years in a row, he had been voted an "All American" analyst by *Institutional Investor* magazine—to financial analysis what a Pulitzer Prize is to journalism.

In November, Gray flew out to Los Angeles to meet with Charlie Knapp before going to Stockton to see key executives at American Savings. Knapp was so keyed up, he practically bounced off the walls as he spoke with the wiry, curly-headed analyst. He started singing a dirty song, an old off-color sea chantey. When his secretary arrived with coffee, Knapp referred to her as his Nazi, meaning that she was well organized and efficient.

"Isn't this funny?" Knapp said. "Here I am being interviewed by Jonathan Gray, and I'm singing dirty songs. But let's get down to business. What would you like to talk about?"

"I'm really out here to understand the company," Gray said. "That's my purpose. This is a very controversial company. I don't have any negative or positive bias. I hope I find that everything is fine with the company.

"I didn't come out here to find out that you are a bad guy or that the company is fatally flawed. I've come to write an objective report, Charlie. That's all I'm here to do. I'm going to go back and objectively study the information and publish my conclusions, positive or negative."

As Gray took notes, Knapp explained his game plan for American Savings. He would continue to expand the company, despite the high-interest-rate environment. American Savings had the ability to gather vast sums of deposits, and he would put them to profitable use. By increasing the company's ability to originate loans, he would book mortgages now and sell them later. If FCA rapidly turned its assets over, the company could avoid the imbalances created when an S&L borrowed short from depositors and loaned long to homeowners. Fees charged for making loans would account for a sizable proportion of profits, as would the development of real estate. It all sounded like a chief executive's typical boilerplate language. What Gray was after was information about the loan losses.

If Knapp and his senior managers had something to hide, they didn't show it. They politely cooperated with Gray. After all, he was a respected analyst whose reports on the company could have a dramatic effect on FCA's stock price, to which Charlie Knapp was extremely devoted. By giving Gray highly detailed information, Knapp and his managers could explain FCA's philosophy and accounting procedures. Perhaps Gray would write a favorable report. Besides, Knapp believed the company had already dealt with the bad loans by selling them.

Knapp arranged to have Gray flown to Stockton on a company jet to meet with Foster Fluetsch and other members of the top-management team at American Savings. As he climbed into the Learjet, Gray was as excited as a little boy. The plane took off much more rapidly than a commercial jetliner. The cabin was like the inside of an exotic sports car. It even had a phone. Gray picked up the phone and dialed his sister Esther, a model and actress in New York. He wanted to be able to say, "Hi, Esther, I'm calling you from a Learjet," but she wasn't home. Jonathan Gray knew he was being stroked by FCA's shrewd chief executive, but he couldn't help but have a little fun. Jetting across California was certainly more glamorous than sitting in a stuffy office in wintry New York crunching a computer.

When he arrived at FCA's Stockton headquarters, he was led to the president, who had one of the loveliest offices Gray had ever seen. It looked like a hunting lodge for Howard Hughes. The room had high ceilings and was decorated with rich wood paneling. A stuffed deer head peered down from a sloping English fireplace.

When Gray expressed admiration for a print of an eagle swooping over the water with a freshly caught fish in its talons, Art Shingler, one of Knapp's senior managers, asked, "You want it? I'll send it to you."

"No, no. I can't accept it. It would not be appropriate for me to accept a gift from the company."

"Are you sure? There'd be no problem sending it to you."

"We're not supposed to accept any gifts. I can't have even

the appearance that I accepted something that might influence me."

He didn't think Shingler was trying to bribe him. He was merely being generous. In fact, Shingler impressed Gray. What Gray liked most about him was his ability to crystallize a complex subject with many nuances and explain it all precisely. Shingler could explain the company's loan-sales program from a financial and accounting standpoint, and pull it all together in a way that made sense. He was like a botanist who could explain every leaf of a plant—the roots, the veins, and how the whole plant was part of a much larger order. Later, Gray would become convinced that Shingler intentionally deceived him, because if Shingler was able to give such a good analysis of the company, he had to know exactly what was going on and then cover it up. Shingler, who was the executive vice president for operations, said he took his reputation seriously and would not have damaged it by providing false information. He said he always related the facts as he knew them at the time.

As Shingler pointed out to Gray, FCA wanted to avoid the cost of owning, managing, and selling property that had been foreclosed because of delinquent loans. Instead, the company offered foreclosed property and delinquent loans to real-estate syndicators and other investors at prices that would bring speedy sales. To facilitate the transactions, the company also provided loans to the buyers, securing these with mortgages on properties the investors already owned. The company had accounted for them as sales on the installment method. Since the SEC had disagreed with FCA's accounting procedures, the company complied with the agency's wishes and did not list these as sales but as assets subject to sale.

If Shingler was the academic, Foster Fluetsch was the charmer. A friendly man by nature, Fluetsch was the kind of executive who believed work should be fun, and he liked to think of his employees as an extension of his family. In the old days, when State had been just another small S&L, Fluetsch used to have the employees out to his home for a barbecue. He would sponsor Easter-egg hunts in which the workers searched not for colored eggs but for miniature booze bottles used on airlines. He liked to rule through love, not fear.*

Gray said he needed access to the key data in the S&L's computer, and Fluetsch asked the analyst what he hoped to accomplish.

"I believe I will be able to gain some insight into whether you are making good loans or bad loans," Gray explained. "That's really the issue here. I want to know not how many bad loans you have but when they were originally produced. I will be able to project your ultimate underwriting experience."

Fluetsch complied with Gray's wishes, giving Gray access to volumes of data on loan originations and purchases, foreclosures, delinquencies, slow loans, fee income, and assets, broken down by several different categories, such as residential and commercial construction. Gray had precise information covering several years of the company's operations.

What Fluetsch failed to mention, however, was that he had already come to believe the company was getting out of control, growing much too quickly. Indeed, he had recently led an unsuccessful management revolt in which Knapp upbraided his executives for their lack of fortitude.

Although he was concerned about the S&L's loan losses, Gray took some solace from the company's history. When he controlled American Savings, Mark Taper had tight underwriting standards. His company was known for its high-quality loans. If FCA's former State Savings had bad loans left from before the merger, these could be offset to some extent by this "Taper paper," which could be sold quickly to cover a cash crunch brought about by rising interest rates. This was important since FCA had made one of the most aggressive bets on a decline in interest rates of any major U.S. financial institution.

Having accomplished his objective in Stockton, Gray flew back to Los Angeles and had dinner with Knapp and several

---

*Among other things, Foster Fluetsch fostered flatulence. He had two stakes in his yard that he referred to as "farting posts." At one, an employee who released a long sonorous burst received $150. At the other post, employees were paid $100 if they passed their gas silently. The name Blazing Saddles for the jet partnerships referred to the scene in the Mel Brooks movie in which a group of cowboys amuse themselves around the campfire after filling up on beans.

business associates. Gray can't recall the name of the restaurant, but it was one of the glitzy places in the west end of town. What Gray recalls quite clearly is that Knapp complained about the treatment FCA had received in the *Wall Street Journal.* John Andrew, a reporter in the Los Angeles bureau, had written a number of hard-hitting stories the previous summer after the SEC had forced the company to restate its earnings.

"Maybe we should get someone to break his legs," Knapp said.

Gray thought he was kidding, but the comment startled him nonetheless. That just wasn't the kind of thing the chief executive officer of a major American company said in front of a securities analyst. But Gray let it pass. When dinner broke up, he and Knapp were still on friendly terms.

But the relationship quickly degenerated into open antagonism when, seven weeks later on December 28, Gray published his report. It was a 150-page bombshell that painted a portrait of a financial institution with a huge crater in its loan portfolio. In fact, Gray had to check his math several times before releasing the report because he couldn't believe the scope of the difficulties at FCA. It was frightening.

According to his calculations, the longer loans had been in the portfolio, the worse they appeared to be. Problem loans produced in 1982 represented 5.4 percent of assets, but the proportion rose to 13.6 percent for 1981 loans and 18.8 percent for loans made in 1980. Gray thought the ultimate loss could approach 30 percent. As a rule, a problem-loan ratio of 20 percent is devastating; for every $100 millionin loans, American Savings would have $20 million in problem assets, money the company might never see again; problem loans eat up capital. If Gray's projection was true, the bad loans would devour American's capital in a hurry.

Gray pointed out that the company appeared to have improved its lending record. But American Savings had doubled its loan portfolio to $9.7 billion in the first nine months of 1983, not counting the First Charter acquisition. The analyst observed that there was no guarantee the recent improvement in loan underwriting would continue, adding that it might take a year or more to see how many of the new loans would go into default.

If interest rates declined in 1984, as Gray had predicted, FCA stood to make enormous profits. The company's operating earnings would rise because of increased demand for loans and because it could sell its assets in the secondary market at a premium. Gains on loan sales would act as a cushion against potential loan losses.

However, should rates rise quickly, FCA could experience an increase in problem assets and be unable to sell enough loans to offset the drag on earnings. At the same time, earnings from normal operations would get squeezed. Therefore, Gray concluded, FCA was a "double leveraged" speculation on a decline in interest rates. Investors should buy the stock only if they thought interest rates would fall. Otherwise, steer clear of FCA.

Jonathan Gray was proud of his report. He knew he had been thorough. He thought he had been fair. Gray's report certainly was controversial as far as the company was concerned, but he hoped Charlie Knapp would respect his conclusions.

Despite the time he devoted to the study and the in-depth nature of his report, Gray saw only a snapshot of the problems developing at FCA. Indeed, the federal regulators believed the strengths of Mark Taper's American Savings would overcome the weakness at Knapp's State Savings. In reality, the reverse was true. As it continued to pay high interest rates on deposits, American Savings put the money to use obtaining assets of questionable value, but that allowed the company to continue reporting new growth and higher earnings.

As he pyramided his way to success, Knapp was sowing the seeds of his own demise. Sloppy management and poor investment decisions made to further the company's growth plan almost guaranteed a serious decline. Eventually these weaknesses would catch up with him. Although it is almost axiomatic in business that sustained rapid expansion is a self-destructive game plan, growth was FCA's guiding light and would remain so as long as Charlie Knapp was in charge.

Neither Jonathan Gray nor the SEC's investigators could detect the harm lurking at FCA, for no other institution had been built to such an extent on systematic and virulent deception.

As one financial analyst who crossed swords with Knapp put

it, "Southern California is full of good con men. Charlie Knapp just happened to be the best."

Indeed, he and his managers were beguiling in the diabolic methods they employed as they stretched FCA's influence in the financial system. But like a superpower suffering from strategic overexpansion, Financial Corp. was weak at the core. Even worse, Knapp was a menace as a leader, for as the company expanded, his policies consistently weakened the company's foundation.

Knapp had a simple plan. He was transforming FCA into a financial powerhouse capable of large and daring mergers. With his intricate knowledge of finance, he was quick to make a great intuitive leap: If you played your cards right, you could take a sleepy little S&L in a farm town like Stockton and conquer the world. The former investment banker saw all too clearly that the new game in corporate America was takeovers, and the key ingredient was either leveraged buyouts (LBOs) or stock swaps. LBOs were out since they don't work at financial institutions as they do with manufacturing or related concerns. That left stock swaps.

In order to conduct stock swaps, a company's shares had to command a sizable price in the marketplace. And that meant developing not only high profits but economies of scale. To get economies of scale that would support enough earnings to lead to high stock prices, the company had to grow. Thus was hatched a plan to make FCA bigger and bigger every year.

Unfortunately for the nation's taxpayers, growth entailed not only risk but a culture at FCA that rewarded disregard for rules and regulations, self-deceptions, misinformation, extremely aggressive interpretation of accounting procedures, and a total disregard for prudent management. Knapp was far too clever a man to make crazy loans on cocktail napkins. No, if he was to grow, he had to have an infrastructure in place that could get hundreds of millions of new assets in the doors each month and make FCA's stock soar.

Hundreds of millions of loans were granted each month, not despite their poor quality but because of it, for these shaky assets carried high nominal returns. This strategy could be implemented by hiding the nature of the loans, loaning customers the money they needed to repay the loans, accepting overly generous property appraisals, and forcing other borrowers to take bad credits off the company's hands until the heat was off.

At this point, Knapp's personal life began to cloud the picture. Following the death of his son Alex, Knapp was increasingly driven, frustrated, and confrontational, according to Fluetsch. As Fluetsch explained it, FCA grew rapidly in the months between the merger's announcement and consummation because Knapp didn't want to be the "poor cousin" to Taper's larger company. After the merger, there was no stopping Charlie Knapp.

Fluetsch also said that Knapp had little understanding of or respect for the elaborate regulations governing S&Ls. Shingler had been told to "push the envelope"—an old test pilot's term for derring-do—to their legal limits. With Knapp as the guiding force and star salesman; with Shingler, the pontifical son of a car salesman, pushing the financial buttons; and with jolly Foster Fleutsch's unmatched skill at closing a loan, FCA romped through the financial community. In so doing, however, the company was laden with hidden time bombs, traps that would take new management years to uncover.

At times, Art Shingler thought Charlie Knapp was a certified genius. He just wanted to slow the hard-charging chairman down a little bit. American Savings had just gone through the trauma of a complicated merger, and it was bulging at the seams.

Most corporations would take a breathing spell, get all the financial and computer systems consolidated, and make sure the employees understood their new roles in the combined enterprise. Not Charlie Knapp. He was already hungry for new challenges.

With his expertise in finance, Shingler had seen firsthand the adverse impact FCA's growth had on its capital base. Much of its need for capital had been solved with the merger. Now that he had absorbed Taper's company—and its capital—Knapp wanted to continue his old game plan. He wanted to grow several billion dollars by taking the large deposits the salesmen were gathering and using them to book new loans and/or purchase them from other institutions. Art Shingler didn't think American Savings or FCA could handle the additional strain.

He couldn't fault Knapp's logic, though. From his own studies of the U.S. financial system, Shingler thought the best time to make mortgage loans was when interest rates were high. That way, the company booked loans with big yields. Unfortunately, most financial institutions experienced a cash crunch when rates rose and couldn't make a lot of loans, partly because demand declined. Charlie Knapp found the solution. By hiring his own deposit salesmen to tap large investors, he assured himself constant access to deposits that he could use to make loans with exceptional returns.

Knapp focused on "strategic profits," obtaining assets in adverse economic conditions that could be sold at enormous profits when good times returned. Art Shingler had the job of making sure American Savings made it through the rough weather in one piece. At about the time Gray was finishing his scathing report on American's loan problems, Shingler prepared to suggest that FCA adopt a new and simpler growth strategy.

The son of a Chevrolet dealer in Pasadena, Shingler was born in south Georgia, just nine miles from the Florida border, and still had a trace of a soft southern accent. A tall, easygoing man, Shingler also had the earnest air he had acquired as a student at Nazarene schools.

He had arrived at FCA almost by accident. When he was off hunting elk in Colorado in late 1979, his wife learned of an ad in the *Wall Street Journal* about an S&L looking for a chief financial officer. Shingler seemed more than qualified for the job. He was the chief financial officer at Central Federal Savings in San Diego, had been an investment officer at Denver-based Western Empire Financial, had worked for several years as an auditor for Peat Marwick Mitchell (a Big Eight accounting firm), and had a master's degree in finance from the University of Southern California. His wife signed his name to a letter and sent in Shingler's résumé.

After half a dozen interviews with Charlie Knapp, Foster Fluetsch, and other senior executives at old State Savings, Shingler got the job and started in January 1980. Like a rickety hot rod driven too hard for too long, State Savings had a lot of mechanical problems when Art Shingler came on the scene. Not one of the S&L's branches could reconcile its books. Monthly financial statements came out late and then contained countless flaws. In an industry that prided itself on harnessing the computer, employees at State Savings still calculated some interest charges and fee disbursements by hand. Although he made many improvements, such as getting the accounts to reconcile at the branches, Shingler felt he never had the time to catch up. He was always solving problems on the fly. And in fact, the company's back-shop operations continued to degenerate, getting worse as the company's growth accelerated, the result of sloppiness throughout the management ranks.

Shortly after the merger was completed, Shingler figured FCA was bound to blow a gasket someday. There had to be a simpler way to add new assets that didn't stretch the company's technical abilities to their limits. In the fall and early winter of 1983, Shingler talked with a southern California financial consultant about trading mortgage-backed securities. He claims he also spoke at length with Arthur Anderson, FCA's auditors, about his concept and how the company would account for the trades. He said the accountants signed off on the plan.

At a high-level management meeting in early 1984 at FCA's Los Angeles headquarters, Shingler made his pitch. The strategy sounded complicated but actually was quite simple. As Shingler envisioned it, FCA would grow by acquiring mortgage-backed securities issued by the Government National Mortgage Association, a quasi-federal agency that purchased loans from lenders, pooled the paper, and sold it in the secondary market. In late 1983 and early 1984, these "Ginnie Mae" securities sold at a mere fraction of a point less than American Savings could get on its loans. Loans always carried the risk of default, but Ginnie Mae securities were gilt-edged paper actively traded on Wall Street.

Ron Struck, a senior FCA executive, had been abreast of Shingler's plan and told him it "sounded risky as hell." When Shingler explained he had discussed the subject with FCA's accountants at length, Struck said he told Shingler that "you better get a second opinion" because in all likelihood he or they were dead wrong.*

---

*Shingler said he did not recall the conversation but added that Struck could very well have made those comments but he would have paid them no heed because he did not consider Struck a "player" within the organization.

Shingler thought buying the securities would allow the company to avoid the loan problems while satisfying Knapp's intense lust for growth. The fact was, even without the risk of default, loans booked at this stage of the company's history would pose an enormous burden on the system. Mortgages entailed a blizzard of paperwork that American Savings simply couldn't handle. Under the plan Shingler presented, growing quickly would require little more than a few phone calls and some bookkeeping entries in the computer. Shingler's pitch proved convincing. Knapp approved the plan. Yet the chairman caught Shingler unprepared. Knapp also wanted to continue lending.

After the meeting, FCA developed a securities-trading program with the forbidding title of Dollar Roll Reverse-Repurchase Agreements. It worked like this: American Savings would take some of its deposits and buy the Ginnie Mae securities. In turn, it would take the securities to a Wall Street broker-dealer and sell them with the agreement to buy them back a short time later. Essentially, FCA was borrowing from the broker-dealer and using its own securities as collateral. The difference between the price at which FCA sold the securities and bought them back represented interest on the borrowing.

The beauty of it was that the company could take the money it borrowed on its own securities and use that to buy additional Ginnie Maes, thus pyramiding its way to an enormous portfolio. If rates fell, FCA would make a bundle because the price of Ginnie Maes would increase. There was another advantage. Unlike a brokerage house, an S&L would not have to mark the securities to the market value if rates rose against the firm. That way, the company would not have to show a loss on a poorly timed securities sale. Instead, the securities represented a borrowing, not a purchase and sale of securities, according to Shingler's research and the consultant with whom he spoke.

In reality, however, accountants differed widely on dollar-roll transactions. Some believed that if the securities the company sold and agreed to buy back were the same ones or "nearly identical," the transaction represented a borrowing. Others believed that if the pools of securities were "similar" but had different yields or principal amounts, the transaction was a sale and purchase. Accordingly, with a sale and purchase, an S&L might have to show gains or losses from the trades on its profit-

and-loss statement, which would affect its net income and earnings-per-share.

Art Shingler proved to be too aggressive for his own good. With Knapp's approval, he pushed the accounting rules to their limits, and this would be a fatal mistake. Fluetsch said neither he nor Knapp understood that the securities used in the dollar-roll program would be tied up and unavailable for use in a cash crunch such as a series of sudden withdrawals. In addition, the program bothered Cirona and other members of the Bank Board staff, who stepped up their scrutiny of the company as a result. But even worse, the SEC would have a great deal to say about the way the company accounted for these dollar rolls, raising questions that would cut to the core of the company. Art Shingler didn't know it then but would learn much to his horror that he had just helped FCA chart a disastrous course.

At first glance, Foster Fleutsch seemed like the kind of man you wouldn't want to anger. He stood six feet one inches, weighed 250 pounds, had black hair, a full beard, and an intimidating stare. His thick hands had a powerful threatening look. They looked like bone crushers. Actually, though, Foster Fluetsch was a sensitive, easygoing family man who put his hands to use making floral arrangements. He was an art lover who painted as a hobby and also raised large Japanese goldfish in a pond in the backyard of his million-dollar home.

A native of Merced, a small town in California's Central Valley, Fluetsch, the son of an insurance agent, began working in flower shops when he was in the fifth grade, a part-time job he kept through high school. Although he was a mediocre student with a C-minus average, Fluetsch somehow was accepted at Stanford University, where he enrolled shortly after turning 17.

Stanford did not have an undergraduate business program, so Fluetsch decided to major in economics to be prepared for the business world. With all those diagrams, calculations, and abstract concepts, the course work proved difficult. Fluetsch continued taking art courses until he finally decided to switch his major, picking up a minor in economics.

After college, he became a banker, working as a teller in Redwood City, a suburb of San Francisco. He joined State Savings in 1959 and returned to Merced. Fluetsch's winning personality helped him rise quickly through the ranks. In 1964, he moved to the main office in Stockton and became a senior loan officer. He was named a vice president in 1970, started a company day-care center in 1971, and became president in 1972.

At times, he could be tough. He once foreclosed on his own mother's mortgages. She had to pay her bills just like everyone else. In fact, he foreclosed on her rental property the weekend before Thanksgiving, which put a real damper on the holidays, but he couldn't afford to risk an accusation of favoritism.

He was the top man at the company during the time American zoomed to daring new heights and booked hundreds of millions in questionable loans. Although Charlie Knapp had become chairman in 1975, Fluetsch often thought of State Savings as his own company. Knapp was a classic delegator and relied on Fluetsch to handle the day-to-day operations. He built a loyal staff and was a popular business leader in Stockton, where the S&L was one of the largest employers.

Fluetsch would later say that he clearly made mistakes, that he failed to get his arms around all the loans and the shoddy paperwork, that he could have been a tougher manager and fired those who failed to perform. He acknowledged that there were a lot of bad loans. But he justified many of those loans by saying that the company had decided to stay in the lending market while financial institutions were turning their back on the real-estate market.

This avoids the obvious issue of competency. Other financial institutions choked off their lending because they couldn't make money. And many lenders said they would turn down a loan because of poor credit risk, only to hear that the borrower would get funding from State Savings. Bill Crawford, who later became California's S&L commissioner, was a competitor who said he refused projects that seemed ill-advised but were approved by State when Fluetsch was president. Tony Frank, whose company would later try to buy FCA, said it was common knowledge in the industry that State was making bad or improper loans. In response, Fluetsch said that American clearly made some bad loans but that there was no fraud at FCA. Mistakes, yes; fraud, no.

Although Knapp and Fluetsch worked well together, the two men began to differ in their vision of the company shortly after the merger between State and American. At a three-day retreat in September 1983 at a resort near Monterey Bay, American's senior managers decided it was time to curb the company's growth and concentrate on building capital.

Fluetsch said he presented the group's decision to Knapp at an executive-committee meeting in October. The FCA chairman lost his temper, attacked the group for its shortsightedness, and said essentially that those who did not believe in his philosophy should leave the company. Fluetsch resigned the next month. But Knapp talked him into staying, saying he would make him chairman of the S&L. Fluetsch became chairman, and Shingler replaced him as American's president on January 1, 1984. Despite the management change, American Savings failed to improve as FCA senior executives made decisions that hastened the company's decline and furthered their own financial well-being.

Charlie Knapp's ambition knew no boundaries. Not only had he risen from relative obscurity to create the largest S&L in the nation in just a few years, but he was now ready to move beyond his industry and had his eyes on a sexy financial company.

A new California law enabled Knapp to seek new conquests. On January 1, 1984, liberal legislation deregulating state-chartered S&Ls took effect. Called the Nolan Bill, this law was widely blamed for exacerbating the thrift crisis in California by allowing thrifts to invest in speculative ventures. Under the new law, California thrifts could invest up to 5 percent of their assets in the stock of other companies.

Knapp intended to take full advantage of the new legislation. He was going after American Express, the travel-services company with $39 billion in assets, 55,000 employees, and operations in 130 countries. Although a huge and glamorous enterprise, American Express could not escape the vagaries of fickle investors.

The stock market reacted strongly to news in late 1983 of financial difficulties at the company's Fireman's Fund subsidiary, one of the nation's largest insurance firms. Fireman's Fund had inadequate reserves for claims and also had low investment income. As a result, the subsidiary became a drain on American

Express, which had to build reserves at Fireman's Fund. Following the news, the price of American Express stock tumbled in the market, falling from a 1983 high of $49.50 to a low of $27.625 in early 1984.

Charlie Knapp saw the trouble at American Express as a rare opportunity, and in December he began buying a huge block of the company's stock. The investment made a lot of sense to Knapp, beyond the prospect of a quick killing; Knapp wanted to broaden FCA's investment base. That same month, he told financial analysts in New York that he wanted to invest in as many as sixteen financial-services companies, including such stellar insurance and brokerage firms as Cigna Corp., USF&G Corp., Aetna Life & Casualty Co., and Merrill, Lynch, Pierce, Fenner & Smith, Inc.

Knapp had told Jonathan Gray and some high-level FCA executives that he would like to take over Merrill Lynch, one of the largest brokerage houses in the country, in a leveraged buyout in which much of the company would be sold back to the managers at regional offices.

FCA also began buying stock in Walt Disney Productions, the movie and theme-park company, while Disney was embroiled in a bitter takeover battle. In January, Knapp continued buying American Express stock. His purchases heightened speculation that FCA's chairman hoped to acquire as much as 20 percent of American Express and that he wanted to engage in joint marketing efforts with the better-known company.

Although he said he intended to remain a passive investor and not seek a role in management, Knapp's investment made the senior managers and the directors at American Express uneasy. FCA purchased 10 million shares of American Express stock for $290 million. On January 16, Knapp signed an agreement not to purchase any more than 4.9 percent of American Express stock without its board's approval.

He had in fact intended to purchase up to 20 percent in the company because accounting rules would allow FCA to count as its own profits 20 percent of the earnings at American Express, money that could be used to make FCA even bigger.

That January was unusually cold in New York, but on the twenty-second floor of the General Motors building on Fifth

Avenue, the Bernstein & Co. conference room was blisteringly hot. Charlie Knapp was seated at a round conference table, fuming as though a solar flare had erupted from his personality. If Jonathan Gray had had a voltmeter, he could have measured the electricity in the air.

"Charlie, did you see the report?" Gray asked. "Whether you agree with it or not is one thing, but I hope you'll feel it was thoughtful, a well done job."

"Jonathan, I'll tell you what I think of your report," Knapp replied, looking Gray straight in the eye. Knapp then took a copy of the black-bound strategic analysis and like a graceful basketball player, gave it a hook shot over his head and into the garbage can behind him. "That's what I think of your report."

Gray's pulse quickened. "Look, Charlie," he said, trying to soothe the angry chairman, "if I were your doctor and you came to me for a checkup and I found a spot on your lung, I would try to convince you of the seriousness of the matter. You've got to get control of your loan quality. You've got to find out if these numbers are accurate."

"We don't have a loan problem. We've sold all our bad loans. We told you that. We explained that to you very carefully. You either didn't understand what we told you or you weren't listening."

"You haven't sold those loans, but whether you have or not, if you're writing all these bad loans, how can you have thirty percent of all your loans no good and only four percent capital? How can you survive with four dollars in capital for every hundred dollars in assets, and thirty dollars of every hundred dollars in loans you make are no good? How can you escape that?"

"We don't have that kind of a loan problem. I don't know where you got your figures. I don't know who you've been listening to, but this is totally ridiculous."

"This is an emergency, Charlie," Gray said. "There's no way you can survive that kind of underwriting experience. You've got to check it immediately, or it is going to do you in."

"How many times do I have to tell you that we don't have a loan problem," Knapp practically shouted. "You don't know what you're talking about, Jonathan."

"Charlie," Gray said, "if I were you, I would be shaking in my boots or shitting in my pants."

Gray was shaken. In all his years as an analyst, he had never had such an angry confrontation with the chief executive officer of a company he covered. But it would not be his last showdown with Knapp.

Several weeks later, Jonathan Gray walked into the lion's den at a banquet room of the Intercontinental Hotel. Following a presentation to the New York Society of Securities Analysts in February 1984, FCA sponsored a dinner attended by dozens of prominent investment bankers, financial analysts, and mutual-fund managers.

With Brooke Knapp, Charlie's attractive and vivacious wife, seated to his left and Charlie Knapp on his right, Gray began to feel uneasy. He didn't know if it was intentional, but he seemed to be getting the good-cop–bad-cop treatment from the Knapps, and he had little appetite for such behavior. Brooke was very sweet and friendly with him, while Charlie either ignored him or made slighting comments.

Later, Knapp said, "I want to toast Jonathan Gray, the enemy in our midst."

Gray decided not to spar with Charlie Knapp. Knapp denied making the toast, saying Gray's account was "stupid. I never said anything like that," Knapp continued. "I think he had an enemy mentality. He's an argumentative individual. He was one of the best analysts around. That would not be my style, and back then I was pretty arrogant." Gray would not rise to the occasion. He could make his points more effectively in other arenas.

Shortly after the dinner, Jonathan Gray began calling Bernstein clients and encouraging them to sell their FCA stock. He told them he was concerned about the quality of the company's loan portfolio. He also became a source for negative newspaper and magazine stories about troubles brewing at FCA. And Gray also talked with the SEC about some of his suspicions.

Knapp wanted Gray to keep quiet. Three weeks after the dinner for securities analysts, Knapp mailed a strong rebuke to Gray, marked "personal and confidential."*

---

*Knapp would later say he did not recall sending any such letter to Gray. However, a copy of the letter was obtained by the author.

Knapp told Gray that one of his greatest strategic mistakes in running FCA was to assume that Gray had an open enough mind to understand that American was not a traditional S&L. Believing Gray would understand FCA's unique nature, company officials provided the analyst with specific business plans and showed him the corporate book. As a result of his misunderstanding the true situation, Gray was doing significant damage to FCA, Knapp said, adding that the analyst's lack of insight had actually increased despite all the information he had received from the company.

Even in his critique of Gray, Knapp's sense of salesmanship shone through. He said that it was hard to argue with his company's record of performance, one he said would continue, and added that in time, perhaps even Jonathan Gray would come to understand the success that lay ahead for FCA.

Chapter 6

Too Big to Fail

When Ed Gray had started as head of the Bank Board in the spring of 1983, he still had that free-market optimism that marked so many members of the Reagan administration. Within a few months, however, he became convinced that the easy access S&Ls had to wholesale funds provided by professional money brokers could destroy an entire industry.

In August, he heard a briefing by staff members of the FSLIC, showing that a disproportionate number of defunct thrifts had raised funds from money brokers, many of them Wall Street firms that took large pools of funds from institutional investors and broke them down into $100,000 deposits, which were federally insured. The thrifts then squandered much of the money on bad assets, leaving the federal insurance fund to clean up the mess. Ed Gray may not have possessed the sharpest financial mind in America, but he quickly saw the potential hazard. With brokered funds, a small S&L could become a big time bomb overnight.

Limiting brokered deposits not only would have reduced the chances for excessive and imprudent growth at new S&Ls but would have limited competition. The limits would have served as a barrier to entry, thus protecting profits at established firms.

Although many observers have repeatedly blamed brokered deposits for much of the industry's debacle, especially the looting by fraudulent operators, in reality the hot money was merely a symptom of a deeper malaise. Deregulated interest rates were part of the real problem, and they underscored the eternal chase for profitable investments. The only way new thrifts could entice brokered money was to pay higher rates on deposits.

Congress and the regulators had deregulated thrifts in part to protect them against disintermediation, the transfer of money from thrifts and banks to funds that paid higher rates of return. That a correlation, no matter how strong, existed between busted thrifts and brokered money didn't prove the cause of the disaster. As long as thrift executives were free to pay whatever interest rates they chose to attract new federally insured money, trouble would always result, especially if thrift owners had to put up little of their own money to obtain or operate a franchise. Rather than limit competition from mutual funds, so as not to cheat the consumer out of a few percentage points of interest, Congress instead deregulated the savings industry—and very nearly destroyed it.

Deregulation was not the cause of the crisis but was rather a part of a much larger dynamic weakening America's financial system, directly linked to overexpansion and the mismanagement of the American economy in the postwar era prior to Paul Volcker, as a succession of political leaders sought to maintain the nation's superpower status. Thus, federal budget deficits ballooned as the nation's financial institutions withered, and these were not isolated incidents. In the meantime, foreign competitors, particularly the Japanese, strengthened their hold on the global financial arena. Deregulation was thus part of the much larger economic mismanagement that had begun decades earlier and continues today.

For its part, the brokered-money issue actually overshadowed the poor job the regulators were doing at identifying problem institutions and taking corrective action. S&L executives had every incentive to lie, cheat, steal, and exercise generally bad judgment. These institutions had been founded to pay small rates on passbook savings and write home loans. But in the new environment for banks and thrifts, growth was glorious. The lending market was increasingly competitive, with returns on home loans declining as interest rates rose. Years earlier, thrifts made money by taking interest-rate risks. They charged loan customers more than they paid savers and hoped the cost of funds wouldn't rise. With the spread between mortgage rates and deposits falling, thrifts turned to credit risks, that is, shaky loans. In the investment world, the higher the risk, the greater the potential reward.

Brokered deposits merely recognized the new reality of the financial-services industry. Rather than build new branches and hire workers, banks and thrifts could instead harness the telephone and the computer. The hot money signaled the failing of the deregulated system. With little capital in the company to absorb losses and check abuses, thrift executives could jack up rates, sell an insured product to investors, put the money in risky ventures, close their eyes, and hope for the best. If trouble ensued, they could always raise rates and attract new deposits. The regulators had only a few hundred poorly paid examiners in the field to spot problem institutions and only limited authority in correcting abuses and mistakes.

In fact, American Savings under Charlie Knapp plunged into a regulator's worst nightmare, a multibillion run, without having resorted to brokered money. Rather than cut brokers in on the riches at American, Knapp hired his own telephone sales force.

As Gray would soon learn, brokered funds were an efficient source of deposits in volatile economic times. High interest rates threatened to reduce or even eliminate a thrift's profits. By using brokered money, thrift executives, especially newcomers to the field, could at least cut their overhead for branches and labor. A company without a strong branch network had little incentive to install one. Branches cost millions for the real estate, equipment, and personnel.

Brokered funds were safe as long as thrift managers acted prudently and legally. As long as they were free to pay whatever interest rates they chose, thrift executives would have access to new deposits, whether brokered funds or not. They could always take a lesson from Charlie Knapp and turn to telephone sales.

Gray still believed in deregulation, but there had to be limits. With brokered money, S&Ls didn't really compete in the free market. They gambled with federally insured funds. If enough of them bungled the job or broke the law, the insurance fund might go out of the business of bailing out failed associations.

He made thwarting the use of brokered funds a major priority of his administration. Later that August, he forged an alliance with William Isaac, chairman of the FDIC, which provided deposit insurance for commercial banks, and in January 1984, the two men proposed low ceilings on deposit insurance for brokered funds at thrifts and banks. Wall Street quickly criticized the joint plan.

A federal court would later strike down the simplistic regulations the two men had proposed, but Ed Gray had found an issue behind which he put the full force of his strong personality. Like an evangelist warning of fire and brimstone at the end of a sinful life, Ed Gray made it sound as though brokered money were the root of evil in the S&L industry.

At a lawyers' seminar sponsored by the National Council of Savings Institutions on January 31, 1984, in Washington, Gray warned the audience that a day of reckoning was coming to the S&L industry. With what turned out to be uncanny foresight, he said money brokers could so undermine the S&L system that a taxpayer bailout might someday become necessary.

Brokered money was like "a spreading cancer on the federal deposit insurance system," Gray declared.

"Does it make any sense," he asked, "to expect these (relatively) tiny insurance funds to underwrite the vastness, the enormity of risk posed by such (deposit) growth in the future?

"In my view, allowing this to happen could either result ultimately in destroying the funds themselves, or by threatening to exhaust the resources of the insurance funds sooner or later, the situation would require substantial infusions of funds from the U.S. Treasury, and hence the nation's taxpayers."

But while Ed Gray was busy making speeches and proposing new regulations, Charlie Knapp was plunging ahead with his aggressive growth schedule, swelling FCA's size in no small measure because of his access to the wholesale market for funds. Gray was worried about S&Ls using brokered money, but Knapp's deposit salespeople proved far more efficient than even the largest Wall Street firms. After the FCA management meeting early in January, Knapp and his senior managers had decided to continue obtaining loans in bulk while buying the Ginnie Mae mortgage-backed bonds. Even before Gray and Isaac could get a proposal together, Knapp had outmaneuvered them by going directly to larger depositors.

Knapp's strategy provided strong evidence that limiting an S&L's use of uninsured or brokered funds to a set percentage of the company's assets would have been a better regulation. The Gray–Isaac plan was practically a ban on brokered funds, which seemed to raise important legal questions. However, limiting wholesale funds to 5 or 10 percent of total assets almost surely would have passed any legal challenge and would have stopped Charlie Knapp in his tracks.

In fact, the Bank Board had previously adopted a regulation limiting brokered funds to 5 percent of assets, but this was removed during the early halcyon days of deregulation. What was needed was a regulation that gave S&Ls flexibility in raising funds, especially if they needed to obtain money quickly for unexpected heavy withdrawals, but protected the public and the federal insurance fund from unsound and dishonest business practices. By the time the courts ruled on the Gray-Isaac plan, it would be too late. Charlie Knapp's American Savings would become so large so fast and so full of bad and questionable loans that it was beyond repair. But for the last several weeks, a quietly determined bureaucrat in San Francisco was working behind the scenes to restrain Charlie Knapp and contain the damage he could cause.

James M. Cirona was easily underestimated. Medium in height and build, he wore conservative suits and kept a low profile as he worked the long hours required by his demanding job. As the president of the San Francisco Federal Home Loan Bank, Cirona seemed content to stand in the shadow of a board of directors that included some of the most powerful S&L executives in the country, men like Herb Sandler of World Savings, Tony Frank of First Nationwide, Jim Montgomery of Great Western Financial, and Doug Clark of Glendale Federal.

Shy and reserved, Jim Cirona did not flaunt the considerable power at his disposal. Nonetheless, the man who ran the largest of the twelve district banks in the Bank Board system, making him arguably the second-ranking regulator in the system after Ed Gray, had a strong independent streak and spoke his mind.

The son of a Sicilian tailor who worked in Manhattan's garment district, Cirona had majored in economics at Cornell University, and after graduation, enlisted in the army (a popular lieutenant during his stint as head of a bread-baking unit, Cirona still wears a low-priced Bulova watch his men gave him as a farewell present). After the army, he took a job at Ithaca Savings and Loan Association in upstate New York because he figured he would end up running it some day. The company had only $10 million in assets and ten employees. Cirona learned every aspect of the business and did become president. Ithaca Savings grew steadily to about $55 million in assets, but with the industry's changing economics, Cirona could see the company probably would not survive on its own. He merged the firm with the much larger First Federal Savings in nearby Rochester, taking a job there as head of real-estate lending.

Cirona spent a lot of time traveling the country working on problem loans, which gave him hard-won insight into how bad assets can hobble a financial institution. His talent for leadership flourished, and he eventually became First Federal's chairman, president, and chief executive officer.

By June 1983 when he joined the San Francisco Federal Home Loan Bank, Cirona knew enough to be jolted by the applications piled high on his desk. They were from state-chartered S&Ls seeking federal insurance, and it was Cirona's duty to review them.

He picked up the first folder in the stack, did some quick calculations, and realized that by utilizing financial instruments and accounting rules allowed under state and federal regulations, a company with very little starting capital could end up with more than $100 million in assets within a year. The thrift could claim net worth of $1 million and through brokered funds could raise more than $100 million in deposits. It was an absurd level of leveraging, like starting a nuclear war with a pack of matches. Then the company could invest the money in real-estate developments, stocks, and junk bonds, areas where S&L managers had little expertise. Even worse for Cirona, Larry Taggart, then head of the state department of S&Ls, was giving the applications extremely quick approval. As the federal government's top man in California, Cirona wanted to put the brakes on state applications.

On this issue he found a sympathetic listener in Ed Gray. Cirona wanted to deny the new S&Ls federal insurance. So did Gray. Like Cirona, Gray was concerned about S&Ls growing too quickly without enough capital to protect the insurance fund if the companies later failed. Cirona and Gray thwarted federal insurance for the new thrifts, effectively preventing them from opening shop, even though they had obtained a charter from California's S&L's commissioner.

Charlie Knapp's shop soon came under Jim Cirona's watchful

eye. Cirona sensed trouble at American Savings within a few months of the merger. He had a number of concerns, covering a wide spectrum of American's operations.

At the top of the list was the business plan American Savings was supposed to submit to Cirona under conditions imposed by the Bank Board when FCA's merger was approved. Cirona wanted comprehensive information about the company's strategy—how it generated deposits, the rates it paid on deposits, its growth in assets, and the controls the board of directors had placed on management. Cirona's staff had been pressing company officials for the business plan and had had difficulty getting it. When the company finally filed the report a few months after the merger, it was a scant three pages that fell far short of providing the kind of precise details the examiners needed to track the company's health.

There were other disturbing trends. Despite the controls the Bank Board had placed on American Savings, the company's growth seemed out of control. By the end of 1983, FCA had more than $22 billion in assets. From 1975 to 1980, FCA averaged less than $200 million in new assets a year and through 1982, had never grown by more than $3 billion in a single year. Now, in the spring of 1984, FCA was adding more than $1 billion in new assets each month.

With his background in real estate and problem loans, Cirona also worried about the quality of American's new assets. Back in December 1983, American had received a supervisory letter from Cirona's staff, criticizing the company's underwriting procedures and the way it appraised real estate, and also questioning the level of slow and problem loans and lending commitments. These shortcomings were discovered in examinations separate from the problems Cirona saw in the business plans but pointed up the same issue of management largess.

There were questionable and improper business practices as well. In a highly unusual maneuver, FCA filed an application with the San Francisco bank in early March so that American could loan about $34 million to the holding company's employee stock-ownership plan (ESOP). The ESOP intended to use the money to purchase FCA common stock as part of Knapp's deliberate attempt to maintain a high price for his company's shares. FCA withdrew the application a week later and was warned that because the ESOP was an affiliate of the company, federal regulation prohibited the transaction.*

The ESOP deal showed the extent to which Knapp and his managers would go to avoid or undermine regulations when they stood in FCA's way. Under Knapp, FCA would report profits when losses had occurred, would fund loans that would almost certainly damage the company in the future, would resort to chicanery with borrowers, and would lie to the regulators. All of this ensured that the stockholders who believed the company's financial statements were headed for a rude surprise.

Cirona was also worried about the wildly speculative nature of the dollar-roll program at FCA, especially since interest rates started spiraling upward again in early 1984. The rate on three-month Treasury bills rose from 8.9 percent in January to 9.7 percent in April, which meant that FCA could be losing substantial sums on the securities in its portfolio.

But Cirona's hands were still tied by the regulations, and there was little he could do to stop Knapp, who had the advantage in their adversarial relationship. The rules and regulations were designed not only to safeguard depositors but to protect S&L managers against unreasonable or arbitrary actions by the regulators. For this reason, an S&L executive could stall for months, could pretend to be taking corrective measures, even as problems continued to escalate.

Indeed, this often happened at failed S&Ls and would crop up repeatedly as the industry's death toll rose in the 1980s. The regulators would warn an S&L's senior managers and board of directors to improve underwriting of loans, to increase the size of charge-offs for bad assets, to quit loaning so much money to a single borrower (often someone with ties to the company), or to stop squandering assets on such things as art collections. But in dozens of cases, like that of American Savings, the S&L's

---

*The ESOP later bought 2.3 million shares of FCA common, but FCA's managers assured the regulators that American had not financed the purchase. In fact, the company had devised a loan that evaded the rule. Financial Corp. formed a subsidiary called American Savings International, which was chartered in the Netherlands Antilles. The offshore subsidiary loaned the ESOP the money for the transaction, which also was prohibited under the Employee Retirement Income Security Act of 1974, which covers the funding and operation of most nongovernment pension and benefit plans.

health would decline rapidly as its managers or lawyers sought to convince the regulators that they had improved the situation or that nothing had been wrong in the first place.

In the case of American Savings, Cirona had little basis for obtaining a cease-and-desist order at this point. The merger had been approved only a few months earlier, and Knapp's team could claim that some of the deficiencies resulted from difficulties in bringing the two units together smoothly. That would buy them some additional time.

Nevertheless, Cirona wasn't going to sit by and watch Knapp take unbridled risks in his jurisdiction. He decided the moment was right for a little chat with Charlie Knapp, to let him know he was on the case. One evening that spring, Cirona and Pullen met Knapp for a two-hour dinner at a quiet restaurant in North Beach, San Francisco's popular Italian district.

As Knapp explained his plans for FCA, his view of the S&L industry, and the future of financial services, Cirona sized him up as a supersalesman given to hyperbole, a man with a global view who glossed over the critical details of his business.

"We've had a lot of trouble getting information from your company," Cirona said. "You gave us business plans that had only sketchy information."

"I admit we've been a little remiss," Knapp said. "But we're going to correct that."

"You were allowed to do that merger subject to certain conditions. You agreed to those conditions. And you are going to live up to them."

"You know, Jim, you're right. We've been given a great opportunity, and we aren't going to do anything to mess that up. We're going to get things straightened out. We're going to maintain our net worth. We aren't going to pay high rates on deposits. We're going to watch our lending."

The meeting ended with Knapp's strong assurances that he would address the regulator's concerns, but Cirona remained uneasy. There were simply too many problems at American Savings. They couldn't be corrected with glib promises. The nation's largest thrift was obviously in trouble. It was unraveling quickly, maybe too quickly to stop. Even if he could get a cease-and-desist order, it might already be too late. There were almost certainly heavy losses in the bond trading and in many of the loans on American's books, losses that could surface all at once and cause a run on the institution. Although Cirona didn't have the ammunition to prevent Knapp's reckless methods, he could at least be prepared for the worst.

Within weeks of his meeting with Knapp, Cirona instructed his staff to get ready for a liquidity crisis that could blow through the Federal Home Loan Bank like a hurricane. He feared that a run at American Savings could force the company to borrow heavily from his bank. Cirona had the bank's credit officers meet with American's senior managers to discuss their contingency plans. He arranged to have the San Francisco bank borrow from other district banks and got the staff ready to raise rates on deposits to attract funds from member thrifts.

Moreover, the San Francisco bank arranged to sell notes to obtain additional funds if those were needed. Cirona's staff also began meeting with John Balles and his senior team at the Federal Reserve Bank of San Francisco to see if FCA could borrow directly from the Fed. Jim Cirona wanted to be fully prepared for the debacle shaping up at American Savings.

While Cirona and other regulators were trying to restrain the nation's largest thrift, a rescue team of federal banking officials was desperately trying to save one of the nation's largest banks in an event that had a dark foreboding for American Savings.

A conflagration erupted at Continental Illinois Bank on May 9 when Asian investors wired for the return of their money. The Chicago-based bank that had once been hailed for its aggressive lending practices and fast-growth strategy lost $1 billion in deposits in what seemed like microseconds.

Despite the feverish efforts of federal regulators and other large banks to restore calm at Continental, the panic continued. To prevent the run from spreading to other large U.S. banks, the FDIC agreed to inject $4.5 billion in new capital at Continental. The largest run and the biggest banking bailout in history occurred in just eight days.

Under the government's bailout plan, the FDIC pumped in new capital and assumed an 80 percent ownership of the company. Not only had Continental Illinois paid high rates for CDs and collected billions in wholesale funds, but it used the money to buy $1 billion in loan participations from Penn Square and to loan at least another $1 billion to companies that later went broke.

Located in an Oklahoma shopping center, Penn Square had plowed billions into wildly speculative energy loans just before the depression in the oil patch. Many of those loans were sold to big-city banks like Continental Illinois and Seafirst Bank in Seattle, which was later bailed out by Bank of America. Penn Square was placed in receivership in July 1982, and Continental's senior managers maintained that the loans they bought from the shopping-center bank were good credits.

Although the situation was not yet that perilous, FCA also faced a loss of confidence. Investors were beginning to cool on the once-popular company.

For the first quarter of 1984, the corporation claimed net profits of $44.2 million, a dramatic 47 percent increase from the year before. But the high profits did little to lift FCA's sagging stock price. From a 52-week high of $32.75, FCA common had steadily declined to $15.75 by mid-May, even though the company's employee stock-ownership plan had recently purchased some 2.3 million shares improperly. FCA's stock was worth less in the market than its $18.36 a share in stated book value, or what the stock would be worth if the company was liquidated.*

Although net income soared, FCA earnings-per-share sank by some 30 percent, reflecting the greater number of shares circulating in the market because of the merger with First Charter. The higher earnings were more than offset by the greater number of shares circulating in the market. Lower earnings-per-share helped drive down the stock price. Investors had other concerns about the true value of the company's stock. Jonathan Gray continued urging Bernstein customers to sell FCA because of the severe loan problems at American Savings, and other analysts and money managers also worried about whether FCA was as healthy as it appeared on the surface.

These were only suspicions. Jonathan Gray's analysis, although thorough, uncovered only a portion of the problems piling up at American Savings. None of the federal regulators

*As the stock price fell, so did Charlie Knapp's personal net worth. At $32.75 a share, his FCA stock had been worth $47.8 million. On paper, he had lost nearly $25 million in just a few months.

in San Francisco or in Washington had a true picture of the company's weaknesses, which served to increase their concern. And perhaps no one at the company understood exactly what was going wrong. While conducting the bond trades and booking the new loans, the company had swelled by several billion dollars in just a few months. With so many loans coming in from around the country, not even American's top managers could keep track of the company's true financial condition. Boxes of loan documents were being flown in from around the country as FCA was busy trading mortgage-backed bonds on Wall Street, bonds that were declining in value even though the company was reporting profits.

Uncovering all the facts would be difficult. There was still no concrete evidence of the full scope of the inevitable losses. As much as anything else, what worried Jonathan Gray, Jim Cirona, and some Bank Board staff members in Washington was Charlie Knapp's attitude. Knapp was supposed to shore up FCA's weaknesses, improve the company's capital base, and slow the growth. He had done just the opposite and showed no signs of changing or even listening to the voices of caution.

Knapp remained optimistic and bucked the negative attitude affecting FCA's stock price. "I believe our shares are undervalued when you look at the long-term prospects," he told the *Wall Street Journal* in a story that appeared May 14.

The announcement came in conjunction with one proclaiming a bold plan to issue $225 million in debt and use the proceeds to purchase 25 percent of FCA's stock at discount prices. Undoubtedly the stock price would rise once FCA snapped up such a large block of its own shares.

Exchanging debt for stock had become a popular practice as companies took advantage of the U.S. tax structure. Dividends paid to investors were taxable since they represented corporate earnings, but interest on debt was a deductible expense. Under the plan, as interest rates rose, FCA's debt payments would fall at a time when S&Ls came under pressure from higher operating costs and lower loan volume. As interest rates fell and income rose, FCA's debt burden would rise at a time when it could better afford the expense.

Not only would the debt issue increase the company's stock price, but it would improve its net-worth position as well. American had stated net worth of about 3.5 percent, failing to meet the 4 percent level required by the government. Subordinated debt could be included in the calculation of net worth, so FCA could improve its capital base, come within federal guidelines, and shore up its stock price, all in one tidy package.

There was just one catch. Assuming that they had the authority to issue the debt, no one at FCA bothered to check with the Bank Board before launching the offering. But the Bank Board had a much different attitude about the new debt and told Knapp not to proceed until the regulators reviewed the proposed issue and approved the transaction. This also heightened concerns about FCA's health. The company needed to raise capital but was being blocked by the regulators, which meant that the company would not comply with its federal mandate. In the climate that had been created by the collapse of Continental Illinois, FCA was now being viewed with increasing skepticism by the regulators, analysts, and stockholders. And FCA's competitors kept up their criticism, suggesting that Knapp was heading for a nosedive.

To Preston Martin, the parallels between Continental Illinois and FCA were frightening. Both companies continued making risky loans at breakneck speed, despite repeated warnings by the regulators. And with its high proportion of hot money, American Savings was at least as vulnerable to a wire run as Continental, maybe even more susceptible. If a strongly capitalized commercial bank like Continental Illinois could go down, was there any hope of protecting a rickety thrift like American?

The Fed vice chairman had been watching FCA and Charlie Knapp for more than two years and had plenty of sources in the S&L industry. Martin was the former chairman of the Bank Board, had served as California's S&L commissioner, and before joining the Fed in 1982, had served as head of Sears Savings. While at Sears, he heard dozens of stories about FCA's unconventional business practices and its penchant for buying loans in bulk, loans that Martin figured most financial institutions would have avoided because of their poor quality.

A few weeks after the run at Continental, he could contain himself no longer. From his sources, including officials at the San Francisco Federal Reserve, Martin drew a picture of a company in serious distress, one that was short of capital and low on cash. He suspected that FCA had filed inaccurate financial reports, statements to make the company seem healthier than it was.

Although he wanted to see Knapp removed from FCA, as a practical matter, there was little the Fed could do since the central bank has direct jurisdiction over only commercial banks. Not only that, the experience with Continental had shown the difficulty of removing senior management at a troubled financial institution. Volcker himself had pressed for Anderson's ouster, but until close to the end, the board stood behind the embattled chairman. The Fed's strongest weapon against FCA was to threaten to prevent it from borrowing at the discount window if it needed emergency funds to cover huge withdrawals. That seemed unlikely, given the consequence of a run at a $30-billion thrift.

Nevertheless, in early June, Martin summoned Knapp to a meeting at the Fed in Washington. Martin and his aide Bill Taylor met Knapp in a second-floor conference room down the hall from where the Fed's board of governors convene to make policy decisions affecting the direction of the American economy.

"You can't proceed like this, Charlie," Martin said. "It's unsafe and unsound. You're growing too fast. You're funding the growth in a way that you can't sustain. You've got some questionable assets on your balance sheet. You're doing these reverse repos. It's going to catch up with you."

"I appreciate what you're saying," Knapp replied. "We can handle our loan problems. Our scheduled assets are manageable. Our reserves are adequate. You know as well as anyone that interest rates are historically high. When they come down, and they will, we'll make a lot of money on our loans and our securities."

"As the lender of last resort, the Fed has to be concerned about your safety and soundness," Martin said. "And frankly, I don't like what I see. Your financial position is weak. Your liquidity is especially weak. I'm worried about your liquidity. I have some real concerns about your financial statements."

"We have adequate reserves," Knapp countered. "We have a positive cash flow. We have outside auditors look at our books. We're a publicly held company. Our financial statements conform to generally accepted accounting principles."

For every point Martin raised, Knapp seemed to have a ready reply. Martin pressed on, hitting Knapp where he found him most vulnerable.

"Charlie, you're going out on an awful limb. Do you really want to stand behind these financial statements? Don't you think it's in the best interests of your stockholders to change your policies? You have a responsibility to those people."

When the meeting broke up half an hour later, Martin decided that jawboning alone wouldn't get the job done. He thought he'd better get some help from another federal agency that could put additional pressure on Knapp, so he made an appointment to see John Shad, chairman of the SEC, a couple of days later.

Martin went over FCA's balance sheet with Shad, telling the SEC chairman of his concerns about the company's net worth, the accuracy of its financial statements, and the accounting treatment used in its risky dollar-roll program. Shad and his key aides seemed receptive. They already had FCA's financial statements and were suspicious following the decision in 1983 to have the company restate its earnings. Martin wanted Knapp out of office, and now he thought he had a powerful ally.

At the same time, the Bank Board staff in Washington now had serious doubts about FCA's continued viability. The debentures that would be issued under Knapp's financing plan would double the company's outstanding debt and make it difficult for the firm to cover the interest payments. Eric Hemmel, head of the Bank Board's office of policy and economic research, whose job it was to review the application for the financing plan and make a recommendation to the Bank Board, took an especially dim view of the debentures.

Hemmel had been skeptical of the 1983 merger with First Charter. Then new to the Bank Board, he had no analysis to back up his feeling but was worried about Knapp's penchant for taking big risks. Hemmel feared that the merger would simply allow Knapp to double the size of his gamble. Knapp's continued growth and his dollar-roll bond trades confirmed Hemmel's suspicions that American was a dangerous institution. Before making a recommendation on the financing plan, he asked FCA officials to provide additional details, but these did not allay his concerns. On the contrary, the more he probed, the more it seemed to Hemmel that FCA was gravely ill and needed to be restrained for the good of the financial system.

At a June meeting in Washington, Knapp encountered sharp questions from the Bank Board staff. From the questions, it appeared the staff thought FCA was an extremely weak company that could fold.

"We're too big to fail," an exasperated Knapp declared. "If we go down, we'll take the whole system with us."

Some staff members thought Knapp was threatening them and became even more suspicious of FCA's instability. On June 12, Hemmel recommended that the Bank Board reject the application. He questioned FCA's ability to service the debt. Hemmel and the staff who worked for him based their analysis on two key points: The $225 million would put American Savings under pressure to pay additional dividends to the parent company, which could weaken American's net worth, and FCA's financial problems could eventually force American Savings into insolvency.

Couching his recommendation in bureaucratic lingo, Hemmel wrote, "In my own judgment, in light of the enormous losses American would face with a relatively modest up-tick in interest rates, additional pressure on the association to up-stream dividends to the parent, simply to facilitate a paper-for-paper transaction, would be injurious to American's operations."

As a thirty-day deadline for approving the transaction approached, Bank Board staff members kept asking for additional information. Finally, though, the Bank Board decided not to reject the application outright but to attach a number of severe restrictions that they knew left Knapp little choice but to cancel the offering. The regulators now required FCA to maintain 4 percent net worth each quarter, rather than at year end, to slow its growth to the industry average and to throttle back on its practice of making long-term fixed-rate loans.

In late June, FCA canceled the debt offering, and company officials scrambled to find new sources of funds. The company had already postponed the debentures three times, and the price of FCA stock languished, falling to $13 in the third week of June.

For the most part, they had been acting separately, each with his own concerns, but now some of FCA's strongest antagonists would begin working in concert. Hemmel would remain in constant communication with the Fed, Jonathan Gray would feed information to the SEC, and the SEC staff would be in contact with the Bank Board regarding FCA's dollar rolls and financial statements. This loose confederation was turning up the heat on Knapp.

But a major turning point clearly was the company's decision to shelve the debt plan. That spread concern about FCA's health throughout Wall Street. Institutional investors saw the move as an acknowledgment that the Bank Board lacked confidence in the nation's largest S&L and that something was wrong with American Savings. Coming on the heels of the collapse at Continental Illinois, some fund managers decided not to take a chance and quietly began removing their deposits. Within weeks, they would have lots of company as other customers scrambled to remove their money in a deposit run the likes of which had never been seen in the history of the S&L industry.

Within weeks, Knapp became frustrated with another critic who questioned his company's health. Now the feud between him and Jonathan Gray reached a fever pitch. While FCA officials tried to gloss over the company's quick decline, Gray told anyone who would listen that investing money in FCA was a dangerous game. As the company's problems mounted, Gray was inundated with calls from business reporters around the country who were publishing negative stories.

Following damaging quotations attributed to Gray in the *Los Angeles Times* business section on July 25, the analyst received a phone call from Mark Dodge, FCA's senior vice president and top in-house lawyer, warning him of the hazards of making such critical comments. Dodge followed up the phone call with a strongly worded letter dated July 27, reminding Gray that such statements could be a violation of state law, punishable by a term in the state penitentiary, creating the suggestion that Knapp would prosecute.

The letter warned Gray against making "gratuitous comments about deposits, depositors or liquidity, unless you have specific and verifiable information on that subject to report. Further, any statements about FCA going out of business are totally irresponsible."

"As you well realize, financial intermediaries function on depositor confidence," Dodge continued. "Further, as you know, loss of confidence is contagious and is rarely contained once eroded."

Gray could scarcely believe what was happening. He was a financial analyst, free to talk to the press, and now he was being threatened with imprisonment. But sending the letter to him in the first place proved that the company was desperate, a fact that Gray kept in mind as he continued talking with the media about FCA's poor health.

He had gotten away with it for years, but Knapp had finally thumbed his nose at the regulators one time too often. His warning that the company was "too big to fail" was transmitted to Ed Gray. No one, but no one, threatened Ed Gray.

By August, Gray was convinced that Knapp was a menace to the system. He was not only angry about the warning but felt betrayed because he had approved the merger on the condition that Knapp would restrain himself.

Knapp stood for everything Gray opposed in the S&L industry. He was one of the new breed of risk takers, a maverick who borrowed funds short-term by paying high interest rates and then lent the money out long-term. On the one hand, his company was vulnerable to a sudden swing in interest rates that would virtually guarantee substantial losses. On the other hand, if his investments turned sour, that would bring big losses as well. Either way, the government's insurance fund was at risk.

This was the very kind of situation that so bothered Ed Gray. Under deregulation, he was seeing too many S&L executives shooting craps with federally insured money. His awakening had come just five months earlier when he had seen the enormous damage that a company could sustain (and in turn cause the FSLIC) with excessive risk taking based on easy access to wholesale deposits. Empire Savings and Loan of Mesquite, Texas, had grown some seventeen-fold in two years. Gray had seen a videotape that detailed dozens of uncompleted construction projects financed by Empire. The Bank Board seized Empire that day.

Empire was small pickings compared with FCA. The company's American Savings unit alone would wipe out the FSLIC. Although many of the deposits were uninsured, in practical effect, the government could not let depositors lose billions in investments. In this regard, Knapp was right. FCA was too big to fail. But the Bank Board lacked the resources to bail the company out. That would mean turning to the Federal Reserve for help.

On August 2, an angry Gray summoned Charlie Knapp to his office. It was the first time the two men had met face-to-face. Gray was fully prepared for the showdown. He had outlined his thoughts on a yellow legal pad and had compiled a list of problems at FCA, complete with supporting documents.

Seated at one end of a wooden dining-room table that Gray used for conferences, with Knapp at the other, the Bank Board chairman began his harangue. It would last nearly fifteen minutes. As Gray ran down his list of FCA's deficiencies and Knapp's weaknesses as a manager, Knapp sat in stunned silence. His aides said he had tried several times in the past few months to arrange a personal meeting with Gray but had never heard from Washington on his requests. Knapp had hoped to spend several hours with Gray and smooth over their differences. Instead, he couldn't get a word in as Gray hammered away at him.

"You have violated each and every one of your agreements. You have operated in an unsafe and unsound manner. You have grown far beyond what you should have. The Securities and Exchange Commission says you have overstated your earnings.

"You have placed the FSLIC in great jeopardy. You have placed the entire savings and loan system in great jeopardy. As far as I am concerned, I am going to do everything in my power to make sure you leave that company. And I am going to do everything in my power to make sure you leave the system."

Chapter 7

The Gang of Four

On August 15, 1984, a Wednesday, a strong cool breeze blew through Los Angeles. The city still basked in the positive international publicity showered on it during the recent summer Olympic Games. The games had gone smoothly, despite a boycott by the Soviets and other Eastern-bloc countries. And Peter Ueberroth, the president of the Los Angeles Olympic Organizing Committee, was still the toast of the town and was already being touted as a possible candidate for public office.

What hardly anyone knew, however, was that Ueberroth was being considered as a potential replacement for Charlie Knapp, whose back was to the wall now that his company was in the headlines with extremely damaging disclosures.

After days of intense negotiations between FCA's senior executives and the SEC's staff, the agency's commissioners had ordered the corporation to restate its earnings on July 14. The company had until August 14 to file its 10-Q earnings report with the agency, and FCA filed the report at the last possible moment.

The new financial statements showed that FCA had incurred staggering losses from trading the Ginnie Mae securities under the dollar-roll program that Art Shingler and his southern California consultant had developed.

Instead of the formerly stated profit of $31.1 million for the three months ended June 30, FCA had lost $107.5 million, one of the largest quarterly losses in the thrift industry. For the first six months of the year, the company lost $79.9 million rather than making the $75.3-million profit it had reported. FCA had been prepared to fight the SEC's restatement request and had drafted two separate documents to submit to the agency when Knapp decided to file the one that complied with the government.

The monumental reversal occurred because FCA, the company that pushed accounting rules to their limits, never took possession of the mortgage-backed securities and did not have registered ownership when it entered into the repurchase agreements with its dealer. As a result, the SEC said the transactions should be counted as sales and not borrowings. Accordingly, when interest rates rose, as they had for the first six months of the year, FCA lost money as the value of the securities plummeted.

The SEC statement revealed other fundamental weaknesses. Everywhere the examiners probed, they found sensitive tissue. The deficiencies included

- Questions about American Savings' liquidity, meaning its ability to meet short-term cash obligations like deposits. American Savings had fallen below the liquidity level required by the Bank Board in July and said it expected the situation to continue through August.
- As of June 30, American Savings had net worth of only 2.92 percent, slightly below the 3 percent required for the rest of the industry but well below the 4 percent level mandated for FCA. To come up to the correct net-worth standard, FCA would have to issue some $327 million in equity, namely stock, or sell subordinated debt.
- Stockholders' equity had fallen by $228 million in six months because FCA had purchased 2.2 million shares of its own stock. The attempt to reinforce the stock price had hastened FCA's demise. Selling stock was virtually impossible at the currently depressed price. The company had filled an application with the Bank Board to issue $400 million in new debt. Given the attitude in Washington, issuing debt also seemed highly doubtful.
- Problem loans had soared. The twenty-two-page report showed that loans delinquent sixty days or longer and foreclosed property totaled $1.5 billion, a staggering 43 percent increase in just six months.
- The company disclosed that it remained under investigation with the SEC for some of its business deals with real-estate developers back in 1980 and 1981, and that it might have to restate earnings for those years as well.

Charlie Knapp stepped into the blinding glare of television lights at a company press conference. Though he looked tan and fit from a yacht trip in the Caribbean, his jocular air was gone, as was his usual bantering with the press.

Just three months earlier, at FCA's annual meeting, Knapp had acted cocky and caustic, publicly chastising the Bank of America for turning FCA down on a $5-million loan. He said American Savings was the envy of the industry because it had made so much money in 1981 and 1982 while other thrifts struggled for survival.

"We're happy people," Knapp had told the shareholders, "and nobody likes happy people."

Now, as he took tough questions from the media, Charlie Knapp did not look like a happy man. Asked about speculation that Ed Gray, the Bank Board chairman, was searching for his replacement, Knapp denied it. Nevertheless, he acknowledged that a change in the FCA chairman's office might be necessary, saying, "It took one style of management to build this company, and it's going to take another to manage it."

The grim financial news shocked investors, and FCA's stock got slaughtered in the market. The price plummeted that day by more than $2 a share, to close at $5. Market analysts also credited concern over FCA for much of the 15-point decline in the bellwether Dow Jones Industrial Average, which suffered its biggest setback since the midsummer rally had begun more than a month before. In related trading, the price of American Express fell $2.50, to close at $31, because stockholders feared FCA would sell its 4.9 percent interest.

The drubbing continued on Thursday. FCA stock fell another 62.5 cents, to close at $4.375, as 3.5 million shares traded on the New York Stock Exchange and one block of a million shares sold at $4.25.

That same day, shareholders began filing suit. The first to file for damages was Nessim Husni, who owned 100 shares. As defendants, Husni named Knapp, FCA, and the company's auditors, Arthur Andersen. On Friday, four more suits were filed, alleging that the defendants had violated federal securities laws and entered into a plan to inflate artificially the price of FCA stock. The company had no comment on the suits.

Aggravating the crisis, as deposits poured out the door, the company was simultaneously being asked to honor contracts to fund new investments. For years, FCA had earned substantial fees by selling loan commitments (promises to make mortgage loans or to buy them from other institutions in the future). At the worst possible time, the day of reckoning had arrived. Now the company was being hit from both sides of the balance sheet at once—from depositors who wanted their money back and from customers who were demanding that they be allowed to borrow. The company was a hemophiliac being asked to donate blood.

Behind the scenes, Knapp was losing the support of his board. Before going on a month-long vacation to the Soviet Union, Charles Offer, the company's founder, called Knapp and suggested that the chairman step aside.

"Why don't you find out what the SEC has against you? If you can't deal with them, then you ought to bring someone else in. Why don't you call Peter Ueberroth?" he asked, alluding to Ueberroth's familiarity with FCA's operations, having served as a director of Century Bank, FCA's former subsidiary.

"Ueberroth isn't interested," Knapp replied, according to Offer.*

Meanwhile, FCA officials attempted to quell rumors of a run, but the quiet withdrawals that had begun a few weeks earlier had escalated into a major liquidity crisis that threatened the company's survival. Nervous depositors, especially the large institutional investors with uninsured accounts, withdrew their funds as quickly as they could. With more than 60 percent of its $25 billion in deposits maturing in forty-five days, American Savings was in grave peril. The largest run in the history of the S&L industry had started. And the federal government now had the ammunition it needed to get rid of Charlie Knapp.

Although he had eluded such heavyweights as Ed Gray and

*FCA tried to put the best possible face on the deposit run, making it sound voluntary. On August 13, Knapp told the *Wall Street Journal* in an interview conducted by radio telephone aboard a yacht that institutional deposits declined by $1.4 billion and that that amount was only partially offset by new money from individuals. Knapp claimed American Savings was letting the deposits run off because the rates it had to pay were "too high."

Preston Martin, Knapp was about to be brought down by a relatively unknown lawyer in San Francisco. Dirk Adams and Jim Cirona had been friends since the days when Adams had served as outside counsel to Cirona's thrift in upstate New York. Not long after he arrived in San Francisco, Cirona looked for a new chief counsel and selected Adams, a tall, good-looking man with a baby-face complexion and a propensity for wearing bow ties.

As the crisis heightened at FCA, Adams found himself in one conference call after another with the Bank Board and its staff in Washington. An energetic attorney with a short attention span, Adams was getting tired of the incessant talk, talk, talk about Charlie Knapp and the possible scenarios for American Savings. The Bank Board staff wanted Knapp out, but no one seemed to have a concrete plan for his dismissal. Adams longed for action. With the run at American Savings in high gear, he decided to call Rodney Peck, a lawyer with the prestigious San Francisco law firm of Pillsbury, Madison & Sutro, the San Francisco bank's outside counsel.

As Adams and Peck began, both agreed that the run at American Savings would not end as long as Knapp was chairman of FCA. Adams thought the government could use the liquidity crisis as the basis for seizing the institution, but with Ed Gray still on his month-long swing through Europe to sell bonds and take a vacation, he doubted the Bank Board would undertake such an aggressive move. Adams wondered what legal means the San Francisco bank or the Bank Board had for removing Knapp without taking control of American Savings, which had not yet become insolvent.

The lawyers did the logical thing. They read the laws that governed S&Ls. That's when they stumbled across Section 9 of the Federal Home Loan Bank Act. Seemingly tailor-made for just these kinds of emergencies, the section stated that a federal home loan bank may deny an application for advances, or borrowings, from a member institution, or, if the Bank Board approves, "may grant it on such conditions as the bank prescribes."

"On such conditions as the bank prescribes"! That was it. That was the leverage they needed. They had him. Adams formulated a plan to condition loans to American Savings on Charlie Knapp's resignation. Without credit from the Home Loan Bank, American Savings almost certainly would go under. And even if Knapp himself balked, what board of directors could possibly let the solvency of the nation's largest S&L depend on one man's job?

Cirona endorsed the move, and in another series of conference calls, the San Francisco staff pitched the plan to Washington. Cirona had not received an answer but he nonetheless made arrangements to fly to Los Angeles to attend a meeting of FCA's board of directors. If the plan was not approved, maybe his presence might put pressure on the board members to tell their fighter pilot it was time to eject.

Charlie Knapp wasn't ready to admit defeat. Far from it. As the posse of government regulators bore down on him in mid-August, Knapp calmly formulated a strategy for remaining in power. He decided to form a three-man office of the president, to be shared by Shingler, president of American Savings; Phil Brinkerhoff, now an FCA executive vice president and president of FCA Mortgage Securities, a securities trading subsidiary; and John Darr, who had just joined the firm in June as chief financial officer.

FCA had been operating without a president, and the three would share the duties of chief operating officer. Knapp briefed all three individually before taking his proposal to the board of directors for formal action. Phil Brinkerhoff didn't much like the idea. He had been in frequent communication with the regulators in the last few weeks and doubted that they would accept the reshuffling, which looked like little more than camouflage to hide the presence of the company's true commander.

"I think bringing someone new in who is not closely tied with the past of State Savings will be viewed as a step in the right direction," Brinkerhoff said. "From a political and regulatory standpoint, it's a good move. I think Wall Street will like it. But I don't think it should be a three-man office."

"This will be a way for me to move away from all the visibility of a direct leadership role," Knapp said. "I'll still be here to formulate the strategy, and I think the three of you will work well together."

"Charlie, that's not the point. The regulators won't go for it, and I don't think it makes the best sense. You should just name one person. I'd be more than happy to do the job. If you don't want me to do it, then give it to Art or John. They're certainly qualified. Either of them could run the company."

"I understand what you're saying, Phil," Knapp replied, "but this is what I want to do. We're going to be announcing it to the press."

"As long as you're here, if that's what you want me to do, I'll do it," Brinkerhoff said. "But I don't think it's the right way to go. I don't think the regulators will stand for it."

Soaring sixty thousand feet above sea level at twice the speed of sound, Ed Gray tried hard to relax on the harried flight home from France. Gray had been fortunate enough to get a window seat on the Concorde, which he had boarded at Orly Airport in Paris, and now he watched the sky rush by as the sleek white jet shot through the stratosphere.

As he rushed across the Atlantic to meet with his allies at the Federal Reserve, he thought about how vulnerable Charlie Knapp had become: The SEC had taken action against him; the Bank Board under Gray and with Hemmel's analysis had thwarted FCA's financing plan; Preston Martin at the Federal Reserve was breathing down Knapp's back; depositors were taking cash out of American Savings; and the business press kept exposing the company's enormous weaknesses.

But Knapp still had an escape route. FCA could still go directly to the Fed and borrow at the discount window where financial institutions receive loans at a discount from the collateral they pledge. Gray wanted to keep Knapp away from the discount window if he could. Gray intended to prepare himself for his impending meeting with Volcker and Martin, but as he reflected on the events of the last few weeks, exhaustion from the two-week stint selling Bank Board bonds and the constant conference calls to Washington overcame him, and he fell asleep.

He awoke shortly before the plane landed at Kennedy. A government driver met him at the airport and took him to LaGuardia for the shuttle to Washington. Arriving in Washington a little more than an hour later, Gray stopped at his fifth-floor office at the Bank Board, conferred with aides, grabbed a sandwich, splashed some water on his face, and had his driver take him to the Fed's marble palace.

Four stories tall, of solid Georgian marble, the Federal Reserve Bank, the heart of the nation's financial system, is located at Twentieth Street and Constitution Avenue in northwest Washington, just a few blocks from the White House.

Paul Volcker's office was on the second floor. With its high ceilings and large windows overlooking Constitution Avenue and the Washington Mall to the south, the office had a dignified masculine look. The room was furnished with a maroon leather sofa and chairs, a rich mahogany desk, black cane-back occasional chairs, a large brown rug, and a marble-faced fireplace. A door behind Volcker's desk led to the Board of Governors' conference room where the Fed makes crucial decisions affecting inflation, the direction of interest rates, employment levels, and international trade.

It was an ironic place for a meeting about the safety of the S&L system. With Volcker leading the effort, the Fed had decided in the fall of 1979 to squeeze inflation out of the economy by tightening the money supply, greatly contributing to the thrift industry's misfortunes. Soaring interest rates crippled or killed hundreds of thrifts, beginning in 1980, helping to usher in a wave of reforms designed to help resuscitate the industry. As it turned out, deregulation actually exacerbated the difficulties and was one of the factors leading to the $159-billion bailout of the industry passed by Congress ten years later in the summer of 1989.

Tired from the long journey, Ed Gray had arrived at Volcker's office a few minutes before the 2:00 P.M. meeting was to begin. Just as he had hoped, no reporters had learned of Gray's reentry into the United States. Joining Gray and Volcker were Preston Martin, vice chairman of the Fed, and John Balles, president of the Federal Reserve Bank of San Francisco, the Fed's regional bank covering the West.

The four men discussed contingency plans for dealing with the possible collapse of American Savings. Gray faced a dilemma. He felt his regulatory powers were relatively lax. The Bank Board could issue a cease-and-desist order to stop some of Knapp's business practices, but that would take time, especially if Knapp wanted to challenge it. American Savings still had a positive net worth; its assets were greater than its liabilities. So the Bank Board could not legally place the company in receivership and appoint new management.

Gray told Volcker he wanted to get rid of Knapp and needed the central bank's help. Under new powers that had been granted the S&L industry just four years earlier, thrifts could borrow directly from the Fed, which would make the money available as the country's "lender of last resort."

No thrift had yet made use of this new power, but given its shaky condition, American Savings was an extremely likely candidate. Going directly to the Fed had some clear advantages. As the central bank, the Fed could advance as much money as was needed to ward off a run; the Home Loan Bank system, operating through its district banks, had a much smaller capacity for lending. The district banks financed their loans to member thrifts by selling bonds. American Savings might require billions more than the Home Loan Bank in San Francisco could provide.

The Bank Board chairman implored Volcker not to let American borrow directly from the Fed. He told Volcker that Charlie Knapp was a hazard to the banking system every single day he operated the company. The longer Knapp was in power, the more dangerous he became. Cutting off access to the Fed would almost surely force Knapp to resign or the corporation's board of directors to remove him. Gray opposed a government bailout of American Savings and wanted Knapp to go through the Bank Board system before turning to the Fed.

However, as chairman of the central bank, Volcker had to look at the integrity of the entire banking system. He had some strong concerns about the severe impact the failure of FCA could have on a system already jolted by the debacle at Continental Illinois. It would be difficult to justify allowing panic to spread throughout the S&L industry and possibly to commercial banks just to remove Charlie Knapp as chairman.

Gray continued to press the point with Volcker, saying that he needed his help and that he wanted to install Bill Popejoy as Knapp's replacement. Martin gave enthusiastic support for Popejoy, whom he had known for years and considered a first-rate executive with the kind of marketing muscle American Savings would need to rebuild customer confidence.

A pressing concern for Balles was the poor state of FCA's collateral. Balles and his staff had met in secret through much of the summer with officials at the Home Loan Bank of San Francisco. The poor quality of American's loans had horrified Balles's staff, who wondered how S&L regulators had failed to detect such obvious weaknesses as extremely delinquent loans. If American turned to the Fed for help, the company would go to the discount window in San Francisco.

Since FCA's securities and its best loans would be sold to investors or pledged as collateral at the San Francisco Home Loan Bank, Balles was worried that he could be stuck with a lot of bad paper. To protect the Fed, Balles wanted to give the company a 50 percent discount. That would mean that a $100-million commercial loan could be used to borrow only $50 million.

Finally, after nearly two hours of discussion, the Fed officials decided that American Savings would have access to the discount window. But American would first have to exhaust all other avenues. The Fed would act in its capacity as the lender of last resort. However, the Fed would not advance any funds for which there was not sufficient collateral. American's collateral would be discounted by an amount that was necessary to make sure the money was repaid. FCA may have become the garbage barge of the S&L industry, but Volcker had to let the company dock at the Federal Reserve.

Considering the severity of the situation, this was hardly a bold plan. Once American ran out of collateral, it would collapse. The Fed was not ready to guarantee deposits, which might quell customer fears, especially since so many accounts were uninsured. Nor was the FSLIC prepared to seize the institution, as the FDIC had done with Continental. Knapp was rapidly running out of options. Yet, as Gray would soon learn, removing Knapp did not necessarily mean saving FCA.

Jim Cirona had a saying for cases like this: It doesn't do any good to worry about things. You just have to take action. Now, armed with the Bank Board's approval and accompanied by Norm Raiden, the agency's general counsel, and Dave Serxner, one of the San Francisco Bank's top regulators, Cirona drove from his Beverly Hills hotel to FCA's headquarters in Los Angeles a few blocks away.

The board of directors' meeting was already in progress when Charlie Knapp came out and greeted them. Knapp was reserved but polite as he led his accusers into the boardroom. He ushered Cirona to the head of a long conference table and said, "The meeting's yours."

Sitting in the chairman's spot, Cirona, the steely Sicilian, came right to the point. "We're very dissatisfied with the responses we've been getting," he said. "The company has not been living up to its operating agreement, and we have not been getting the cooperation we need.

"We've got a major liquidity crisis on our hands. The bank has a duty to make sure that the money it loans to members will be repaid. We have real doubts about the company's ability to repay advances given the current management.

"We've come to the conclusion that there has to be a change. Charlie Knapp has to go. In reviewing your application for advances, the bank will consider whether or not there has been a change in management."

Several of those attending the meeting offered slightly different versions of exactly what happened. Knapp's aides insisted that Cirona said the San Francisco Bank would not provide any funds above $3 billion unless Knapp left the company and that the Bank Board wanted the right to dismiss other officers as well. Cirona didn't recall mentioning a specific figure. Some Bank Board officials said that they did not think Knapp was mentioned by name and that Cirona implied Knapp would have to go as well as other members of the management team. Cirona remembered specifically mentioning Knapp but no other officers or directors. He figured that if Knapp left, the rest would take care of itself.

Some of the directors were shocked. How could a regulator dictate to directors that they had to terminate Knapp? Sure, he had made mistakes, but he had built this company. If they questioned the propriety of the remarks, the directors well understood the significance. Without help from the San Francisco Bank, American Savings would perish. There was little hope for a last-minute cure.

When the regulators left the board meeting after about half an hour, Knapp walked them out. For a man about to lose a job that paid him more than $1.1 million in salary and bonus the year before, who had battled the regulators for years, Knapp was surprisingly cordial. He told them to "have a safe trip home."

The next day, August 22, FCA announced the realignment of its senior management, including the three-man office of president. Knapp remained chief executive officer and was supposed to concentrate on strategy and planning. In a one-page letter to shareholders, the company said the appointments were "very positive management promotions."

Jim Cirona didn't see it that way. He thought it was a blatant attempt to sidestep Knapp's dismissal. Well, it wouldn't work. This time the mongoose had the cobra in a death grip. Cirona told Serxner to phone his contacts at the company and tell them the realignment was unacceptable. Knapp had to go.

Chapter 8

The End of an Era

Thick drops of sweat poured off Bill Popejoy as he put a fresh coat of paint on an old barn in the blazing August sun. Fixing up his father-in-law's farm hadn't been exactly what he had had in mind when he decided to take time off from the treadmill of running troubled companies.

He saw no reason to hurry into another job. He was a nationally known executive who could land another job with ease. The key thing was to find just the right spot. A tall, handsome, articulate former athlete, Popejoy moved with confidence and skill among the power brokers of Washington, the money managers of Wall Street, and bank executives throughout California. He had run the Federal Home Loan Mortgage Corporation, had helped Mark Taper run American Savings in the 1970s, and then took on restructurings at Far West Federal Savings and Loan and Financial Federation, Inc.

For the first time since he was a teenager, Popejoy was unemployed, not that he needed the money, having saved his earnings and invested wisely over the years. With a net worth of more than $3 million, Popejoy had made nearly $500,000 from the sale of his home in Beverly Hills. He had two grown sons and a third in college, and his wife wanted him to enjoy life a little.

In fact, he had to admit, he'd been such a gung ho workaholic that he had spent little time with his wife and three sons over the years. He thought of himself as a good father but he wished he had spent more time with his family, and he had decided that a little respite from corporate life would do him good.

At first, traveling to exotic locations, reading a succession of books, and playing tennis around the world, had been relaxing. He and Nancy, a petite attractive woman with chestnut hair, had gone to Switzerland several times, touring the country by car and train. Popejoy had also fallen in love with New Zealand, despite the country's high taxes and what seemed like a disdain for free enterprise, and fantasized about living in the island nation.

Yet, after only a few months away from the challenges of the corporate world, he began to get antsy. Now that he had been out of work for a year, he felt like a freeloader. He longed to find some big project that would engross him and absorb his enormous energy. As it turned out, Ed Gray and Jim Cirona had just the right project for Popejoy.

Bill Popejoy began life like a character straight out of John Steinbeck's *Grapes of Wrath*. His father was part Choctaw Indian, born in Oklahoma and later moving to Texas with his family. During the Dust Bowl that engulfed the Southwest in the early 1930s, the senior Popejoy hit the road in a Model A Ford and joined the great migration of Okies to California. There he became an itinerant fruit picker and went by the nickname "Tex." He would eventually settle in Orangevale, a suburb of Sacramento.

Even as a young man, Bill Popejoy showed a natural talent for managing other people. By the time he was a junior in high school, he was managing three gas stations. The long hours as a grease monkey took their toll on his studies, and his grades began to suffer. He was paying more attention to hot rods and girls than his books. Finally, it got to the point that he was in danger of not graduating. Popejoy decided that he didn't want to be managing gas stations when he was 30 years old. That meant going to college.

Before he did, however, he met Nancy Rice and fell in love. She was a serious student, the high school's head cheerleader and the senior homecoming queen, and shortly after graduation, he married her. Ten months later, a son was born; he was named Parry, in honor of Popejoy's hero, Parry O'Brien, the great shot-putter who medaled in the 1952 and 1956 Olympics. Popejoy worked his way through college and graduate school, getting a master's in guidance and counseling. He spent the next several years in labor relations in the defense industry before embarking on his career in finance, which turned out to be his true calling.

After a series of rapid promotions, he became, at age 35, president of the Federal Home Loan Mortgage Corporation, commonly referred to as Freddie Mac. A quasi-governmental agency that bought and sold residential mortgages, Freddie Mac had been chartered by Congress in 1970 to help ease a national housing crunch. With assets of nearly $6 billion, it was pushing real-estate financing into new areas. Running the government corporation was quite a responsibility for a young man who just a few years before had been an anonymous labor-relations worker.

Freddie Mac was designed to increase the availability of money for home lending by buying mortgages from S&Ls and selling them to institutional investors. This generally entailed turning the mortgages into investment paper, called mortgage-backed securities, which was sold in the secondary market. A secondary market for mortgages had existed for years, but it was cumbersome because an S&L would frequently sell its paper directly to a company across the country.

But with the work of Freddie Mac and other housing-related agencies, a smooth secondary market developed. Lenders could now sell their mortgages easily. In so doing, they would collect a fee on the sale, and they could even continue to service the loans for investors for an additional fee. Once they sold the mortgages, the lenders could use that money for additional investments, including home loans that could once again be sold to investors.*

Although he could not envision the full extent of the success of the secondary market, Popejoy knew he was at the center of something important. A few years earlier, he hadn't known a basis point from a bowling ball. Now, he was giving speeches on the future of real-estate finance to rooms filled with thrift executives who were older and more seasoned than he. Bill Popejoy had to admit that he had done pretty well for himself.

Popejoy's success caught Mark Taper's attention. In the

---

*By 1986, lenders sold some $300 billion in mortgages in the secondary market. The dollar amount of all mortgage-backed securities issued that year exceeded the 1986 borrowings of the federal government and all U.S. corporations combined. As the secondary market grew, so did the amount of housing credit. By 1985, home loans outstanding totaled $1.7 trillion, compared with the enormous national debt of $2.2 trillion.

spring of 1974, the aging financial genius, whom Popejoy had met during a customer call at American Savings, phoned him at home one Saturday to offer him the job of president of his savings and loan. Though flattered, Popejoy was cautious to the point of being smug.

Popejoy knew of Taper's reputation for going through presidents. One man had lasted some seventy days. Why should he move back to his native California just to be fired a few months later when he had such an exciting and glamorous career going in Washington?

Taper proved persistent, though. He sent an emissary to Washington, who told Popejoy the old man would give him an employment contract. He convinced the hotshot young executive to fly to the coast and meet Taper in person. Despite their differences in age and background and the old man's reputation as a tough negotiator, Popejoy and Taper hit it off. Popejoy accepted an offer as president and chief operating officer of both the holding company and the S&L. He received a five-year contract and an annual salary starting at $125,000. Not bad for a kid from Sacramento who had nearly flunked out of high school.

For a while, the relationship worked. Popejoy put in long hours, racked up big earnings increases, and worked with Taper at his home on Sundays; frequently, he and Nancy would go out with Taper and one of his dates. Taper liked to say that he thought of Popejoy as his son.

But as time passed, Popejoy grew more frustrated with Taper's constant meddling, the son struggling with the overly domineering father. Taper continually undercut Popejoy's decisions, making him look like a fool in front of his subordinates. Popejoy wanted to expand, add branches, gain more assets, push into the new areas of finance he had seen developing in Washington, but Taper wanted to hold the line on costs. Popejoy had the title, but he wasn't really running the company; Taper wouldn't let him. Every major decision had to be approved by the old man.

Finally, Popejoy had had enough, and one Sunday he told Taper he was leaving when his contract expired. In a bid to keep Popejoy, Taper said he would relinquish the title of chief executive officer and bestow it on Popejoy. But that didn't help much. In fact, within a few months, the situation had gotten worse. Taper wouldn't, or more likely couldn't, let go of the reins of power at a company he had founded and still controlled.

On June 19, 1980, American Savings announced that Popejoy was departing and that Taper had assumed his duties. Popejoy had served for five and a half years, longer than any other president at First Charter. And though he never lost respect for his old boss, who continued to call him on his birthday for years afterward, Popejoy would never forget the frustration he had suffered while working for Mark Taper.

Shortly thereafter, Popejoy became president of Far West Federal Savings and Loan, which was owned by the Belzberg family of Canada. The move was a mixed blessing. The company was losing money when he arrived, but by the time he left eighteen months later, Far West was back in the black. On a personal level, however, Far West was a little like American Savings. As long as he ran a family-owned company, he would never have a free hand in management.

In December 1981, he became president and chief executive officer of Financial Federation, a Los Angeles–based S&L holding company that would shortly announce record losses of $32 million. What's more, with the industry in so much turmoil and the company facing a shareholder lawsuit after the 1981 losses, Fin Fed was a tense environment. When Popejoy arrived, the conservatively run company had an organization chart that resembled a maze. Fin Fed had eleven separately chartered thrifts operating under eight different names and seventy-one branches in fifty-nine California communities.

Within months Popejoy merged the eleven thrifts into a single company called United Savings and Loan Association. He embarked on a plan to take advantage of deregulation and move the thrift into more aggressive lending and other investments. By the time the company was sold to Great Western Financial in July 1983, Fin Fed had earned a profit for 1982 and was registering record earnings for 1983. Popejoy had begun to think of himself as the S&L industry's Lee Iacocca.

After the sale went through, he spent the next several months traveling with Nancy. He then put together an investment group to buy a derelict savings and loan in northern California. But nothing came of the negotiations with the regulators at the San

Francisco Federal Home Loan Bank. Feeling frustrated, Popejoy left again for Switzerland and an extended tour of Europe. The couple was motoring through Ireland when Nancy received word that her father, Clyde Rice, was gravely ill. The Popejoys flew home to Sacramento, and Rice entered the hospital for exploratory surgery. Since his childhood, Popejoy had been close to Rice, who had become like a second father. The doctors said Rice had cancer of the colon and gave him only three to six months to live. Bill Popejoy spent the next several weeks at his father-in-law's farm, helping out as best he could. It was a good place to reflect on past accomplishments and plot his future.

He was painting his father-in-law's barn in the intense heat and trying in vain to kill his thirst with a beer when the telephone rang. Charlie Knapp was on the line. They were not friends, but the two men had known each other for years as leading executives in the S&L industry. Popejoy also had served as chairman of the California League of Savings Institutions, an industry trade group, in 1982 and 1983 when Knapp was racking up record profits, acquiring American Savings, and bragging to anyone who would listen.

Popejoy wasn't completely surprised by the call. Shortly before Knapp phoned, Popejoy had received another call from a friend in Orange County, telling him that his name had surfaced in press accounts mentioning possible candidates to replace the embattled Knapp.

"Bill, I'm going to be leaving FCA and American, but I plan to stay on as a consultant and director," Knapp began. "I'm interviewing people to replace me, and I would like to talk with you. We already know each other, so we can handle this by telephone. Would you be interested in the job of chairman of FCA?"

"Well, Charlie, if you are really leaving, I would certainly be interested. But I need to know a little bit more. I know you guys are having a lot of problems. What's the situation there?"

"The situation is that they have been after me for years."

Knapp didn't say who "they" were, but Popejoy assumed he meant the regulators and the company's critics.

"It just isn't worth it anymore," Knapp continued. "Bill, I want you to know that you'd be my second choice. Dave Stockman is my first choice," he said, referring to the controversial budget director during President Reagan's first term.

Popejoy felt a flash of anger. Here he was, soaking wet with sweat, and some guy was on the line telling him he was the second choice for one of the toughest jobs in the industry.

"Well, hell, Charlie, go with Dave Stockman."

"No, I can't hire Stockman," Knapp said without elaborating.

The FCA chairman then launched into a long emotional diatribe about what he had tried to do as he built the company from a small association in Stockton into the nation's largest thrift, how he was misunderstood and was being treated unfairly. Popejoy felt more like a captive audience than an executive being interviewed for a high-level job.

Finally Knapp said, "Bill, it's a big salary, six hundred fifty thousand a year, options for a hundred thousand shares of stock and a five-year contract."

"God, that is a lot of money."

"The job's worth it," Knapp said. "It's a big job."

"Sounds like quite a challenge. I'm certainly interested."

"Good. But as I'm sure you can understand, I still need to talk with several other people."

The two men left it at that: Popejoy was under consideration. The next day, he got another call about FCA. This one was from Jim Cirona, whom Popejoy had gotten to know while serving the previous year as vice chairman of the Home Loan Bank in San Francisco. In fact, Popejoy had headed the search committee that hired Cirona.

"Bill, are you interested in running FCA?" Cirona asked.

"Yeah, Jim, I am."

Popejoy prepared himself for a long conversation, thinking that Cirona would want to discuss the atmosphere at FCA and what the regulators thought of the situation. Instead, Cirona said, "Thank you," added a few terse sentences, and was off the line.

"What the hell is going on here?" Popejoy asked himself after he hung up. Just exactly who, if anyone, was running FCA these days? He was confident he could handle the job, though he knew the company was in a lot of trouble. The company had bad real-estate loans, not exotic investments in oil rigs in Venezuela. Popejoy knew real-estate lending inside out, and even though he had been away from American for four years and it was decidedly a different company, he figured it couldn't have changed that much.

And deep in his heart, there was another reason why Popejoy wanted to return to American, one that had nothing to do with the generous salary. Popejoy had struggled in Mark Taper's shadow when he ran American Savings. Now he would go back as chairman, the head man, the undisputed leader. Maybe it was the wrong motivation, but Bill Popejoy wanted Charlie Knapp's job partly because he still had something to prove to Mark Taper. And something to prove to himself.

David Stockman was in fact offered the job, but Ed Gray expressed strong reservations when Stockman discussed the matter with him. Stockman seemed inclined to take the job, pointing out that Knapp had offered a great deal of money, according to Gray.

But Gray wanted someone who knew the S&L business and who could start immediately because American was borrowing heavily from the Federal Home Loan Bank and could go under at any moment. Stockman would have a lot of loose ends to tie up in Washington before he could move to the West Coast. Even if he could be on a plane within a week, an extremely short departure time, given Stockman's enormous duties as budget director, that might not leave enough time to save the company. And the White House wouldn't want to lose a budget director with Reagan's 1984 reelection just around the corner.

Gray thought it was a crazy scheme, one of the wildest he had ever heard. Sure, Stockman was famous and carried a great deal of respect in the financial world, but that hardly qualified him to guide a large thrift through the turmoil of a major run. Gray made it clear that he wanted Popejoy for the job, even going so far as to tell Stockman that if he became chairman of FCA, he would want Popejoy to work alongside him. Stockman discussed the offer with other members of the Reagan administration and his personal advisers, and turned the job down.

Now that Stockman was out of the picture, Gray focused on Popejoy, in whom he had great confidence. Popejoy had impressive credentials. He had run American Savings and was familiar with its operations; well known in California, he was bright and articulate, just the kind of guy who could inspire confidence in a beleaguered institution losing hundreds of millions in deposits.

Gray's assistant, Ann Fairbanks, took it upon herself to call Knapp personally and tell him that the Bank Board chairman would accept no one but Popejoy. When Gray found out about it, he became angry and told her not to do it again. The Bank Board couldn't legally force a company to hire a particular executive as chairman. But Fairbanks, worried that Knapp's last act would be to pick someone other than Popejoy just to defy Ed Gray and the Bank Board, ignored Gray and phoned Knapp again to say Popejoy had to be the replacement.

She may have exceeded her authority, but Ann Fairbanks had the right instincts. Knapp was searching for a certified corporate star and was unenthusiastic about Popejoy, whom he considered the quintessential narrow-minded S&L executive who lacked the creative flair to run FCA and American Savings.

Knapp was making plans to leave, but he would not go gently. Far from it. He engaged in a high-stakes showdown with his board of directors. Although he was not on a committee of directors negotiating with the chairman, Phil Brinkerhoff said Knapp had two main conditions for his departure. He wanted it to look as if he had left of his own volition, and he wanted $2 million.

In the abstract, $2 million seemed like a lot of money. But the company couldn't afford to get involved in a lawsuit in the midst of a major run that could bring destruction at any moment. Compared with the prospect of losing a $32-billion company, $2 million looked pretty cheap. The board voted to give Knapp his generous send-off.

Now that Knapp was preparing to leave, the directors had to decide on his replacement. Phil Brinkerhoff had become Bill Popejoy's biggest booster within FCA. Popejoy had hired Brinkerhoff as a lawyer for Freddie Mac several years earlier, and the two men had stayed in touch over the years. Once Brinkerhoff learned he would not succeed Knapp, he started pushing for Popejoy.

Popejoy had returned to his salmon-colored Spanish-style town house in Newport Beach from his father-in-law's farm a few days after his initial contact with Knapp when he got a third call about the chairman's job. This time it was Brinkerhoff, who asked Popejoy to join him and two other members of FCA's board for dinner.

Popejoy first stopped by Brinkerhoff's office at FCA headquarters.

"Phil, what's going on here? I'm a little puzzled by all this. Am I being interviewed or what?"

"No, Bill, it's not really an interview. I think they want to hire you. I think they have to hire you. It's just a matter of some of the directors' getting to know you a little better."

"I'm anxious to meet them too. What am I getting myself into here, Phil?"

"I'm not going to kid you, Bill. It's a very difficult situation. We're losing hundreds of millions in deposits every day. We're scrambling to come up with collateral. We've been borrowing from the Federal Home Loan Bank. We may have to borrow from the Fed. The relationship between the Bank Board and Charlie was not good. The employees are worried. Morale is very low."

"What's the situation with Charlie?"

"I think he'll be leaving within a few days. The board is still working out the details. He wants to make the announcement himself."

Popejoy didn't mention his earlier conversations with Knapp and Cirona.

"Bill, I'm sure the board will like you," Brinkerhoff said. "It'll be good to work with you again."

Popejoy thanked Brinkerhoff for the support, and the two men left for their meeting. Brinkerhoff and Popejoy joined Don Reynolds, Knapp's PR man, and Charles Young, chancellor of the University of California at Los Angeles, for dinner at the Regency Club, a private club at the Murdoch Plaza.

Reynolds and Young seemed defensive about what was happening to FCA, and Popejoy got the impression that they thought the government had given Knapp a raw deal.

Popejoy filled them in on his background, his history in the mortgage business, his tenure at Freddie Mac, and his experience running American Savings under Mark Taper. He also told them what he had learned about the industry while at Far West and Fin Fed, and what it takes to turn a company around. But Popejoy had his own questions. He wanted to know about the strained relations with the Bank Board and the company's direction.

Young explained that FCA's basic strategy was mortgage banking, to make and buy loans while interest rates were high, hold them until rates went down, then sell them at a profit. Popejoy tried to explain that that wasn't mortgage banking but a speculative play on interest rates. Young seemed uninterested in Popejoy's description of mortgage banking as an enterprise in which you merely act as a conduit between the borrower and investor, and don't take an interest rate position, so Popejoy just smiled and listened as Young described mortgage banking at FCA.

The directors told Popejoy that the salary was indeed $650,000, plus stock options and a five-year contract. Popejoy said nothing about the salary. He wasn't about to negotiate money when the offer already sounded more than reasonable. He told them he wanted to be the chief executive at FCA.

Popejoy was the first to leave, and the directors discussed their impressions of him.

Reynolds seemed particularly underwhelmed with Popejoy. "I guess that's going to be the next CEO," Reynolds said. "We've got ourselves a caretaker."

Brinkerhoff cautiously defended his old friend, reminding Reynolds and Young that Popejoy really knew the S&L business and was acceptable to the regulators.

"You watch. He'll do exactly what he's told," Reynolds said, implying that unlike Knapp, Popejoy would go along with the government. "Mark my words. It's the end of an era."

After twelve extremely tense days in which the company's future was in constant jeopardy, partly because Knapp remained in charge, the beleaguered chief executive gave the board his resignation on Monday, August 27. The next day, he received his $2 million separation pay. The money was wired to his account at the Century City branch of First Los Angeles Bank, according to a lawsuit the company later filed against Knapp.

Tuesday morning, FCA announced Knapp's resignation to the press and released a copy of a letter he had written to the company's shareholders. Once again, he was dishonest with the company's investors. The tone of the letter made it sound as though his departure was part of the natural order of the universe.

Knapp said it was his "voluntary" decision to resign. "It takes a particular entrepreneurial style of management to build a company and another style to preserve and run an organization when it becomes as large and complex as Financial Corporation of America and American Savings," he continued.

"Quite obviously, my resignation from active management is a difficult decision, but in end result, it is made with the very best interests of the company in mind. What has added greatly to the emotional difficulty are the letters, telegrams, and direct personal contact from so many employees and shareholders pledging total support and lending their much-needed encouragement during these embattled times."

Then again, he had $2 million worth of encouragement. He could afford to buy just about any kind of solace he needed. He had repeatedly ignored the warnings of his colleagues in the industry and the regulators, and now that his company was on the precipice, he had a wonderful going-away present.

With his $2 million in separation pay, Charlie Knapp walked out of FCA's headquarters, leaving others to clean up the mess he had created. Not only had Charlie Knapp engineered a huge merger, built the largest thrift in the country, run a company that booked millions in bad loans, used questionable accounting methods, and gambled on interest rates, but he was seeing another woman on the side. For nearly a year, he had been dating a woman nearly fifteen years younger than he. Lois Hamilton was a striking blonde B-movie actress, who, like Brooke, also was a pilot. Soon, the two would go for a long cruise aboard a 120-foot yacht before embarking on another ill-fated business venture marked by allegations of questionable conduct.*

* * *

---

*Information about Knapp's relationship with Lois Hamilton prior to his leaving Brooke appeared in a lengthy page-one story in the *Wall Street Journal.* The story was also highly critical of Knapp's business affairs after leaving FCA. Asked about the story, Knapp said the entire article was "totally inaccurate" but claimed not to have read the section regarding his relationship with Lois, who is an officer in his company. Knapp said the two met "a couple of months" before he left FCA, adding that Lois, whom he later married, is a "staunch Catholic" and a "no-fool-around lady."

Late that Tuesday afternoon, Bill Popejoy got another high-level phone call at his Newport Beach town house. This time it was a conference call from the full board. Each of the directors introduced himself to Popejoy, who was asked if he wanted to be the chairman and chief executive officer of FCA. Foster Fluetsch would remain chairman of American Savings.

Popejoy said yes, he wanted the job. He was then asked if he could be on a company plane that evening to fly to Washington to meet with the members of the Bank Board. The company was negotiating an operating agreement that would severely restrict its activities and call for an orderly reduction in American's size. He was told that senior executives would fly to Washington with him and that they would brief him on the status of the run. There was no time to waste; he had to hurry. The company was in total disarray—its life could be measured in days. The new chairman of this chaotic enterprise had just been hired by telephone.

Book Two

Staying Alive

Chapter 9

Capitol Flight

The Learjet lifted off the runway at John Wayne Airport in Orange County and streaked through the tailwinds to the east. Bill Popejoy was off and running. His destination was clear. But the chances for success seemed highly questionable.

As the company plane slipped through the smog that ringed Los Angeles, Financial Corporation of America was sinking, losing as much as $500 million in deposits a day, $62.5 million an hour, $1 million a minute. The nation's largest and most aggressive S&L floundered like a battleship shot full of holes. The crew members kept plugging the leaks, only to find additional damage. The ship could sink at any moment.

Bill Popejoy sat in the aircraft's pressure-filled cabin, listening to two of his key executive officers, Art Shingler and Phil Brinkerhoff, brief him on the scope of the run and how the company was selling loans, securities, and other assets to meet the cash drain. Despite the grim news, Popejoy seemed relaxed and ready for duty, as though he actually relished the tough challenge ahead.

What he heard was enough to daunt any man. FCA was borrowing money and selling assets at breakneck speed. In July, the month before Popejoy was hired, FCA had borrowed nearly $300 million from the Federal Home Loan Bank of San Francisco because institutional investors had removed nearly $1.4 billion in deposits, or 6 percent of the company's deposit base, and American Savings could raise only about $800 million in retail deposits to cover the withdrawals. Later that same month, the company had sold nearly $500 million in mortgage-backed securities.

But in the ensuing run, the moves were like applying a Band-Aid to a severed artery. By Monday, August 13, FCA had borrowed an additional $500 million from the San Francisco Bank, bringing its total government borrowings to $1.4 billion, double the June 30 level. Five days later, on August 20, the day before Jim Cirona told FCA's board that Knapp would have to leave, the company sold 7 million shares of American Express stock in what was then the second-largest trade in volume in the history of the New York Stock Exchange. FCA received $223.3 million, representing the fifth-largest trade in the Big Board's history in dollar value. By August 28, the day Popejoy was hired, FCA had borrowed some $2.49 billion from the Federal Home Loan Bank and would certainly need additional funds to stay alive.

Shingler, who had been in Washington earlier in the summer negotiating with the SEC, gave Popejoy details of the meetings and the impact the earnings restatement of August 15 had on American Savings and its cash flow. Since then, American's smooth-talking deposit salespeople had encountered constant rejections from the company's customers, many of whom said they were glad to hear from American Savings because they wanted to withdraw their money.

As head of FCA's mortgage-securities unit, Brinkerhoff had supervised the effort to find loans and package them for resale. Since FCA faced the constant danger that it would not be able to find enough collateral to match the enormous deposit outflows, Brinkerhoff's team engaged in a frantic search through the loan files to find enough assets to keep American afloat. Indeed, as Popejoy would learn more fully in a few days, the situation was so bad that a squad of federal examiners had gone to Stockton to aid in the effort. Brinkerhoff told Popejoy that in FCA's search for billions of dollars worth of collateral, each day brought another brush with death.

Beyond the critical short-term priorities, Popejoy had to keep in mind the conditions of a stringent operating agreement that FCA had just signed that day with the Bank Board. Faced with the threat of extinction, FCA had signed away much of its freedom.

The twelve-page agreement stipulated the following:

- The Bank Board had the right to request the resignation of any director or company officer at American Savings or

FCA, the holding company. Furthermore, both companies were forbidden from hiring as consultants any of those who were purged. The Bank Board also had to approve any director or officer hired by FCA or American Savings.

- American Savings was required to have 4 percent net worth and to adopt a plan to sell assets to increase the company's liquidity to repay debts owed to the Federal Home Loan Bank and other creditors. Neither American nor FCA could pay a dividend on its stock without the written approval of the Bank Board.
- Senior managers at FCA and American Savings had to meet at least monthly with the Home Loan's bank's supervisory agent in San Francisco and Bank Board officials. The executives also had to submit whatever reports the supervisory agent requested. Neither American nor FCA could give its senior managers a pay raise without the written approval of the supervisory agent, Jim Cirona.
- Both American and FCA had thirty days to submit a business plan that called for the orderly reduction in size of American Savings. Both companies had to submit annual budgets to Cirona for his approval and engage in quarterly reviews with him.

If FCA or American failed to adhere to the conditions of the agreement, the companies would immediately comply with a cease-and-desist order, requiring them to uphold every aspect of the pact. In essence, the company's board of directors and shareholders had ceded many of their rights and powers to the Bank Board. American Savings had just become a high-priced ward of the federal government.

As the corporate jet neared Washington, the FCA executives discussed what might happen in the meeting with the regulators. In the final days of Knapp's tenure, the relationship between the company and the government had been frosty at best. Popejoy knew he had to forge a strong relationship with Gray and the rest of the Bank Board to have any chance of salvaging the company. Brinkerhoff thought the atmosphere would ease now that Popejoy was chairman. Nevertheless, there was no guarantee, given the size of the run at American, that Popejoy wouldn't end up serving as chairman for a day.

"Look," Popejoy said, "we obviously still have a very tough situation here. We'll just have to work at it every day.

"If we've done the best that we can, that's all that we can ask of ourselves. There's nothing more we can do. If we make it, we make it. If we don't, we don't."

When Popejoy and his team arrived at the Bank Board at 1700 G Street in northwest Washington at 9:00 P.M., they expected to find only a few people on duty. Instead, it seemed that every light in the building was on, and the new FCA chairman found himself welcomed by a phalanx of government officials.

Ed Gray and the rest of the Bank Board were anxiously awaiting the arrival of Popejoy and his team. No one knew whether Popejoy could save the company, for with so many deposits above the federally insured limit of $100,000, survival remained in doubt as long as depositors felt there was a chance of loss. All the same, Popejoy was their best hope.

If American Savings folded, it could take the federal insurance system with it. FSLIC had only $6.3 billion in reserves, compared with American's total deposits of more than $24 billion, more than 50 percent of which were federally insured. If American Savings became insolvent, FSLIC couldn't pay off all the depositors. No insured depositor had ever lost a dime in the entire fifty-year history of the system. The first time would be a devastating blow because a chain reaction of panic might spread throughout the entire thrift industry.

After brief introductions, Popejoy's team split up. Popejoy met with Ed Gray, Don Hovde, and Mary Grigsby, who had recently replaced Jamie Jackson on the Bank Board, while the other FCA executives conferred with the board's staff. The staff had assembled a task force to deal with the liquidity crisis and wanted to obtain new information about deposit withdrawals and how the company was raising collateral.

Now that Knapp was gone and the Bank Board was more receptive to the company's needs, American's senior managers dropped their guard and provided as much information as they could. During the final days of the Knapp regime, the relationship between the company and the government had been adversarial. Knapp did not respect the regulators, and some company directors were angry with the government for being what they felt was heavy-handed. In this tense environment, understandably, there was mistrust on both sides. Popejoy brought a new cooperative attitude. Both he and Brinkerhoff were longtime Washington insiders who were willing to work closely with the government to save the company.

Meanwhile, Popejoy was meeting privately with each member of the Bank Board and collectively with the group, reviewing his own career history, American's financial condition, and the hostile environment facing the company. Hovde particularly was impressed with Popejoy. He thought FCA's articulate chairman exuded confidence and integrity. And to his credit, Popejoy didn't try to fool anyone. He knew as well as they did that the liquidity crisis might kill the company. He was planning to fly to New York the next day to convince Wall Street investors to stick with FCA. Popejoy thanked the members of the Bank Board for giving him the opportunity to serve as FCA's chairman and said the company would cooperate in any way it could. He said he would do everything in his power to keep American Savings alive.

Midnight had passed before Popejoy prepared to leave for his hotel. Suddenly, Ed Gray remembered that the new red-white-and-blue plastic insignias he had ordered for the Bank Board had arrived that very day. Ever the marketing man, Gray thought it would make a good public-relations ploy to take a photograph of the Bank Board chairman shaking hands with Popejoy in front of the agency's seal and distribute the picture to the media.

Gray was excited. What better way to show that the government was backing American Savings? The symbolism was perfect. One of his aides found the staff photographer, the seal was pinned to the wall in Gray's fifth-floor office, and Gray, Popejoy, and Cirona posed in front of it. A few days later, in an effort to build customer confidence, Gray phoned Popejoy and suggested that FCA run the picture in newspaper advertisements. At first, Popejoy resisted, thinking it a hokey idea. But Gray pressed the matter, and Popejoy went along.

Cirona, however, wanted no part of the advertising campaign. A government official had no business being so cozy with the head of a company he regulated, and he told Popejoy he wanted to be cropped out of the photo.

His refusal to participate also reflected his belief that American had already suffered irreparable damage. From here, the best public policy was to perform what he called an "open-door" liquidation. The most prudent course was to protect the industry's insurance fund by keeping American alive for the time being and then slowly wind it down. The company would sell off whatever assets it could, such as loans and branches, and allow deposits to decline with the overall reduction in size. Once there was nothing but bad assets left, the government would take over. The flap over the photo was the first time Cirona would disagree with the strategic vision of Popejoy and Gray. But it would not be the last.

The next day, Popejoy flew to New York to meet with key investment bankers on Wall Street. Shingler flew back to Stockton; Popejoy wanted him to help rally personnel so they could find collateral from the loan files to pledge for borrowings from Wall Street. He wanted people working around the clock over the upcoming Labor Day weekend. American could take advantage of the holiday by finding assets to sell while depositors were away on vacation and couldn't wire for the return of their money.

Popejoy spent Wednesday and Thursday in New York, talking with such firms as Merrill Lynch, Prudential-Bache, First Boston, and E. F. Hutton. As with the meetings in Washington, Popejoy introduced himself and his senior managers. He told them American had the backing of the Bank Board, that it needed to borrow heavily to meet its deposit drain, and that it had adequate collateral to back the loans. The plan he revealed to them, one that Knapp had begun shortly before leaving office, was to accelerate an effort to convert loans into mortgage-backed securities that could be easily sold and used to obtain billions in loans needed to keep American from going under.

Some Wall Street firms pledged their support. Others wanted nothing to do with FCA or its loans, whose value had been questioned by the SEC, by one of the street's top thrift analysts, and by respected financial reporters.

In fact, a damaging article in the *Wall Street Journal* appeared on Thursday, August 30, while the new chairman was still in New York meeting with the investment bankers. Many investors, institutional depositors, and thrift-industry executives applauded Popejoy's hiring, the paper reported. However, the article made it clear that this same group also thought Popejoy's presence alone would not stop the run. The *Journal* quoted some sources as saying that even a federal guarantee of FCA like the one given Contintental Illinois would not be enough to cure the company's ills. In a particularly damaging quotation, Robert Citron, the treasurer and tax collector in Orange County, Calif., which was practically in the company's backyard and soon would become Financial Corp.'s home base, said he was going to withdraw all $155 million his agency had on deposit with American Savings.*

"I am an elected government official with a fiduciary duty to protect the public's money," Citron said. "If things don't work out at American, they [taxpayers] will ask 'Why did you do it?' "

"Nobody wants a loser on their list," said Ronald Lee, president of Golconda Financial, a broker of certificates of deposit based in El Monte, California.

Ed Gray read the *Journal* article with more than casual interest. Not only did the story illustrate that American had entered into a crucial two-week period in which nearly 25 percent of its deposits would mature, but it also said the regulators were drafting contingency plans that might include a guarantee of all uninsured deposits. The Bank Board couldn't guarantee uninsured deposits at American because it didn't have the funds to do so.

Gray was in an awkward position. The Bank Board had not considered guaranteeing all deposits. In fact, the operating agreement the agency had signed with FCA didn't even promise that the Home Loan Bank would continue lending money to American Savings. The document said only that the government would consider making additional loans only after American changed its business practices. But Gray could not deny the story either. That might make it sound as though the Bank

---

*Popejoy relocated FCA to Irvine in Orange County.

Board were not fully behind American, possibly escalating the crisis. As it turned out, the article was good public relations because it made it seem as if the government would protect the depositors, which would help restore calm.*

That same day, Popejoy disclosed that American had borrowed nearly $2.1 billion from the Home Loan Bank in San Francisco, the first indication of the run's size and scope. Popejoy also said he intended to bring about a sharp reduction in American's fixed-rate lending. Although he offered no timetable for implementing his plan, he said he eventually wanted fixed-rate loans to account for only 10 percent of American's portfolio. That amounted to a complete repudiation of Knapp's strategy. At the time, 90 percent of American's loans had fixed interest rates, written under Knapp's wild-eyed growth formula of booking loans and selling them when interest rates declined. Clearly, American Savings would be a different company under Bill Popejoy.

For Popejoy to get control of the company, he would have to have new executives in command, people he could trust. His first priority was to stop the run. Later, of course, when the crisis was behind him, he could adopt a full-fledged restructuring. But right now there was one management change that could not wait.

The new FCA chairman was still in Washington when he phoned Foster Fluetsch and told him that he wanted to discuss his status with the company. Fluetsch knew what that meant: He was about to be fired, and he was devastated. He had been with the firm for twenty-four years and had assumed that Knapp was the only executive who would be forced to leave. It wasn't much leverage, but he told Popejoy that he thought his management contract gave him half his annual pay for ten years as severance.

---

*The need for good public relations figured in a dispute two weeks later between Gray and Treasury Secretary Donald Regan. Regan had told reporters the government was not considering a guarantee of uninsured depositors. What followed was an exchange of nasty notes between the two men in which Gray chided Regan for his comments and Regan responded by suggesting that perhaps Gray had not done all he should to contain the worsening situation at American Savings.

A few days later, Popejoy and Fluetsch met in American's offices in Stockton.

"Foster, we're in a crisis," Popejoy said. "The company needs a new image. We have to restore confidence. The management here is associated with the problems that caused this run. You and Charlie are at the top of that list. I need your resignation."

Fluetsch, who had favored hiring Popejoy to replace Knapp, disagreed. "If you keep me on, there's a lot I can do to help solve the problems," he replied. "I know this company better than anyone. I have the loyalty of the employees and the executives here. I've always worked well with the Federal Home Loan Bank."

Popejoy continued to insist on Fluetsch's resignation, and Fluetsch realized he had no option. Even worse, Fluetsch had learned that a paragraph in his contract provided that his ten years of half pay applied only after he turned 65. Now Popejoy was playing hardball, and Fluetsch knew why. The Bank Board members were angered over Knapp's $2-million send-off and did not want him to receive a handsome separation package.

Nevertheless, Fluetsch wasn't about to resign without some economic protection. He felt he had earned the money, and he had no plans for his future professional life, so he negotiated over his severance pay. Popejoy offered Fluetsch half his annual salary of $290,000 and full health-care coverage for five years. Forty-five minutes later, the matter was settled. Popejoy had begun to clean house.

On September 4, FCA announced Fluetsch's resignation. Before departing to paint pictures near the coast of Santa Cruz, the former florist drafted a statement that urged American's employees to "continue to support your new leaders as you have me for so long. I am proud of you and have confidence that I have left the company in good hands."

Chapter 10

Liquid Assets

Phil Brinkerhoff could feel the pressure building as he stepped into the "War Room." Today, the day after Labor Day, would bring the toughest test of his abilities and might even determine whether American Savings could remain solvent.

FCA's securities-trading center had been dubbed the War Room because Brinkerhoff and his subordinates were under siege as they sought to find loans and securities to cover the outpouring of deposits. The traders were in constant contact with the Bank Board, Freddie Mac, Wall Street, and the company's major investors. A large easel depicted in different colors the amount of deposits coming due on particular days, how much collateral American had available, and when and where the loans or securities were to be delivered.

Just as hot money had fueled American's fast growth, it now hastened its swift descent. Depositors who were searching only for the highest return had little or no loyalty to American Savings.

The situation was particularly ironic for Clark Coleman, who had been hired just four months before as a trader. While working at competing banks and thrifts, Coleman had sometimes taken advantage of American's high interest rates. Coleman would funnel some of his institution's money into high-yield deposits at American, earning as much as two points above what his own bank or thrift paid its depositors. Now, as Coleman helped try to rescue the company, his former employers were pulling their money out of American Savings as quickly as possible.

As Brinkerhoff stood in the trading center, multiline phones constantly blinked, and the computer screens glowed with the symbols and numbers of the bond-trading business. The last few weeks had brought one Herculean test after another. He was like an air traffic controller monitoring a blizzard of near-misses.

In one dire example ten days before, one Wall Street firm had wanted to back out of an agreement to loan American $900 million backed by Ginnie Mae mortgage securities. That sent the normally calm Coleman into a frenzy. Far more than $900 million was at stake.

If American did not receive the money, the thrift would be unable to pay off the securities contracts that were coming due at other Wall Street firms. Once American defaulted on a single contract, Wall Street probably would immediately dump the company's mortgage-backed securities that had been pledged as collateral for borrowings from investment houses. American would be crushed in an avalanche of securities sales.

Coleman practically foamed at the mouth as he shouted at a Wall Street trader. "Goddammit," he screamed, "this is bullshit. This is total bullshit. You guys promised. Goddammit, you gave us your word. In this business your word is your bond. And you know that."

"Now, wait a minute," the trader said. "Calm down, Clark."

"Calm down, my ass. Everything is riding on this deal. You knew that. You knew that. We all verified the numbers. Everybody agreed that you would take the bonds. And now you want to pull out at the last minute. I can't believe this. If anybody goes down in this organization, you will be implicated along with them."

John Darr, one of the company's three presidents, was in New York at the time, firming up support from Wall Street. Darr and high-ranking officials from other investment houses talked to the firm's top brass, imploring them to complete the transaction because American Savings, the Bank Board, and the nation's financial system depended on it. Later that day, the company relented, and the deal went through.

Other complications surfaced often. The chart used to show the flow of money at American wasn't useless, but it was highly inaccurate as a forecasting tool. For instance, the chart would show that $200 million might come due on a particular day, but American would actually lose $350 million. What the chart made all too clear was that more certificates of deposit had been withdrawn every day since the run began than actually came due. With FCA's troubles constantly in the news, depositors were willing to pay a penalty to withdraw their funds early. They could afford to lose some interest, but they were not willing to sacrifice a single cent of principal.

Brinkerhoff's team was doing all it could to cover the withdrawals. In the last week of August, FCA finally completed an unusual transaction that had started several months earlier. The company borrowed $2 billion from Freddie Mac, Popejoy's old company, by pledging home loans as collateral with an agreement that FCA would repurchase the loans in the future. Freddie Mac in turn was converting the mortgages into government-guaranteed mortgage-backed securities. It was the first time the agency had loaned money to a thrift secured by mortgage loans rather than government-backed securities.

Freddie Mac sent its own team of examiners to go through American's tainted loans, and working around the clock throughout the Labor Day weekend, dozens of FCA employees, investment bankers, and federal examiners had scoured the Stockton offices of American Savings, looking for loans that would qualify as collateral.

At most financial institutions, identifying collateral is a routine matter of pulling loan documents from the files and taking them to the federal government or private investors. But the rescue workers at the thrift's Stockton offices stepped into an administrative nightmare. Miraculously, they raised nearly $1.5 billion over the weekend, money that kept the company from sinking under the tidal wave of withdrawals.

The long weekend gave American a badly needed respite, time to find new sources of funds without fear that the money would immediately evaporate. But as a consequence, the deposits that would have come due on Monday, when the thrift was closed for the holiday, now expired on Tuesday. As Brinkerhoff calculated it, American faced withdrawals totaling more than $700 million by the end of the next day.

Brinkerhoff relied heavily on Vic Indiek, the trading unit's executive vice president. Like Brinkerhoff, Indiek was a former president of Freddie Mac and was close to Popejoy. Indiek was frequently on the phone, trying to motivate the deposit sales staff, attempting to restore their sagging morale, telling them to ignore the damaging publicity and negative feedback from customers. He ordered them to find new deposits, and find them fast. Between them, Brinkerhoff and Indiek had a decade's experience at packaging loans for sale in the secondary market. Along with Popejoy, they had extensive contacts throughout the investment community and the federal government. But time, not lack of experience, was their greatest enemy.

As Brinkerhoff's team struggled to keep American alive, Bill Popejoy, the confident can-do executive, burst into the War Room. He wanted a quick update to see how Brinkerhoff's staff was coping with the run.

"What's your plan for the next week?" he asked.

"Our plan for next week is that we have eight-hundred million maturing by tomorrow," Brinkerhoff said. "I am up to one o'clock tomorrow. It will take every available resource we have to get through tomorrow."

"Look, Phil, I know you guys are under a lot of pressure. This isn't easy. It's tough on everyone. You guys have done a great job. But we have billions in deposits coming due next week, and we have to plan for that."

"We can't predict what will happen beyond one day at a time. We just don't have the ability. Long-range planning is an hour. Once I get through today, I will look at tomorrow. And then I will look at the next day and the next day after that. There are no plans for next week."

Bill Popejoy was amazed that a company he thought he knew so well had degenerated past pandemonium into near anarchy.

If he had visited American's offices in Stockton before going to Washington and Wall Street, he might not have shown so much self-confidence. Once he started surveying the offices located in dozens of buildings throughout Stockton, Popejoy was nearly overpowered by disbelief. In his entire professional career, he had never seen so much disarray.

The back-shop operations of American Savings were nothing short of a labyrinth. If someone had set off a bomb inside American's loan offices, it might have resulted in a more logical filing system. Unable to cope with the volume of loans the company had written and purchased from around the country, the back-shop workers had simply stacked boxes of files anywhere they could. Unmarked boxes had been placed in the bathrooms and janitors' closets.

Added to that were thousands of loan files that lacked sufficient documentation. Essential paperwork, such as appraisal forms and property deeds, were missing. The company was receiving checks from some customers but could find no record of having granted them a mortgage loan. Other customers who were mailed dunning notices and threats of foreclosure had responded with copies of canceled checks; yet no one could find a record of payments. There were unmarked boxes of crucial "trailing" documents that came in a few weeks after a mortgage loan was completed, but no one could find the original loan documents.

Popejoy mustered every available body to help sort through the loan files to find the collateral that could keep American from failing. The San Francisco Home Loan Bank sent a team of examiners and paralegals to help certify the quality of the loans. Lacking faith in American's assets, the Home Loan Bank hired appraisers to perform spot checks of properties to make sure the buildings actually existed.*

Clearly, Popejoy realized, he had to get his own people up to Stockton, people whose judgment he trusted. He knew a lot of good real estate, lending and administrative experts he could call. He would have to hire them to help out, have them examine the properties on which mortgages had been written so he could draw a bead on the severity of the loan problems. Popejoy remained optimistic, though. With any luck at all, fixing the company's back shop operations would go a long way toward saving the company. Maybe the loan troubles at American weren't as bad as they had been portrayed by the press. Perhaps instead, many of the loans would prove to be sound once he got the Stockton offices running smoothly.

---

*Ironically, the Home Loan Bank's help nearly resulted in disaster. To centralize the collateral, Home Loan Bank personnel had nearly $10 billion in loans placed in the basement of one building. That way, the loans could be grabbed in a hurry. The federal examiners didn't know it, but the building they chose was located near a river that occasionally flooded. The basement was below the water line. Flooded loan documents would bring a whole new meaning to the term *liquid assets*. American Savings might literally sink if its assets went under water. After water was discovered on the floor one day, the loans were moved to a safer location.

Stockton wasn't the only scene of bedlam. American Savings was overwhelming the Federal Reserve Bank of San Francisco by delivering billions in collateral to the Federal Reserve's discount window.

Located at the end of Market Street just across from the Hyatt Regency Hotel and a major stop on the city's cable-car route, the regional bank was in a conspicuous spot. Not only did hundreds of tourists mill about just across the street from the bank every day, but newspaper photographers and television camera crews could easily stake it out.

Because of this, American Savings officials, who were bringing collateral to the Fed's discount window to establish a line of credit, at first brought loans to the bank in the backseats of their cars. They arrived at night and came in through the back door.

The Fed officials had been shocked at the poor quality of the collateral. Through a team hired to perform spot appraisals, they rejected hundreds of American's loans as unsuitable. The team found properties supposedly more than halfway completed for which the foundations had barely been laid, and the Fed's internal team found a plethora of shoddy paperwork such as loan files that lacked appraisals or any record of insurance on the property.

The company brought so much paperwork to the Fed's discount window that the bank's personnel couldn't keep up. San Francisco Fed executives called Washington and asked for extra workers to man the discount window. And once examiners from Federal Reserve banks in Chicago and New York arrived, they had them working almost around the clock.

After surveying so many rotten loans, the Fed's managers became convinced that American would fail. They didn't think there was any way the company could move fast enough to cover all the withdrawals. The Fed officials kept in frequent communication with American Savings, the Home Loan Bank of San Francisco, and the Federal Reserve Board of Governors in Washington. Every day, they monitored American's transfers of funds—how much money flowed out and how much was wired in from Wall Street and other locations. Every day they telecopied an update to Preston Martin, the Fed vice chairman.

As they watched the flow of funds at American, the San Francisco Fed officials noticed that every time it looked as though the company was ready to run out of collateral and collapse, which was almost every day, money miraculously appeared.

By mid-September, the Fed's senior executives had to hand it to Popejoy. He was emerging from the maelstrom. Popejoy's experience at Freddie Mac, packaging and selling loans, was paying off. American Savings seemed to be selling its way to solvency.

Despite the efficient securities sales, American Savings needed more help. In September, Popejoy told Ann Fairbanks that the company required sizable new deposits. The deposit-gathering staff couldn't raise enough money, and he did not want to rely solely on asset sales and borrowings from the Home Loan Bank. That meant using brokered funds. It was the fastest and most efficient source of fresh cash. Popejoy wanted to use the proceeds for general corporate purposes and to repay some borrowings from the Home Loan Bank of San Francisco. Repaying the debt would serve as a show of strength and would help restore faith in American Savings.

This left Ed Gray with two difficult choices. He could swallow his pride, or he could let American Savings fend for itself. Gray had continued to speak out about the evils of brokered money in the months before the trauma at American. If anything, he had become even more convinced of the threat it posed to the thrift industry, and he battled Wall Street over the issue.

Investment houses strongly opposed the restrictions Gray wanted to place on brokered funds. Brokering money was a good business. The brokerage companies could tap the financial markets for investment money, break huge pools of funds into increments of $100,000, and place them in federally insured institutions, earning a handsome fee on a riskless investment. Stockbrokers could also offer federally insured certificates of deposit to their retail customers.

Merrill Lynch, one of the country's largest brokerage firms, wasn't about to let Gray go forward without a fight. In February, the company sent letters to 500,000 of its customers who purchased certificates of deposit, telling them to write their representatives in Washington condemning the "sledgehammer rule" proposed by Gray and Bill Isaac, his colleague at the FDIC.

The crusade soon became embarrassing for Merrill Lynch. After a Washington press conference, Edson Mitchell, managing director of Merrill Lynch Money Markets, Inc., talked to reporter Stephen Katsanos, of *Washington Financial Reports*. Katsanos in turn passed to the Bank Board what he said were Mitchell's comments.

Mitchell was quoted as suggesting that Merrill Lynch had someone following Ed Gray and that Gray's interest in the brokered-fund issue was colored by his close connection to California thrifts, adding that the company knew because "we have put some people in to follow his movements."

Ed Gray fired off an angry letter to Merrill Lynch, accusing Mitchell of impugning "not only my personal integrity but my professional integrity." Merrill Lynch replied that the quotations were "inaccurate." Gray sent copies of the correspondence to every member of the House and Senate banking committees, where the subject of brokered funds was still an important issue because a federal court had not yet struck down the proposed restrictions.

Now Merrill Lynch would have the last laugh, however. With the run at American Savings building steam, Gray had little choice but to turn to brokered deposits for help. He approved the use of brokered funds at American Savings, proving the point that brokered money was the most efficient means of attracting new deposits. In addition, he sought help from the very firm he had been battling with, Merrill Lynch, for Dick Pratt, the former Bank Board chairman was now a senior Merrill official and was helping Popejoy keep American from going under.

At the Bank Board's request, according to Gray, Pratt began putting together a $1-billion package of insured certificates of deposit. At the last moment in late September, Pratt called to say the deal had fallen through because he had been overruled by his superiors. Ed Gray later blamed Treasury Secretary Don Regan for the loss of support at Merrill Lynch. He claimed Dick Pratt told him that Don Regan, the former head of Merrill Lynch, was the reason the company pulled out. Regan denied it, saying Gray was "mistaken in his account."

In any case, Gray and Fairbanks hit the phones, calling a variety of investment firms, and finally Prudential-Bache Securities agreed to lead a syndicate of five firms that would offer the CDs, primarily through the retail market. With this support, American took the $1-billion package to the market on October 1 in multiples of $1,000 with maturities ranging from six months to seven years. The liquidity crisis was drawing to a close, but many challenges still lay ahead, as Bill Popejoy would soon learn.

Unlike a war, the siege at American Savings had no crucial turning point, no decisive moment of action that could be credited with saving the company.

It may have been Knapp's ouster, followed by the hiring of Bill Popejoy. It could have been the fast action on the part of Brinkerhoff's team or the ability of Cirona's staff to keep lending money to American, although in smaller amounts and at higher rates than Popejoy wanted.

The picture of Ed Gray shaking hands with Popejoy also helped, as did Freddie Mac's decision to come to the company's aid. During the run, FCA paid a dividend on its common stock, an action that had to be approved by the federal government and was viewed as a sign of support. Wall Street pitched in and continued to loan money to American. The deposit salespeople kept dialing for dollars.

By standing firm in the face of what seemed to be insurmountable obstacles, American Savings survived an onslaught that would have killed many other financial institutions. The company came close to folding several times but never missed a payment to creditors or depositors.

With Popejoy in command, American fought through a $6.8-billion run. Unlike Continental, American never received a direct injection of funds from the federal government. The company ultimately borrowed $3.3 billion from the Home Loan Bank of San Francisco, $6 billion from Wall Street, $2 billion from Freddie Mac, and established an $800 million line of credit with the San Francisco Federal Reserve.

Hundreds of anonymous workers throughout the company, the federal government, and Wall Street toiled countless hours to keep the nation's largest S&L from collapsing. Gradually, the run subsided, and by October, it was clear that American had survived the second-largest run in the history of the United States. Nevertheless, the company resembled a once-proud city that had been shelled into near submission. Now Bill Popejoy faced a daunting question: Could he rebuild American from the rubble?

Chapter 11

The Ax Falls

Although Popejoy's two previous corporate restructurings had seemed difficult at the time, they were minor in comparison with the tough challenges ahead at FCA. Even before the run had subsided, Popejoy began to formulate his plan. He would turn the company upside down, go after waste and inefficiency with an ax. But one of his first major changes thrust him into open conflict with an adversary outside the company.

In mid-September, a few weeks after learning of the horrendous administrative problems facing him, Popejoy had received a visit at his fifteenth-floor office from two worried executives at American Savings who had damaging information about the company's prospects for recovery.

The executives, both based in Stockton, told Popejoy they had reason to believe that American had unrecognized loan losses due to foreclosures and delinquencies of about $70 million in just one segment of the portfolio. A careful check of all American loans might reveal even larger losses, although the executives couldn't be sure how much.

Popejoy remembered that conversation a short time later when he met with senior executives at Arthur Andersen, the Big Eight accounting firm that had served as FCA's outside auditors for a decade. The FCA chairman had gone to Washington for another fence-mending session with the Federal Reserve and the Bank Board. He also had a meeting scheduled at the Securities and Exchange Commission, the agency that had twice called FCA's earnings into question.

Before going to the SEC, Popejoy wanted to confer with FCA's accountants. He was worried about the size of American's loan losses; a $70 million hit was a lot to swallow. At a breakfast meeting at the Madison Hotel in downtown Washington, Popejoy asked the senior Arthur Andersen staff if FCA's reserves to cover future loan losses were adequate. No, he said he was told. American might need to reserve an extra $15 million or $20 million.

That sounded awfully low to Popejoy. He had seen the poor condition of the loan files for himself and had the warning of two senior American executives about large losses in just a segment of its asset base. If he had had any doubts about his tentative decision to replace Arthur Andersen as the firm's accountants, that breakfast meeting erased them.

Shortly after returning to Los Angeles, Popejoy began looking for new auditors. On a philosophical level, he believed a company should not retain the same accountants for more than five years. Otherwise, a cozy relationship developed, and the company might not get the most accurate and objective information.

In addition, because the SEC had questioned the accuracy of the company's financial statements, Popejoy felt it was time to bring in another firm that would have an unbiased view. The SEC's investigation into 1980 and 1981 lending practices was continuing, and FCA was still in a dispute with the Bank Board about the accounting treatment for hundreds of millions in problem loans. In the last week of September, Popejoy went public with his plans.

"We have simply decided that it is appropriate to make a change at this time," Popejoy told the media, though in fact no replacement firm had yet been selected. "This decision by our board does not result from any accounting disagreement with Arthur Andersen."

Sheldon Ausman, an officer at Arthur Andersen's Los Angeles office, said that he was surprised by the decision, adding that FCA "just called us up on Thursday and read us the press release." Soon, FCA's workers would be just as stunned by Popejoy's actions.

On October 12, the bloodletting began. As part of his recovery plan for FCA, which was under pressure from the federal government to retrench, Popejoy unveiled the layoff of 1,500 of its 7,500 workers, a 20 percent reduction.

The deepest cuts were to come from management, staff,

administrators, technical and loan-production personnel, many of whom were located at American's offices in Stockton. FCA also eliminated all "frills and nonessential expenses." Popejoy decided to sell 475 company cars, 5 corporate jets, and 41 condominiums that had been used by American staff members, particularly executives. In all, these changes were estimated to save some $32 million to $35 million a year.

The new chairman shared in the sacrifices, taking a 20 percent pay cut, from $650,000 a year to $520,000, but retaining his stock options and performance bonuses. Fifty-nine other senior managers accepted the same salary reductions.

Nevertheless, Foster Fluetsch was furious. The company was being dismantled before his eyes, and he was powerless to prevent it. Fluetsch said he was upset because many of his friends at American Savings would lose their jobs. Even worse, FCA made the announcement to the media before warning the workers. Fluetsch blasted FCA for its "unchristian" behavior. He said the company's management should have had the good grace to tell the employees first.

Still a popular business leader in Stockton despite his dismissal from American Savings, Fluetsch, the hometown hero, denounced FCA's new leaders for the "inept and unprofessional" way they released news of the impending layoffs. "There must have been a better way to handle it," he said, adding that FCA's executives "had better start thinking about the people." Telling the media first was "shortsighted on the part of management and shortsighted on the part of anybody who has the least sense of human values."

Unchristian? Shortsighted? No sense of human values? That was a pretty strong rebuke to a man who considered himself a people-oriented manager. Popejoy was in a war, and in war there are casualties. Besides, he would not have adopted such drastic measures if Fluetsch had had the foresight to be frugal.

Popejoy defended his action plan, telling the *Stockton Record* that the company would have preferred to tell individual workers first, but "premature press coverage" had forced him to make the announcement to the media.

Ironically, FCA had relatively low overhead for a company its size. General and administrative expenses, a measure of efficiency in the thrift business, were about $100 million a quarter in 1984, about half that of some competitors. However, these costs had surged a startling 64 percent from January to August, reflecting the hiring of new workers needed to cope with American's rapid growth, and Popejoy wanted a sharp reversal of that trend.

Bill Popejoy had a bit of Mark Taper in him, after all. Although it might not be cheaper in the long run, selling the cars and planes was essential, Popejoy thought, because they portrayed the wrong image for American Savings. The jets were just an unneeded frill at a company that had come close to crashing. While less convenient, commercial flights went everywhere American workers needed to go.

Company cars were also unnecessary and established counterproductive differences in status. With so many cars, American required a whole staff to keep track of the vehicles. And petty differences among the staff arose over who got the nicest car with the fanciest stereo. From an administrative standpoint, it was simpler and more efficient to give car allowances to those employees who needed them and then let the workers decide what they wanted to drive.

Securities analysts saw FCA's cuts as a sign that Popejoy would make good on his pledge to shrink the company. He promised that despite the cutbacks, FCA would have ample corporate muscle and would remain an aggressive competitor.

The cost-cutting plan was just the first stage for Popejoy. He wanted a new board of directors as well. On October 25, FCA announced the selection of six new directors and the voluntary resignation of three others.

From the very start, Bill Popejoy had harbored strong doubts about the accountability between the boards of FCA (the holding company) and American Savings because only one of the outside directors served on both boards. That meant only one board member had direct access to the key management decisions at the holding company's most valuable asset.

Technically, under U.S. securities laws, corporate directors are "control" persons. They not only approve the hiring of senior management but also serve on committees that oversee executive compensation and corporate audits, and determine the size of dividend payments. Selected to protect the shareholders against management mistakes and abuses, the directors have the power to fire a company's chief executive officer if necessary.

The Bank Board also had some concerns about the directors who had allowed Charlie Knapp to grow his company at a dangerous clip and then paid him $2 million to leave. In addition, there were bound to be some mutual animosities among the old directors, some of whom felt the government had treated Knapp and the company shabbily, and new management, who would naturally come in as problem solvers dedicated to fixing past mistakes. So there was little choice but to change the makeup of the board.

The new directors included

- Annelise Anderson, a senior research fellow at the Hoover Institution, a conservative think tank on the campus of Stanford University, had previously served at the Office of Management and Budget in Washington. Her husband, Martin Anderson, had been Ed Gray's boss at the White House, and she had served as a director of the Federal Home Loan Bank of San Francisco.
- Merrill Butler, a highly decorated hero in World War II, a barrel-chested, cigar-smoking real-estate developer, was one of the best in his field. He was chairman and president of the Butler Group and former president of the National Association of Homebuilders.
- Edward L. Johnson was the retired chairman of Financial Federation, Inc., the thrift holding company where Popejoy had worked before coming to FCA.
- Robert M. Barton, an attorney with Barton, Klugman & Oetting in Newport Beach, had served on the board at Fin Fed with Johnson.
- Thomas P. Kemp, brother of conservative Republican Congressman Jack Kemp, was the former chairman of the Coca-Cola Bottling Co. of Los Angeles and the senior vice president of Beatrice Companies, Inc. and president of its Grocery Group.
- J. Ralph Stone, a consultant who had retired as chairman of Santa Rosa Savings and Loan in northern California, was a longtime friend of Mark Taper. He had also served

as president of the California League of Savings Institutions.

Left over from the Knapp regime were Lawrence K. Roos, former president of the Federal Reserve Bank of St. Louis, a limited partner with the brokerage house of Bear, Stearns & Co.; Charles E. Young, UCLA's chancellor (Roos and Young would remain for years); Charles Offer, founder of Budget Industries; and E. John Rosenwald, Jr., a senior Bear, Stearns partner.

In addition to these changes, Popejoy moved to reshuffle the American board as well. He wanted all the outside board members at FCA to become directors at American and would make the American board members "directors emeritus," to serve as a shadow advisory group. In other words, he was easing the American directors out gracefully.

The new board wasted little time settling an old score. As one of its first official acts, the board decided to sue Charlie Knapp for the return of his $2-million severance pay.

The matter had been coming to a head since September 26 when at a meeting of the old board, Popejoy read two letters from the regulators, seeking return of Knapp's severance payment. Two months later, at a November 27 board meeting, Popejoy told the directors that the Bank Board felt FCA's decision to pay Knapp to leave in the midst of the liquidity crisis was inappropriate.

John Rosenwald, the investment banker who had served as a director when Knapp was chairman, said he understood why Popejoy advocated trying to recover the money, but he thought the severance payment had been correct under the circumstances because the company was under enormous pressure to get rid of Knapp.

Annelise Anderson, the Hoover fellow who was one of Ed Gray's friends, had her doubts as well. She noted not only that the previous board had voted to give Knapp the money but that the former chief executive had already received payment. It would be difficult to get the money back.

Popejoy was persuasive. He said the Bank Board felt strongly about the issue and had continued pressing him to take action against Knapp. Popejoy said he had already written Knapp, demanding the return of the money, which Knapp declined to do. When it came to a vote, he received the backing of the new board. Despite her doubts, Anderson decided to support Popejoy. To avoid any misunderstanding a no vote might bring, Rosenwald decided to abstain. So did Phil Brinkerhoff and Charles Young, both of whom had been directors under Knapp when the old board approved the separation package. With these three abstentions, the board voted unanimously to sue Knapp.

FCA then filed suit in state court, charging that Knapp exercised "undue influence" over the company during the depositor panic. Knapp was accused of "taking unfair advantage of FCA's economic necessities and distress then well-known to him."

Art Shingler no longer fit in at the new American Savings. Whether he could have survived the company's overhaul is doubtful. As American's current president and former chief financial officer, he was closely identified with American's financial weaknesses and low-grade loans.

Shingler also made the mistake of quarreling with Ken Krause, one of Popejoy's most trusted aides. A former marine sergeant who still handled tough assignments as though he were storming an enemy bunker, he often joked that he had become FCA's "hatchet man." He thought Shingler moved too slowly and was too generous in granting severance pay to American Savings workers fired under Popejoy's downsizing plan. After one vitriolic argument, Krause offered to resign and later called Popejoy to complain.

In early December, Popejoy called Shingler in Stockton. "I need to talk with you," he said.

"That sounds pretty ominous."

"I'm afraid it is."

"Well, I'm a big boy. Let's have it."

"We're going to have to let you go. But I want you to fly down, and I want to talk about it face-to-face. Let's meet this afternoon."

At the follow-up meeting in person, the two men negotiated Shingler's separation pay. He received $500,000, or two years' salary. Shingler said he warned Popejoy that the government's calls to whittle away assets would result in insolvency and that firing the managers from the real-estate-owned department was a mistake because Popejoy would need those people to identify problem loans.

On December 14, FCA announced Shingler's resignation and said Popejoy would replace him as head of American Savings. The company also announced a restructuring of both the holding company and the thrift into four operating divisions: administrative, financial, legal, and lending.

Two weeks later, Phil Brinkerhoff resigned. Like Popejoy, Brinkerhoff had a strong urge to become the chief executive officer. Although the two men had worked well together and Brinkerhoff still considered himself Popejoy's friend, his desire to run things had not diminished.

Brinkerhoff had intended to stay at FCA until his three-year contract expired and then leave. But an executive-recruitment firm contacted him about the top spot at Financial Corp. of Santa Barbara (no relation to FCA in Los Angeles). Located in the seaside resort community ninety miles northwest of Los Angeles, Financial Corp. of Santa Barbara owned Santa Barbara Savings & Loan Association, an unhealthy thrift attempting to recover from a long string of losses. John Darr had recently resigned from FCA in Los Angeles as well. With Brinkerhoff, Darr, and Shingler gone, Charlie Knapp's three-man office of president was closed, leaving Bill Popejoy firmly in control.

Chapter 12

The Miracle Man

Bill Popejoy was quick to realize that plotting a safe future for American Savings would require more than reducing overhead and realigning management. He had to get a handle on the size of the company's real-estate losses, for additional loan losses would undermine all his hard work. And he had to start rebuilding American's horribly depleted capital base and restore its tarnished image.

One of his first opportunities for discovering the size of American's loan problems came in a luncheon with Jonathan Gray, the analyst Charlie Knapp had threatened with imprisonment. Gray, who had known Popejoy for years, had met with him several times while Popejoy worked for Mark Taper as president of First Charter. He found Popejoy a bright and likable executive greatly overshadowed by Taper, who seemed to talk to the young president as though he were his grandson.

In mid-September, Gray was scheduled to be in California to meet with Bernstein clients. He called Popejoy and suggested that the two men talk about the company's health. They met at a hotel restaurant on the western end of Wilshire Boulevard. Still trim and athletic-looking at 46, Popejoy ordered a chef's salad.

Popejoy was concerned about the harsh comments Gray had made about FCA's weak condition and wanted to learn firsthand why Gray was so downbeat about FCA's prospects. If Popejoy could convince him that the company was much stronger than the analyst thought, if he could bring Gray into the fold, it would make his life much easier by cutting down on negative publicity.

"I don't think we have serious loan problems," Popejoy said. "I think it is a servicing problem. I think they are getting checks that are being paid, but they are not recording the checks in time. It looks like they have a lot of loans that are not performing but in fact are."

"Bill, you're kidding yourself. American has got a lot of bad loans. I've never seen anything like it. The SEC found something like four-hundred million dollars in bad loans. My guess is the number is closer to something like five-hundred million."

"Jonathan, how would you know? You've never made a mortgage in your life."

"I was out to visit the company last November," Gray said, handing him a copy of the report he had earlier given Charlie Knapp. "I did a very careful analysis. Let me show you what I have found."

Gray walked Popejoy through the extensive calculations and pages and pages of numbers he had put together in his critical examination of American's loan portfolio. Popejoy couldn't believe Gray's attitude. What did he know about loan problems? He was an analyst, not a lender. He had spent such a short time in Stockton going over the financials. Popejoy, on the other hand, had dozens of seasoned professionals pouring over the books. No one but Gray was projecting such staggering losses.

Popejoy had predicted it would take three to five years to restore FCA to health, an estimate that had not counted on a half-billion dollars in loan losses. Half a billion in bad loans? The amount was inconceivable. Even if Jonathan Gray had used a computer for his research, that wasn't the same thing as first-hand experience with real-estate mortgages.

Gray stood by his study, stating that poor loan quality would cast a dark shadow on FCA's future. Two weeks later, with the announcement of Arthur Andersen's dismissal, an upbeat Popejoy said FCA's liquidity was steadily improving and that investors had a greater belief in the company's viability.

In contrast, Jonathan Gray led securities analysts who said they expected FCA to take writedowns in the real-estate portfolio. Although FCA's stock had steadily gained from a low of about $4 to a high on Friday, September 24, of $8, professional stock speculators were also anticipating trouble and had been shorting FCA stock. ("Shorting" stock is an agreement to sell shares you do not own because you expect the price to fall, allowing the sale of stock at higher prices than it will cost to purchase them to fulfill the contract.) A lot of short sellers were interested in FCA. In fact, the number of FCA shares sold short had increased 40 percent to 7 million shares between August 15 and September 15.

"The stock is an excellent short," said Jonathan Gray, still clinging to his belief that the loan portfolio was a shambles. He speculated that FCA would soon take sizable writeoffs. "Liquidity is a short-term issue. The long-term question is the loan quality."

A month later, on the same day that FCA announced the selection of new directors, the company also produced some long-awaited upbeat financial news, reporting a profit of $1.2 million for the third quarter of 1984. That was a meager amount, based largely on such nonrecurring gains as securities sales and withdrawal penalties from depositors during the run. But it was a profit, nonetheless, and Popejoy was glad to have it. He would take all the positive publicity he could get.

Combined with the results of the first six months, the company's nine-month deficit stood at $78.4 million, compared with net income of $116.1 million for the similar period in 1983.

FCA's assets had actually grown in the third period. That was partly the result of the loan commitments that Knapp's regime had negotiated as one plank in FCA's growth strategy. Now, as the company was trying to cut back, Popejoy found that American was a balloon expanding on its own. In many instances, Popejoy and his senior managers had no choice but to honor the commitments to make and buy loans that had already been issued. The company originated $2.84 billion in new mortgage loans in the third quarter and bought an additional $2.95 billion.

Some clear warning signs emerged from the financial statements. Reserves against loan losses leapt 37 percent, to $90.5 million. The company had capital of $781.8 million, or only about 2.4 percent of total assets. FCA had only sixty days remaining to make its year-end requirement of 4 percent net worth mandated by the Bank Board.

With bad loans still on the rise, if American met the net-worth requirement, it would be a miracle. Then again, to keep from going under, American Savings would require a lot of miracles from Bill Popejoy.

* * *

As he moved ahead with his recovery plans, Popejoy wasn't content to let FCA's reputation rely on the release of good news. The company needed a fresh image, and that required good public relations and a new advertising campaign.

Soon enough, Popejoy found himself seated in a film studio on Sunset Boulevard, filming a television commercial. He was uncomfortable and fidgeted in his seat. First of all, maybe it was a macho thing, but he didn't like wearing makeup. He felt overwhelmed by the size of the studio. Then again, a pushy woman had cut off part of his shirt sleeve, and as the script rolled across the camera on the kind of teleprompter device that news anchors use, Popejoy flubbed his lines. Perspiration soaked his coat. Someone handed him a Coke, but he was shaking so badly, he could hardly hold on to the drink.

Finally, he relaxed, looked straight into the camera, and delivered his most important line: "My money is with American."

At first, Popejoy hadn't wanted to appear in the company's commercials. He thought other executives who became corporate pitchmen were probably on an ego trip, and he didn't want to seem like them. But after he thought about it, he decided the advertising campaign would be an important kickoff for a company that desperately needed to improve its standing with the public. Customers should know that American had weathered the storm and that new management was in charge. Iacocca had done the same thing at Chrysler, and it had worked.

The My Money Is with American campaign was a perfect fit for Popejoy, the handsome articulate chairman with salt-and-pepper hair and a baritone voice. Filmed in black and white, the commercials portrayed him as a sincere financier, the kind of man you could trust with your life's savings and still sleep at night. When he saw the edited version of the commercials, Popejoy liked the way he came across. Maybe he would be another Iacocca after all.

Unfortunately for Popejoy, positive publicity was short-lived. On December 18, just three weeks after FCA posted a third-quarter profit, the company went public with bad news.

Armed with some preliminary information from a task force

reviewing American's real-estate portfolio, Popejoy predicted FCA would take a big hit in earnings for the fourth quarter but said he did not yet know how much. He said FCA would show a loss for the fourth quarter, in part because of "substantial" increases in the reserve for loan losses and because of a $6.3-million loss on the sale of 896,900 shares of Walt Disney common stock. Other problems resulted from high severance costs and a virtual standstill in lending volume.

The fourth-quarter losses, Popejoy said, meant FCA's chances of meeting the 4 percent net-worth level mandated by the Bank Board were "nonexistent."

The day after Christmas, Popejoy met with the members of the Bank Board and Jim Cirona. He told them American could not reach its net-worth requirement. A new real-estate task force had not yet finished its report on bad loans, and just two weeks earlier, FCA had hired an outside real-estate consulting firm to help. Although he did not know the size of the real-estate losses, he was sure the company's capital position would only get worse.

Ed Gray was worried about the seriousness of the net-worth situation. But there was nothing he could do. The Bank Board couldn't grant a waiver on such a sensitive issue at a time when Gray wanted to force others to improve their capital levels as a safeguard for the federal insurance fund. He had been adamant with Knapp about the 4 percent level, and that figure had been clearly stated in the agreement the Bank Board had reached last August when Popejoy was hired.

Under the terms of FCA's operating agreement, the Bank Board could get a cease-and-desist order if American's net worth fell below 4 percent. In addition, failure to meet the terms of the agreement meant that the loans from the Federal Home Loan Bank were in default. The Bank Board was not about to change its position on the capital issue, even if American was still weak from the run.

However, the regulators were willing to give the company more time to regain its footing. The Bank Board members decided the agency would take no action against American Savings because of its weak capital. This was a huge political compromise that would be used to keep the company alive.

Officially, there was no waiver, but in fact, American would never have to live up to its agreement. This also helped Ed Gray. After all, he had approved the merger, and sidestepping the capital issue allowed him to avoid closing the company or taking other tough actions against his handpicked chairman.

Gray knew full well that he could not shut down American. FSLIC didn't have enough money in its reserves to do so. The government also avoided the embarrassment and potential negative reaction of having the loans from the Home Loan Bank declared in default. Thus, he would let American plod along with substandard capital at a time when he was trying to force other thrifts to improve their net worth. Gray wrote a letter of forbearance for American Savings regarding the capital issue, and this letter was printed in the company's annual report. It was needed so that investors and others would do business with FCA without worrying that the regulators would shut down American Savings.

Under strict orders from the federal government, Popejoy began to formulate plans to cut away chunks of American Savings. The most obvious place to start was also the most painful.

American operated 122 branches throughout California, many of them in strategic locations. The southern California branch system was especially desirable because that part of the state, anchored by Los Angeles, had long since passed northern California as a business center. Indeed, southern California had one of the world's largest economies, one that was expected to play an even larger role in U.S. trade by the turn of the century.

Plenty of American's in-state competitors would want to pick up the southern California branch system. But Popejoy thought of a company based in New York that would be especially interested. Citicorp, the nation's largest bank, had just two years before acquired struggling Fidelity Savings of San Francisco, becoming the first commercial-banking company to buy an out-of-state S&L.

Renamed Citicorp Savings and headquartered across the bay in Oakland, the thrift was part of Citicorp's new dedication to national consumer banking. The New York–based giant had for years overlooked the importance of consumer banking. Consumer banking can bring handsome profits because banks and thrifts charge more for credit cards, car loans, and lines of credit than they do for residential mortgages.

John Reed, Citicorp's boyish-looking 43-year-old vice chairman for consumer banking, was on record as having big plans for California. Although Citicorp Savings had only 300,000 customers in the nation's most populous state, Reed said he wanted to expand that number sevenfold. He wanted California to exceed Citicorp's home base in New York where the company had 2 million customers. Reed knew it would take a long time to complete a statewide expansion, but he hoped to gather as many as two hundred branches.

Shortly after the run was under control, Popejoy met in San Francisco with Ed Valencia, a Citicorp officer, to discuss selling American's flagship southern branches. On paper, selling the sixty branches that American Savings had in southern California seemed like a perfect transaction for both companies. American's southern system had about \$7 billion in assets, and charging Citicorp 5 percent of that amount would yield about \$350 million. American Savings would have a quick infusion of the capital it so desperately needed to meet the Bank Board's requirement, and John Reed would have instant statewide expansion.

But the more Popejoy studied the proposal, the more doubtful it became. Rather than help in the recovery, the branch sale would weaken American even further. At the time of the American-State merger in 1983, FCA had used purchase accounting, putting on its books \$1.2 billion for such intangible assets as the company's good name, assets on which it earned no money. Selling the southern California branches would drain FCA of \$500 million of this goodwill, more than offsetting the \$350 million FCA would receive from Citicorp. That would mean hacking away half of American's branch network just so that FCA could lose \$150 million in net worth. Obviously, selling the branches was out of the question under these circumstances, and by late January 1985, the secret Citicorp proposal was dead.

Discovering the adverse impact goodwill had on American's balance sheet led Popejoy to another important insight. The agreement FCA had signed with the Bank Board mandated the orderly reduction in FCA's size, and that too was fraught with problems.

Because of its large number of substandard and delinquent loans and the huge allocation to goodwill, American Savings had to earn nearly double what a healthy financial institution would, just to cover overhead. Reducing American's size meant the company would have to earn ever greater profits on a smaller asset base, a completely unrealistic goal. In other words, Popejoy thought, shrinking meant suicide on the installment plan. His conclusion would be questioned and criticized later, but Popejoy was convinced. American Savings had to grow. Or die.

Chapter 13

And the Good News Is . . .

Vic Indiek was flattered to be emerging as one of Popejoy's most trusted executives. The two men went back a long way, and it felt good to be receiving so much responsibility from his old friend. Yet Indiek was becoming overwhelmed by the mind-numbing complexity of his new job.

He had received this new assignment toward the end of the depositor run when Popejoy came and asked him to head a task force charged with examining American's portfolio of real-estate loans and the property the company owned after foreclosing on borrowers. That meant Indiek's task force would play a critical role in Popejoy's recovery effort because the chairman had to determine the full size of real-estate losses and establish enough reserves to cover them. Without a clear picture of the loan losses, Popejoy could not estimate American's full-year deficit, establish accurate budgets, or provide frank assessments to the regulators or financial analysts closely tracking the company's performance.

Indiek was to live in Stockton during the week throughout that fall and early winter as he supervised the examination of American's troubled assets and then commuted home to Santa Monica on the weekends. A devoted family man who loved to water-ski, Indiek found that American's loan problems left him little time for other activities.

Although much of his career had centered on finance, Indiek was no stranger to the leathery world of real estate or wayward S&Ls. While an auditor at Arthur Anderson in Kansas City, Indiek had specialized in reviewing real-estate and construction companies. After nine years with the accounting firm, he moved to Washington to become the chief financial officer at Freddie Mac where he began working with Popejoy, packaging loans for sale in the secondary market. After Popejoy left to work for Mark Taper at American Savings, Indiek became Freddie Mac's president.

He left in 1977 and took a job in Los Angeles with Watt Industries, a large real-estate developer that concentrated on residential tracts but also built some of the ubiquitous shopping malls of southern California. Indiek was the president of Builders Capital, a joint-venture financing subsidiary, as well as a vice president for the holding company.

With deregulation of the S&L industry starting to take off, Indiek entered the thrift business in 1983, landing a position at American Diversified Savings Bank in Costa Mesa. Indiek put together the business plans and operating strategies for Ranbir Sahni, a native of India and a former airline pilot turned real-estate syndicator, who had a nose for exotic and unprincipled business ventures.

Heading a growth-oriented company in an industry undergoing profound change was exciting at first, but Indiek soon got the impression that Sahni was driving so fast, he was stripping all the company's gears. Indiek's instincts proved correct. American Diversified turned out to be one of the worst-run financial institutions of all time.*

He got out before he became tainted by financial scandal. In early 1984, before the federal government began its crackdown at American Diversified, Indiek joined FCA Mortgage Securities as executive vice president, setting up the trading operation and hiring key staff members. He was still working the bugs out of the operation when American ran aground in August.

---

*According to the Federal Home Loan Bank of San Francisco, in the testimony before the House Banking Committee, American Diversified focused on fast growth by raising deposits through brokered funds and then exploited the investment powers available to state-chartered thrifts in California. Sahni invested insured deposits in such questionable enterprises as windmill farms, ethanol-processing plants, a nationwide paging network, and a facility designed to convert cow manure into methane; there were also sham real-estate deals with friends and business associates. These investments proved disastrous for the company and the nation's taxpayers.

By the time American Diversified was seized by the federal regulators on Valentine's Day in 1986, it had a negative net worth of more than $400 million. Further examination revealed even larger losses. On June 6, 1988, FSLIC became a receiver for the company and paid out a then-record $1.1 billion to depositors.

Indiek's task force consisted of another longtime Popejoy associate, Ken Krause, who later became FCA's chief administrative officer; Alan Bergman, who had been American's general counsel under Popejoy in the 1970s before going into private practice; and Bob Kircher, another real-estate expert. Merrill Butler, the nationally known builder, later joined the group.

Indiek, who was quickly elevated to chief financial officer, was the only FCA employee on the team; the others worked as consultants because Popejoy wanted an independent review by outsiders. The task force had three main goals: identify problem loans and real estate; establish effective administrative controls, and ensure adequate reserves for losses. All three proved difficult.

Aided by Peat Marwick, FCA's new auditors, Indiek's group concentrated on four areas: major problem loans, foreclosed property, construction lending, and investment real estate (the last group consisting primarily of land that American owned and wanted to develop). With hundreds of loans to look at, the task force had a lot of ground to cover.

Many of the properties required additional appraisals. In December, FCA hired Landauer Associates, Inc., a real-estate consulting firm, to conduct a month-long appraisal of single-family homes and commercial properties.

Meanwhile, Indiek had already discovered that he needed a new dictionary to do his job. Under Charlie Knapp and Foster Fluetsch, American Savings had introduced a whole new lexicon to lending, including such odd instruments as "echo loans," "dynamite loans," "see-through buildings," and "trash-for-cash."

Echo loans were those that kept coming back and coming back. With an echo loan, American had granted a mortgage on an investment property that turned out to have overly optimistic cash-flow projections. Thereupon, the loan was restructured, a standard practice at banks and thrifts when customers can't pay their bills. However, the restructuring also turned out to be too sanguine. Some echo loans had bounced back to American several times.

Dynamite loans were those with initial interest payments well below market that exploded two or three years later. For instance, a motel owner's loan might call for payments of $10,000 a month, but he would begin with payments only half that. Three or four years later, the payment would rise to $12,000 to begin recouping the foregone interest and principal. Those kinds of loans could be written in a market with rapid property appreciation or where a company's cash flow grew quickly, but in many cases, the loans went into default because the project did not live up to optimistic projections.

"See-through buildings," vacant office buildings, had deep problems as well. With see-through buildings, American had loaned money to a developer who had failed to sign up any tenants before construction began. The project was developed on speculation that demand would later emerge for the office space. In fact, many see-through office buildings never had tenants; you could see through windows in front and right through the buildings since they had no furnishings or office equipment.

Then there was "trash-for-cash." Trash-for-cash was an innovative marketing plan that American employed to get rid of problem loans. With a trash-for-cash transaction, American would loan money to a developer only after he agreed to take a problem project off the company's hands. For instance, a borrower might seek a loan of $20 million on a $25-million project. American would agree to give the customer a loan for $23 million, the additional sum to be used to acquire problem real estate, a dangerous and highly questionable practice because borrowers were forced to take more money than they probably could afford to repay and use the extra proceeds to pay for American's shaky assets.

With so many categories of bad loans, it seems inconceivable that Knapp, Fluetsch, Shingler, and American's other senior managers could have been blind to the level of assets or the chicanery in the lending operation. True, they may not have known the full extent of the losses, given the shoddy and unprofessional underwriting standards employed at American and the turbulent nature of the lending market following the collapse of oil prices and declining land values. But the fact that so many loans fit nicely into specific categories of problems underscores the extent to which steps were taken at American to hide bad loans from the regulators and investors.

Indeed, the cash-for-trash was not only foolish; it was little more than blackmail. Any prudent financial manager would have to realize that a borrower who was so desperate for money that he would take your garbage loans was likely a poor credit risk. Beyond that, the borrowers were on the hook for more money than the project justified, guaranteeing that in the event of a foreclosure, American would lose much more money than was warranted by standard business practices. Lenders require sizable down payments to protect the company in case of a default. But not at American. Under Knapp and Fluetsch, American's disregarded prudent practices and increased the risk. In addition, the borrowers were essentially forced into the program; if they wanted the money, they had to play American's way. It was little more than legalized loan-sharking.

Besides the troubled assets, Indiek's team also found a maze of computers in the lending operation. It seemed that every employee had a personal computer and acted independently of the rest of the real-estate and lending departments. As a result, just pulling together a detailed list of potential problem loans and properties required long hours of painstaking work.

By mid-January 1985, Popejoy was impatient. FCA's fourth-quarter results were way behind schedule, and the company could not report its financial results without the findings of the task force.

"I need those numbers," Popejoy said in one of his many meetings with Indiek about the real-estate portfolio.

"We can't give them to you yet. This thing is mushrooming. Every time we look, we find another problem loan."

"Can't you give me some projections? I can work with those."

"I can use statistical sampling methods on the residential loans, but I can't do that on commercial property. They're too complicated. Some of these loans are very tricky. The most difficult have the largest losses. Some of the largest loans still need to be checked."

"I know this is hard work, Vic, but we need to get this finished and get it behind us."

"We'll hurry as much as we can," Indiek said. "Right now I can't predict where this will end up."

* * *

Inching its way back to health, American Savings had begun to attract depositors once again, and money had continued to flow in throughout the fourth quarter. At the beginning of the first quarter of 1985, on January 17, FCA announced that its thrift subsidiary registered a $2.1 billion increase in deposits for the period ending December 31, 1984. That represented an 11.5 percent improvement in total deposits and meant that nearly one-third of the $6.8 billion lost during the great run had been recovered.

American Savings had managed to generate $1.1 billion of that amount itself, an important sign of restored faith in the institution. The $1-billion package offering led by Prudential-Bache accounted for the rest of the money.

A mere two weeks later, however, FCA was back in the headlines with bad news. Armed with preliminary information from the task force and Peat Marwick, Popejoy disclosed that despite the increase in deposits, he expected a fourth-quarter loss of $100 million, the worst three-month results in the company's history. In total, FCA was facing a minimum annual loss of $185 million. Popejoy stressed that while this was sizable, it wasn't enough to kill the company.

The reason for the tremendous deficit was simple: The task force had unearthed a number of loans carried on American's books at inflated values. Once the value of the properties was scaled back to reflect its actual worth, American would have to double its loan-loss reserve and charge off other loans altogether.

Nonetheless, over the last few weeks, investors had begun to show renewed confidence in FCA's prospects for survival. This new faith lasted even as Popejoy announced the projected loss, for the stock closed at $11 a share on January 30, up 50 cents. Even Jonathan Gray now rated FCA a "good speculative stock buy."

The task force had found "no wholesale evidence of wrongdoing," Popejoy told the *Los Angeles Times*. "We don't expect there will be any major adjustments in the future. The good news is the bad news is behind us."

Jim Cirona didn't share Bill Popejoy's optimistic outlook. For Cirona, who was becoming one of the most respected thrift regulators in the country, and not just by virtue of running the largest bank in the Bank Board system, the escalating loan losses only fueled his belief that American couldn't survive on its own.

The clash of mind-sets figured in the friction that developed between Popejoy and Cirona. The engaging and loquacious executive found himself locked in a mental tug-of-war with the terse and inscrutable regulator—a Porsche pitted against a four-door Chevrolet. Except that the sports car was running on fumes, and the sedan had a full tank.*

The trouble between Cirona and Popejoy began shortly after the new chairman joined the firm. Although the Home Loan Bank had provided $3.3 billion in loans to American Savings during the crisis, Popejoy felt he got better cooperation from Wall Street. The San Francisco staff seemed overly cautious, treating Popejoy's team with a certain degree of suspicion.

As the run came to a close, Cirona pressed FCA for the business plan the company was required to file under terms of the operating agreement signed with the Bank Board. When Cirona received the business plan on October 1, though, he found it strongly lacking in necessary details and sent a reply to Art Shingler, who was still American's president, stating that he wanted an extensive narrative plan, identifying the company's specific goals and strategic options. He wanted to know the precise steps the company would take to work its way out of its problem and remain a viable thrift.

Popejoy was incredulous. American was struggling to survive a week at a time and was about to announce severe cutbacks in staff and other cost-cutting moves, and Cirona wanted to know his game plan for the next five years.

By December, meetings between Popejoy and Cirona had

*Besides his tough posture on American Savings, Cirona would later emerge as the man who wanted to shut Lincoln Savings, which was owned by antipornography crusader Charles Keating, Jr. Not only was Cirona called on the carpet by five U.S. senators, all of whom had received campaign contributions from Keating and were interceding on his behalf, but Gray's successor at the Bank Board, M. Danny Wall, thwarted Cirona in closing Lincoln by transferring jurisdiction of the institution to another district bank. That action delayed closing Lincoln by two years, by which time thousands of investors lost money buying Lincoln's worthless bonds.

turned icy. Popejoy felt that his staff was doing the San Francisco Bank and the Bank Board a huge favor by keeping American from collapsing. The company needed tough management, and he thought he was providing it.

Cirona, on the other hand, wanted to uphold the operating agreement. Popejoy had known when he signed on as chairman that he would be required to reduce significantly the size of the company's assets and provide a business plan within thirty days. Run or no run, low net worth or not, Cirona wanted the company to make good on its word.

Despite the antagonism, Cirona supported one of Popejoy's key proposals for recovery. On January 8, 1985, American filed with Cirona's staff a plan to purchase $2 billion in retail deposits and related branches from competing institutions. Retail money was a stable source of funds, and American needed to reduce further its dependence on volatile deposits. Cirona agreed to the branch acquisitions as long as American used the funds to replace wholesale funds.

On January 31, however, Cirona recommended against Popejoy's request to pay dividends on common and preferred shares, believing that FCA was not healthy enough to pay dividends to its investors. The tension between Popejoy and Cirona remained just below the surface, waiting for the right incident to set it off.

Up in Stockton, Indiek was discovering that another week meant another $100-million loss. Indiek's task force had turned into a virtual army of auditors, appraisers, and regulators scrutinizing American's loans, and they kept unearthing evidence of enormous failures in the loan portfolio throughout January and February.

With so many problem loans still under examination, Popejoy kept delaying the release of the financial reports. By the end of February, the loan losses reached unbelievable proportions.

Popejoy found it difficult to accept the truth. He was like a man who had checked into a Florida resort only to wake up and find two feet of snow on the beach. How could a company once honored—and sometimes even criticized—for its conservative approach to lending degenerate to such a state of dissolution? American Savings was a great company, one of the best. It couldn't possibly be in such bad shape.

The evidence, however, was incontrovertible. New appraisals showed widespread deficiencies in condominium and office projects in the Sun Belt and parts of California dependent on the energy industry. According to Indiek's task force and Peat Marwick, American Savings would lose a minimum of $400 million for the fourth quarter of 1984. Added to the losses from previous quarters, that would bring the full-year deficit to at least $500 million.

Although the news had not been made public, FCA's stock was dropping fast. By early March, when the financial reports were six weeks late, rumors swept Wall Street that FCA would lose between $1 billion and $2 billion. More than two hundred people were working to correct the loan problems, and American's deficiencies received extensive attention at a housing conference in Utah where some of the nation's best-known lending experts had gathered.

Finally, the SEC and the New York Stock Exchange both wanted to know why FCA's stock price sank on heavy volume on Thursday, March 7. With 1.5 million shares changing hands, the price dropped $1.625, to close at $6.00.

Faced with those two official inquiries, Popejoy disclosed an estimated loss. On Friday, FCA announced that it would suffer a loss of between $500 million and $700 million, five to seven times the size of Popejoy's original projection. But because the announcement was better than expected, the stock actually rallied, gaining 50 cents on Friday. Within hours of Popejoy's announcement, the Bank Board issued a statement of support for American Savings.

"We have full confidence in the American Savings management team led by Mr. Popejoy," the carefully prepared release said. "We are pleased that Mr. Popejoy has sought to identify the problems he and his team inherited. We are also pleased that American Savings is aggressively seeking to address its problems."

A veteran of one mammoth run, Popejoy moved quickly to quell depositor concerns. He ordered extended hours at American's 122 branches so customers could ask questions about the company's health. Longer branch hours would also indicate there was no danger of closing.

FCA's chairman got some welcome support from industry leader Anthony Frank, chairman of San Francisco–based First Nationwide. Frank blamed American's problems on the "recklessness of past management," meaning Charlie Knapp and his band of aggressive lenders. "The industry is pleased," said Frank, because "the problems are over with now and the air is cleared."

Chapter 14

Through the Past Darkly

"This is blackmail," Ralph Stone roared.

"We have to pay them something," said Merrill Butler, who thought it wise to negotiate.

"I don't want to negotiate with them," said Bill Popejoy, trying to forge a consensus among his angry board members. "We should pay them the million dollars. We should be friendly but firm. We have to get a detailed statement."

The senior executives of Peat Marwick, FCA's new auditing firm, had just delivered a stunning ultimatum. They were refusing to finish an examination of American Savings unless the company paid the accountants $1 million right away to cover cost overruns and agreed to cover additional expenses. It was simple: No million, no audit. Without that audit, filing a 10-K report required by the SEC would be exceptionally difficult.

Although FCA's directors were upset, Popejoy didn't want to replace the accountants. He especially didn't want them walking off the job, as senior Peat Marwick officials were threatening to do. FCA's annual earnings statement was already two months late, the audit was nearly completed, and they didn't have time to find another accounting firm.

Moreover, the company had dismissed Arthur Anderson just six months earlier, and the negative publicity of having to replace a second team of auditors with the financial report so far behind schedule threatened to tip off investors that American Savings was in serious trouble once again. Who knew what would happen then? There could even be another run.

It was precisely this pressure that so angered Ralph Stone, a blunt former football star who had won a gold medal at the 1932 Olympics. Stone, a man with decades of experience in the S&L industry, who had once been nominated as chairman of the Bank Board, felt Peat Marwick's demand was unconscionable. In all his years in business, no one had ever held a gun to his head like this. If FCA had to pay the money, he said, the company should drop Peat Marwick. Besides, he said, he was unhappy with their work.

Several directors shared Stone's sentiments. Peat Marwick's bid of $675,000 plus out-of-pocket expenses had been a low-ball one, to be sure. And though there was no question that the audit had turned out to be more complicated than the accountants had anticipated because of the complex nature of American's loan files and the sheer volume of questionable assets, that certainly didn't give them the right to turn around and present a bill several times larger.

The board members, located throughout the country, were discussing the situation in a telephone conference call on March 12, just a few days after Popejoy had announced the preliminary losses of $500 million to $700 million. Popejoy, Indiek, and other senior FCA officials were at Peat Marwick's office on South Flower Street in downtown Los Angeles. They had been meeting with the accounting firm's senior officials, trying to resolve the growing dispute over FCA's bill. Popejoy and Indiek had left the meeting and stepped into another Peat Marwick office where they used a telephone to link up with directors for the board meeting.

William Schulte, the managing director of Peat Marwick's Los Angeles office, had said in a letter dated October 19, 1984, that a fee not to exceed $675,000 for three years covered normal audit items such as financial statements and quarterly reviews. Work related to SEC matters and "special" accounting and regulatory subjects would cost more. Now in dispute at the directors' meeting was the proper amount for Peat Marwick's special work.

At Popejoy's suggestion, Schulte joined the meeting to explain the cost overruns to the directors and was joined by Lesley H. Howe, the partner in charge of the audit department at Peat Marwick's Los Angeles office. The Peat Marwick men faced a gauntlet of questions from the frustrated directors.

"Didn't you review the magnitude of the job in October 1984?" asked Bob Barton.

"We did review it," said Schulte. "We did not rely solely on management's representations."

"Do you have itemized bills for the SEC matters and other work?" asked Annelise Anderson, the Hoover Institution fellow.

"No. This isn't done yet."

"Does it make any sense to pay an unitemized bill?" demanded Lawrence Roos.

"This is normal progress billing without itemization before completing the job," Schulte said. "Once the work is completed, we provide a bill."

"Is it normal to give a triple bill?" asked Charles Young.

Les Howe explained that Peat Marwick had warned of cost overruns many weeks ago. The first occasion had occurred at a January 11 meeting of FCA's audit committee, and Peat Marwick officials requested to discuss it at a February 26 meeting as well. Schulte added that when Peat Marwick had put extra manpower on the job, starting in January, everyone had then assumed the audit expenses would be substantially higher.

"Let's get away from who said what," said John Rosenwald, who challenged Schulte by saying, "You could have expected a lot of work at a troubled savings and loan."

Schulte explained that at the time his firm began the audit, the accountants thought the only real problem at American Savings was in the loan files. To the contrary, Peat Marwick officials discovered serious accounting issues regarding loan fees and booking-fee income. Reviewing accounting practices is a very expensive process, requiring top partners and senior staff.

Schulte conceded that the overrun was unprecedented; had the firm known of the problems in advance, it would have given a more realistic fee. He said the final figure might reach $2.5 million and proposed that FCA pay in installments, beginning with the immediate payment of $1 million.* Peat Marwick had a business to run.

"I hate to say this," Schulte said, "but I have to say this. I have to have a million dollars now, or we can't continue."

A few minutes later, Schulte and Howe departed, leaving the

*The $1 million covered only a portion of the full costs. The total tab facing FCA ran to more than $2.2 million and would eventually rise to $3.26 million.

directors less than thrilled with Peat Marwick's presentation. Popejoy suggested paying the money and asking for a detailed accounting from Peat Marwick. John Rosenwald moved that the board authorize the payment. Bob Barton said he would vote on the motion but preferred to pay $500,000 instead. Once FCA wrote a check for $1 million, Barton warned, it would never see the money again.

Sensing no other option and worried about a loss of depositor confidence if the accountants walked off the job, the directors unanimously approved the $1-million settlement. Later that day, Popejoy ordered a check drafted and sent it to Peat Marwick. In the official statement authorizing the expenditure, the directors justified the payment by citing concerns about shareholders and depositors.*

Three weeks later, on April 1, Bill Popejoy released the financial results for the previous year's fourth quarter, disclosing that the company had lost $512 million in the fourth quarter, bringing the full-year loss to $590 million.

The situation was so grave that FCA omitted its normal annual report to shareholders, sending the much cheaper 10-K instead. Even money-losing companies normally send annual reports, which contain publicity photos, a cheerful letter from the chairman, and other marketing items in addition to financial tables.

Net worth had evaporated. The holding company's net worth had plummeted to $193.7 million, from $925 million at the end of 1983. American Savings had regulatory net worth of $366.7 million, compared with $967.5 million the year before. Furthermore, American Savings had a net worth ratio of 0.5 percent, putting the 4 percent it was supposed to maintain completely out of reach.

In addition, the annual report disclosed that Peat Marwick questioned FCA's future, adding that survival depended on the

---

*For Ralph Stone, the battle wasn't over. From that day on, he tried to deny business to Peat Marwick. He served on several boards of directors, and at every company he represented he tried his best to make sure Peat Marwick didn't get the account. Over the long run, he figured he would eventually cost them more than the $1 million they had bullied out of FCA.

ability to become profitable, the direction of interest rates, and the continued forbearance of state and federal regulators. It further noted that the company's books were so sloppy, the accountants couldn't tell how much of the loss related to 1984 and how much had occurred in prior years.

American Savings was becoming a company of hyperboles. The nation's largest S&L had gone through the largest run of any U.S. financial institution that had not been nationalized, only to register the largest loss in the history of the thrift industry. These were not the kinds of records Bill Popejoy relished.

And another depositor run had indeed developed shortly after the preliminary announcement of a loss. By the time the second run stopped on April 3, American had lost $784 million in deposits, more than one-third the amount it had raised in the fourth quarter of 1984. The new outflow once again jeopardized American's liquidity.

But the heart of the problem lay in the loan files. A lending operation is to an S&L what a diamond mine is to a gem company. Finding so many bad loans was like walking into a diamond mine and discovering that the glittering jewels had been replaced with shards of glass.

Popejoy thought he knew the full extent of the losses. This had to be it. How could it get any worse? As it turned out, this was merely the first in an unending series of surprises. Indeed, Popejoy's inability to provide a true estimate of loan losses would dog his entire administration of FCA and damage his standing with the regulators and his colleagues in the California banking industry. One S&L regulator suggested that under Popejoy, FCA intentionally took a "light touch" in disclosing loan losses, which would make the company appear healthier than it was, thus avoiding action by FSLIC.

But at this point, still enveloped in the aura of optimism, Popejoy was determined to discover how so many bad loans had been sloughed off on American. How could a company that concentrated on real-estate lending, about as safe a business as you could pick, end up shattered? One thing was certain. He was going to find out exactly what had gone wrong—and who was responsible.

* * *

Alan Bergman owed a lot to Bill Popejoy, and he was only too glad to help his old friend once again. Bergman had been a young attorney who also did real-estate work for a southern California chain of discount stores that entered Chapter 11 bankruptcy protection from its creditors. Since there seemed little future working as an assistant general counsel at a bankrupt company, Bergman decided in 1974 to leave the firm and sent an application to First Charter.

Popejoy was in his office late one evening when he interviewed Bergman for nearly two hours. Bergman took an instant liking to the hard-charging Popejoy, who was only 35 but appeared far more mature. Popejoy hired Bergman as First Charter's general counsel, making Bergman the top in-house lawyer at a large and respected financial institution at age 33.

Bergman left First Charter in 1978, worked as general counsel for a real-estate developer, then started a private practice. The firm was doing well by the time Popejoy recruited him to work with Vic Indiek on the real-estate task force, which had recently completed its work and disbanded.

Now, faced with the loss of $590 million, Popejoy decided to form the Past Practices and Procedures Investigative Committee to find out why American was saddled with so many bad loans. If the committee uncovered evidence of gross mismanagement, forgery, or fraud, Popejoy could file a fidelity-bond claim with the corporation's insurance companies, which would have to reimburse FCA.

In late March, shortly before announcing the historic loss, Popejoy phoned Bergman and asked him to chair the committee, which became known as PPPIC (pronounced "Pipic"). Bergman was happy to help. While searching through the loan files in Stockton, he had been disgusted with what he saw. American Savings had once been the most profitable thrift in the industry. Now it was on the verge of insolvency. Sure, the investigation would generate enormous fees for his firm, but Bergman also had the deep moral outrage of a dedicated prosecuting attorney.

"We have to get to the bottom of this," Popejoy said. "The board wants to knows who's responsible for these high losses and if there is any basis for a bond claim."

"I never saw anything like it in my life," Bergman said. "Don't worry. If there's any evidence, we'll find it."

Before hanging up, Popejoy told Bergman he had two other names he wanted him to check out, experts he wanted with Bergman on the committee. Paul Chamberlain was a former FBI agent who had his own investigative agency, Chamberlain International, and Don Mallert was a former auditor for Arthur Young, the accounting firm. Bergman received their résumés, made some inquiries, and interviewed them. Both men had excellent reputations and were considered tops in their fields. Bergman approved, and the committee began the long arduous process of investigating American's purloined loans.

Despite his ungraceful exit, Charlie Knapp wasn't finished with FCA. He still had one more sales job left in him. This time, he wanted to buy FCA's bad loans, those that had gone on the books while he was in charge.

After leaving FCA, Knapp had formed Trafalgar Holdings Ltd., an investment company he hoped to build into a large takeover fund. Before attempting to complete its own financing, Trafalgar had pledged money for other takeovers, collecting a fee in the process.

Actually, Knapp's business was based on the Big Lie. He pretended to have access to an extensive amount of cash when he had little chance of coming up with any sizable amount of money to participate in a major deal. To industry veterans, Knapp's plans to become a major player in the takeover business sounded like little more than a pipe dream.*

At first, the shaky nature of his business went undetected. In February 1985, Trafalgar pledged $100 million for Carl Icahn's $8.1 billion offer for Phillips Petroleum. Trafalgar collected a $350,000 fee just for promising to make the money available. Whether he could come up with the money wasn't made clear because Icahn later dropped the bid.

But in March, Trafalgar was supposed to make $30 million available to Drexel Burnham Lambert, which was financing Triangle Industries' successful $465 million buyout of National Can. At the last minute, Knapp backed out of the deal, returning the

---

*At least one former partner later claimed in a lawsuit that Knapp's Trafalgar was a vehicle for illegal activities, charging FCA's former chairman with racketeering and fraudulent misrepresentation involving more than $100 million.

$150,000 fee to Drexel, whose officials had to scramble to cover the shortfall.

In April, Trafalgar offered to buy FCA's $1.1 billion in delinquent loans and foreclosed real estate. Knapp's associates say the former FCA chairman saw the chance for a big score. Knapp thought Popejoy's team was spending too much time investigating past management and not devoting enough resources to recovering problem real estate. The large portfolio of bad loans demanded immediate action, he reasoned, not additional examination.

Also, Knapp's loyalists at Trafalgar, many of them former FCA executives, figured Popejoy had been too conservative in writing down the loans, creating unrealized profits for a specialist at real-estate workouts. Knapp suspected that Popejoy was aggressive with the write-downs not only to make Knapp look bad but also to portray himself as a hero once he began recovering the loans.

Trafalgar's offer letter called for FCA to provide substantial financing. Under the terms Knapp proposed, Trafalgar would make a $200-million cash down payment, and FCA was to provide the remainder with a ten-year loan at prime rate. Knapp and his partners would buy loans on foreclosed properties at 10 percent above their marked-down value, then sell the properties, and share 20 percent of the profits with FCA.

Although many thrift-industry executives considered Knapp's offer a farce, Popejoy did not dismiss it out of hand. Instead he took the offer to the board of directors, where it encountered a chilly reception.

Merrill Butler, the battle-hardened veteran of the real-estate racket, strongly condemned the offer, viewing it as poorly structured and insignificant. In fact, he didn't consider it a real offer at all, just a letter that gave Knapp the chance to cherry-pick FCA's real estate. He thought the offer was merely a public-relations ploy. Knapp seemed to be saying the loans made under his administration couldn't possibly be as bad as FCA now claimed if he was willing to buy them.

Butler's instincts were almost certainly correct. If Knapp was willing to cross takeover star Mike Milken at Drexel Burnham Lambert (a foolish thing to do in the leveraged-buyout business) by reneging on a pledge for $30 million, how could he hope to come up with nearly four times that amount to buy bad loans? In fact, over the next several years, Knapp would back out of one deal after another but would claim to have the funding needed for each one.

Butler and the other directors decided they would not seek help from Charlie Knapp. Even if Knapp could solve the problems as he claimed, it would be awkward doing business with a man the company was suing to recover the $2-million severance payment. Again, how could Knapp have seriously believed that a board of directors angry enough to sue him over taking advantage of the company would then undertake a huge deal that would require substantial trust? On April 9, the board resoundingly rejected Knapp's "offer."

Alan Bergman's committee had a conundrum to crack and another to create. At this point, FCA faced twelve hundred lawsuits by irate shareholders who claimed the company was guilty of securities fraud related to the huge losses and deposit run that had begun under Knapp. Although they did not know what the committee might uncover, Bergman and Popejoy didn't want the information to become public and used as part of the shareholder lawsuits.

In essence, FCA was attempting to defend itself against charges of securities fraud while trying to discover if there was any evidence of wrongdoing that could lead to reimbursement by its insurance companies. To keep the information confidential, Bergman decided to rely on attorney-client privilege. The committee reported through Bergman, the attorney of the group, who in turn reported his findings to FCA's general counsel.

Although the committee found evidence of questionable business practices shortly after it began the investigation, the group would spend thousands of hours interviewing sources and examining key documents over the next two years. A lengthy secret report detailing some of the committee's allegations about FCA's business practices under Knapp would later be made public.

Although Knapp denied the committee's conclusions, the investigators reported that FCA was in trouble from the day Charlie Knapp took over as chairman in 1975 when it was still called Budget Industries. The previous chairman, Charles Offer, had hired Knapp as a consultant in 1973 to help him with Budget's investment in a resort complex in Padre Island, Texas, one that threatened to bankrupt Budget Industries.

Knapp had to know from the very start that Budget's equity position in the Padre Island Investment Company was worthless and that $9 million in receivables due Budget Industries had a mere fraction of their stated value. Knapp and his executives took FCA's subordinated debt position and converted that into preferred stock. It was more than a desperate move. In fact, had it not later contributed to the company's downfall, Knapp's gambit to avoid bankruptcy might have been considered brilliant. Budget's S&L subsidiary then required some borrowers to buy the Padre Island preferred stock to obtain a loan, the size of which was inflated to cover the cost of the stock. The customers then paid for the stock out of the loan proceeds, the investigators said.

This cash-for-trash strategy worked because the company was the only effective source of funding, either because of the borrower's financial condition or the projected viability of the project. But it was a hazardous course; if the borrower was already having financial difficulties or if the project had questionable investment value, increasing the debt would in many cases simply escalate the size of potential losses.

Nevertheless, Knapp moved forward, and the company did eventually recover some of its investments at Padre Island. Overall, however, the scam at Padre Island only served to delay the recognition of some loan losses and exposed the company to greater potential damage.

Bergman and his team reported that the Padre Island stock cropped up in many questionable deals. Verpet Development Co. was a Los Angeles–based real-estate firm with interests in the California High Desert. On May 26, 1978, FCA purchased 3,312 land-sale contracts with a balance of $18.6 million from Verpet in exchange for $900,000 cash, assumption of about $10.6 million in liens on underlying property, and 4.2 million shares of Padre Island series A preferred stock at $1 a share.

Many of the 2.5-acre desert lots had been developed in violation of state law, and cancellation and delinquency rates were high. As of December 31, 1985, FCA had suffered losses of about $4 million on the Verpet transactions.

FCA's dealings with Perpetual Development Co. were even more costly, according to the investigative committee's lengthy and thorough report. In June 1980, Robert Rippe of Perpetual applied for a sizable loan to purchase eight condominium projects in Los Angeles from the Hanover Group. Once again, FCA invoked the cash-for-trash trade-off.

Rippe wanted $4 million for a down payment on a $9-million deal with Hanover. One of Knapp's associates required Rippe to increase the loan to $6 million. The extra $2 million was used for a $300,000 loan fee, which meant FCA was loaning money to a customer while booking part of it as income. The rest went to buy 1.7 million shares of Padre Island series C preferred stock. FCA also guaranteed Perpetual's performance to the Hanover Group, another expensive blunder.

Within a year, the Perpetual loans went into default. To avoid booking this loss, FCA treated Perpetual as it had the Padre Island cash-for-trash embedded in the loans to Rippe, dealing off the Perpetual loans and collateral to other borrowers.

One of those was Doan Corp., which had real-estate investments in several states. On February 11, 1982, Doan purchased notes and trust deeds from two FCA subsidiaries in exchange for seven loans worth $52.4 million, secured by property in Los Angeles and Riverside counties in California and in the states of Florida and Washington. This deal enabled FCA to avoid recognizing a $2.9 million loss. FCA's S&L subsidiary also took a $1.047-million fee out of the loan proceeds.

One of the Doan loans was an $18-million mortgage, secured by a condominium complex in Hollywood, Florida, known as Diplomat Towers. The appraisal that justified the loan turned out to be grossly high. A 1984 appraisal of Diplomat Towers showed the value as rental property of only $7.4–$9.7 million, far less than the $18 million the project should have been worth if the condos were sold at full retail prices.

Doan's economic travails meant the loan was in default from the beginning. By September 1982, Doan was three months delinquent and was preparing to commence Chapter 11 proceedings. Foster Fluetsch, who wanted to avoid the Doan bankruptcy proceeding and avoid recognizing this as a problem loan, arranged the sale of Diplomat Towers and other properties involved in the dealings with Doan to another real-estate company. As a result of its dealings with Doan, FCA later established a loan-loss reserve of about $11.2 million at the end of 1985, on the Diplomat Towers project alone.

Another complicated and potentially costly deal for FCA was its involvement with the Dunes Casino and Hotel in Las Vegas. Once again, the worthless Padre Island stock was linked to FCA's lending.

In December 1979, State made loans to M&R Development Co., owner of the Dunes, totaling $6.7 million, secured by a first deed of trust on the Dunes. On March 26, 1980, M&R borrowed an additional $16 million. As part of the loan, M&R bought 1 million shares of Padre Island series C preferred stock at $1 a share. M&R's financial statements made no mention of the Padre Island stock, implying it had no investment value.

FCA significantly raised its risk in Dunes with four additional loans totaling $18.3 million. By September 1983, FCA had a total exposure of $42.24 million. By the end of 1983, there was $103 million in encumbrances on the Dunes and other M&R properties. A Nevada bank became the lead lender in a loan participation, and in August 1985 declared the loans in default. On October 17, 1985, the outstanding balance was $75.2 million, with FCA's share valued at $51.5 million.

Bergman's investigators reported other transgressions as well. In fact, they discovered that under Knapp's management, the desire for short-term earnings caused some FCA officers, directors, and employees to operate with reckless indifference for the company's long-term financial health in a variety of ways.

For instance, Knapp and his team generated a high volume of loan transactions, which included purchases from other companies, without taking adequate steps to ensure repayment. Many of the loans even contained false appraisals; information was manufactured to justify a loan that was higher than a particular project would warrant, allowing the company to book larger asset levels and earn higher fees.

In one extremely unusual lending practice, the company would loan money, typically on real-estate construction projects, with a sizable reserve for interest payments. This meant FCA was loaning its customers the money to be used to make payments on the loans. Such loans were self-servicing; the borrower could make payments for an extended period of time, regardless of his financial condition. As a result, the poor quality of some of these loans would remain hidden for several earnings-reporting periods.

In some cases, the borrowers were incapable of repaying the debt without having received the interest reserve. But FCA's State Savings booked loan fees that far exceeded what creditworthy customers normally would have paid. These improvident loans and loan commitments totaled at least $191 million.

FCA also squandered millions in its involvement with San Marino Savings and Loan Association, a southern California thrift the regulators seized in 1984. San Marino was another of the fast-growth thrifts that federal regulators found troubling. With assets of only $2 million at its founding in 1979, San Marino jumped to $668 million in assets by the end of 1983.

In November 1982, FCA's State Savings reached an agreement to buy $100 million worth of loans from San Marino. The agreement required San Marino to deliver such essential loan documents as deeds of trust, credit reports, the appraisal, and title to the property within thirty days from the date on which San Marino obtained the money from State Savings.

Later that month, the two companies signed another agreement under which San Marino pledged that each loan would already have been funded by the time it was sold to State Savings. In fact, many of the San Marino loans did not exist prior to the time State provided the money. State was buying nonexistent loans, and San Marino was loaning out money after receiving it from State Savings.

Over one five-week stretch beginning on December 1, 1982, State Savings funded $81.4 million in loan purchases from San Marino in three large disbursements. In a startling departure from standard industry practice, State Savings took the loans without reviewing any of them. Although the company later examined the documents and required that other loans be substituted for some of those that San Marino shipped to State, severe damage had already occurred. FCA later estimated actual losses and loan-loss reserves in its dealing with San Marino at $25 million.

Not only did Knapp's management team fail to protect the

S&L against dangerous and unsound loans and investments, but they also accepted sizable bonuses that had nothing to do with their performance, FCA's proof of loss said. The bonuses were instead paid as part of an overall plan to prop up the price of FCA's stock.

From 1980 to 1984, several corporate officers accepted unique bonuses used to pay interest on the loans they had taken to buy FCA stock. Indeed, some of the loans had come from FCA with an interest rate of only 4 percent, well below the market rate.

The interest bonuses totaled $726,511.96: Knapp took $227,098.73; Fluetsch, $68,814.91; Edward Marks, an executive vice president, $133.997.33; John Borer, the former general counsel, $104,978.09.

In addition, several officers were buying FCA stock on margin. When FCA's troubles surfaced in the summer of 1984, some of these executives could not meet margin calls from their brokers. Knapp and Fluetsch agreed to pay the executives "special management bonuses" so they could meet their margin calls. Under Popejoy, FCA claimed the $614,154.07 spent on such bonuses to meet margin calls was an improper use of corporate funds.*

Some of the information that Bergman's committee reported would be made public in 1986 after FCA filed a proof of loss with its insurance companies, claiming it had suffered damages of more than $400 million. When the insurance companies refused to pay on the policies, FCA filed suit. The proof of loss became a part of the legal complaint against the insurance companies. However, after years of litigation and following FCA's bankruptcy filing, the proof of loss was scaled back in its scope.

---

*In his defense, Foster Fluetsch later said the money the executives received was an advance on bonuses that would have been paid at some point. They were authorized because FCA was in a war for survival and Knapp did not want any of his key executives distracted from their duties. All the same, the propriety of the program seems highly questionable, and at the very least showed poor judgment. The executives should simply have received their normal bonuses later and then spent the money as they saw fit. Instead, the corporation's assets were wasted improperly bailing out senior executives who had been using their own money to gamble on FCA's stock price. No other investors were offered the same cozy arrangement.

FCA claimed that Knapp and his cohorts had deliberately concealed losses in the loan portfolio. Overstated earnings helped fuel an increase in the price of FCA stock. Furthermore, Knapp was accused of adopting a policy of increasing the size of the company's assets and inflating its earnings for his personal financial gain. The company also claimed in its proof of loss that Arthur Andersen, its former accounting firm, was negligent in audits. Separate from the proof of loss, Arthur Andersen sued FCA, claiming actual and punitive damages of $200 million, saying that under previous management the company fraudulently misrepresented its financial condition. Claiming fraud and negligent misrepresentation, Arthur Andersen sued after FCA reached a settlement in a suit brought by angry shareholders. Andersen had been named as a codefendant in that litigation. The accounting firm alleged that former company officers made materially false statements to the auditors, adding that the truth about FCA's financial condition could not have been determined despite examination of the corporate books.

In October 1986, Knapp sued FCA, claiming defamation of character. The suit sought $100 million in punitive damages and further charged Popejoy's management team with violating securities laws. Knapp's attorney later pointed out to reporters that no proof had ever been provided that Knapp had personal knowledge of the transactions.

For his part, Fluetsch acknowledged that some of the information in the proof of loss was correct, in that the activities occurred, but he said there was no fraud. The money that went to San Marino, for example, was a mistake that would never have happened, he said, had he fired the man in charge sooner. After the San Marino commitments were funded, Fluetsch did fire the executive in question, a man he had known for more than twenty years. On a related issue, he said the regulators wanted S&Ls to sell their bad loans, so it should not have come as a shock that FCA sold some of its problem credits

He blamed many of the losses that resulted after his departure on Popejoy, saying he was too aggressive in cutting off funding on projects that later soured. Fluetsch said Popejoy had every incentive to take large write-offs and make past management look bad.

Although he did not deny the charges in the proof of loss,

Knapp later claimed that because a shorter proof of loss was filed, the original was therefore invalid and inaccurate. He went on to say that much of FCA's problems, particularly in the summer of 1984, culminating in the run on American, occurred because "Ed Gray wanted to put us out of business." He added: "I wasn't a member of the establishment. I was the guy who was flying upside down. Everybody thought I was a little bit crazy."

However, a report later issued by the U.S. House of Representatives would raise the specter of fraud at American Savings by saying the case of American suffered from inaction. The FBI made a "prosecutive recommendation" to the U.S. attorney's office in San Francisco in 1987, but no action was forthcoming, the report noted, adding that the case "inexplicably remains in limbo."

In response, a spokesman in the U.S. attorney's San Francisco office told the *Los Angeles Times* that the congressional charges were not true. The spokesman said the office had not received a complete FBI investigation. As a matter of policy, however, the office could not say if the U.S attorney was investigating the matter or considering indictments. A year after the committee's report was released in 1988, no former officer or director of FCA or American Savings had been charged.

Chapter 15

The Off-the-Wall Gang

Ed Gray could not afford to become preoccupied with rebuilding one company, no matter how large. Instead, he turned his attention to an S&L system that had become a penny arcade for liars and thieves.

Indeed, the second stage of the great S&L crisis had begun. The first stage, which lasted from 1980 to 1982, resulted largely from the severe recession and high interest rates that crippled many lenders. But by early 1985, fraud and insider abuse had become standard practices at hundreds of S&Ls, greatly contributing to the largest financial scandal in history.

The full impact of fraud at S&Ls would not be discovered for years. But a 1988 House Government Operations Committee found that fraud and misconduct played a role in nearly one-third of all commercial-bank closings and three-fourths of all S&L failures. The committee's report also assailed federal prosecutors for not fighting fraud and abuse at banks and thrifts more diligently.

Major misconduct was found at 776 S&Ls, representing nearly one-fourth of the industry, from 1984 through the middle of 1987. By 1988, the committee said, the FSLIC faced a minimum price of $12 billion due to fraud and insider abuse.

The report also pointed out that the Justice Department was short of seasoned professionals who could investigate and prosecute fraud at financial institutions, which results in highly complex cases. In addition, federal regulators and prosecutors failed to cooperate with one another.

Even without widespread fraud and other abuses, S&Ls would have had a difficult time in the mid to late 1980s because of softening real-estate prices. The depression in the oil patch reverberated throughout the national lending market because thrifts from around the country had assets located in Texas, which quickly became the epicenter of the industry's misfortunes.

As land prices fell, borrowers defaulted in droves because homes, condominiums, and office projects simply weren't selling. The flurry of foreclosures led to additional fraud, as many thrift executives discovered that by breaking the law, they could keep their companies in business with the chance that somehow they would recover.

Throughout the industry, S&Ls were jacking up interest rates to attract new deposits, many of which were needed to pay off other customers. The industry was becoming a federally subsidized chain letter. Higher interest rates on deposits increased the cost of business at S&Ls, forcing some of them to cover their overhead with increasingly risky deals that promised high returns if they paid off.

By the spring of 1985, it had become clear to Gray that he did not have enough well-trained examiners to keep up with all the wayward S&Ls under his jurisdiction, and he would soon devise a means to hire additional regulators. Other substantial problems had plagued him all year.

Back in January, a federal appeals court in Washington had upheld a lower-court ruling that said federal bank and thrift regulators did not have the authority to limit insurance coverage on brokered deposits. Limiting brokered deposits in a bid to protect the federal insurance system was one of the key issues of Gray's administration. That same month, he proposed regulations designed to retard the rapid growth of some S&Ls.

Then in February, the Bank Board tacked a special assessment on the premiums paid by FSLIC-insured thrifts. The thrifts now paid an extra one-eighth of one point, designed to provide badly needed extra revenue. Many thrift executives were unhappy with the special assessments, which reduced profitability.

Gray also urged Congress to recapitalize the insurance fund. At a management conference of the U.S. League of Savings Institutions in Washington on March 12, 1985, Gray proposed having member thrifts pay insurance premiums to the fund based on the amount of risk they took with deposits and the amount of a company's real net worth. He warned S&L executives not to suggest that the U.S. Treasury, and therefore the nation's taxpayers, take care of the mounting caseload of problem associations.

"This is the time for courage, a time for leadership, a time for real commitment to preserving the credibility of the deposit insurance fund—the cornerstone of your business," Gray declared. "Nothing is more important to your future."

The job of Bank Board chairman was like being forced to shovel coal into the roaring oven of a runaway train. American Savings was still a pressing concern because of the company's enormous losses and the constant threat it posed to the federal insurance fund.

Meantime, a House subcommittee had ordered Gray to find out how many thrifts were endangered by BankAmerica Corp.'s decision to take a $95 million write-down resulting from fraudulent mortgage-backed securities on which it was the trustee. Many S&Ls held the worthless securities and were in danger of registering large losses as a result.

Even worse, Popejoy's loss projection for American Savings occurred as financial panic was spreading throughout Ohio in a series of scenes reminiscent of the Great Depression. The trouble began March 4, when ESM Securities, Inc., a small government-securities dealer based in Miami, Florida, was placed into receivership under a court order obtained by the SEC.

ESM had borrowed heavily from Home State Savings Bank in Cincinnati, whose executives thought the funds were guaranteed by government securities. But ESM had used the securities as collateral for loans from other institutions. When ESM could not repay Home State, the latter was closed and put up for sale on Saturday, March 9, the same day that many newspapers carried accounts of impending losses at American Savings in California.

The collapse of Home State in Ohio threatened to bankrupt the state's insurance fund. This privately financed insurance system had a mere $136 million to back billions in deposits and was supposed to provide full coverage to customers, regardless of the amounts in their accounts.

Realizing that the insurance fund was woefully inadequate, worried depositors rushed to state-chartered S&Ls to remove their money before the institutions could fail. With thermos bottles, kerosene heaters, blankets, and portable television sets, depositors waited all night outside Molitor Loan & Building Co. in suburban Cincinnati to make sure they could get their money first thing in the morning. In one memorable example, a woman drove ninety miles to close an account for her mother, who survived on Social Security checks and could not afford a loss of her savings.

With so many depositors converging on state-insured thrifts, Governor Richard Celeste ordered all seventy-one Ohio-chartered S&Ls temporarily closed, starting Friday, March 15.

Back in California, American Savings was also under pressure from depositors. It looked as though another run might be developing there after Popejoy handed out the preliminary loss estimate, and the company said concern about the situation in Ohio led to some withdrawals.

In Washington, Ed Gray was at the center of another controversy. Gray refused to provide immediate federal backing for the Ohio thrifts but said he would speed up processing of applications for FSLIC insurance. He came under heavy pressure from some members of the Ohio congressional delegation who argued that the Bank Board should agree to insure the thrifts the state's governor had closed.

Gray sensed he would suffer political damage from a no-win situation. If he let the thrifts into the system without examination, he could be chastised for not doing his full job as a regulator. If he didn't rush to their aid, he would be assailed for not pulling off a speedy rescue.

Gray worried most about the federal insurance fund, itself in serious enough trouble that bankruptcy was a real threat. The agency also was short of examiners, and Gray had been pressing the U.S. Office of Management and Budget for additional funds to hire more supervisors and provide existing staff members with pay raises. Gray was not about to yield to politicians who wanted him to allow new S&Ls in the system without the sort of thorough review each institution was supposed to undergo before it qualified for federal insurance.

Besides, the state-chartered thrifts had had the option of applying for FSLIC insurance but had shunned the federal system. Now, when they were in danger of insolvency and could not rely on their own privately financed fund, they turned to

Ed Gray and the Bank Board for help. He would try to speed up the applications for federal insurance, but he would not bend the rules for the Ohio thrifts. In fact, he wanted higher capital levels.

With the run in Ohio, the court-ordered defeat of his ban on brokered deposits, the higher insurance premiums levied on member thrifts, and his many calls for reform, Gray was quickly becoming unpopular. The strongest evidence of that came on March 22 in a long and critical article in the *Wall Street Journal*. The story portrayed Gray as a regulator closely allied with big California thrifts, an administrator frequently out of the office because of a jammed travel schedule, and an official who was overly concerned with security.*

Bill Popejoy knew his first annual meeting at FCA could be a tough one. Annual meetings at troubled companies often become ugly affairs, with shareholders complaining about the performance of the stock, criticizing the size of dividend payments, and loudly demanding a change in direction. Sometimes they press for the chairman's resignation. Often, corporate gadflys will attend the meetings, soaking up the limelight to ask pointed and embarrassing questions.

But as he prepared to address the shareholders' meeting on Tuesday, May 14, in Irvine, Popejoy wasn't worried. No doubt he could have deflected any challenge to his leadership by virtue of his short tenure at the helm and the number of changes he

---

*An examination of Gray's travel schedule showed that during the previous December and January, he was at the Bank Board offices only three days each month.

Gray also had posted a guard outside his office and installed a bronze-and-glass security door that cost $8,000. The security precautions gave rise to satire at Christmas. Copying an old form of humor from *Mad* magazine, Bank Board staff members made up new lyrics for "God Rest Ye Merry Gentlemen":

God rest ye merry bureaucrats,
Just show me your I.D.
The guards outnumber staffers now,
The chairman loves his privacy, top secrecy.
Oh, we're getting pretty paranoid, paranoid, paranoid.
Oh, we're getting paranoid.

Seeing his integrity questioned stung, but Gray tried to remain philosophical about it. Criticism went with the job, he reminded himself. He figured no one would remember the story in two weeks.

had made. And it was a homecoming of sorts. Ten years ago, he had presided over his first annual meeting at old First Charter. Now he was back, with a bold new strategy to save the company.

Not all of his plans had jelled, but Popejoy was taking the company in several directions at once. He still had Bergman's committee investigating American's past practices with an eye toward collecting substantial sums from the insurance companies. With the new television commercials, he was marketing the company as a safe haven for depositors.

At the same time, he had decided to grow the company rather than cut back as originally required under FCA's operating agreement with the Bank Board. When the Citicorp deal had fallen through a few months earlier, Popejoy had realized not only that he couldn't shrink but that he had to expand. Popejoy's stewardship of the company was now based on the belief, which critics later said was misguided, that he had to grow his way out of his problems. If it didn't expand, the company would fail; without additional assets that earned profits, American would never be able to cover the portfolio of bad loans. Besides new loans, Popejoy also wanted to buy additional branches, which would increase his market penetration and provide a more conservative source of funding.

He also was seeking the help of a group of experts who could help find a way to shore up the net worth of American Savings, still more than $1 billion short of capital. To effect these changes, he would need the assistance of Ed Gray, who he believed had already approved a plan to allow American to add $2 billion in assets rather than continue the program of retrenching. These were the two most important planks in his survival strategy—growing in size and building the capital base.

Considering American's brush with insolvency, Popejoy's first shareholders' meeting was subdued. The new chairman was on solid terms with the shareholders, despite the low stock price, which closed that day at $6.675 a share, up 12.5 cents on the day but down by nearly two-thirds from a 52-week high of $17.25.

Although he was determined to keep the company independent, Popejoy in effect hung a for-sale sign on the company. He told the shareholders he'd welcome a buyer if the acquiring firm could invest $1 billion in new capital to bolster FCA's anemic net worth. But even as he said that, he cast doubt on the opportunity to sell, saying potential buyers would want to study FCA's performance for the next six months or so. The company might make money in the tail end of 1985, he added, but would almost certainly produce a loss for the full year.

Talking with reporters after the meeting, Popejoy said he believed FCA's assets would grow to nearly $30 billion by the end of the year instead of shrinking to the $24.5-billion level the company had previously planned. Popejoy noted that revised business plans called for growth to $29.7 billion, up from $28 billion at the end of 1985's first quarter.

He said FCA had been unable to scale back because interest rates had remained high all year and the company couldn't sell assets at a profit. His off-the-cuff remarks after the meeting generated greater interest than his formal speech to the shareholders and were highlighted in news accounts. A sharp reversal in strategy at the nation's largest S&L was an important business story. But before the story could unfold, he would need the help of a crusty old veteran of the S&L industry.

Bill Crawford was being asked to help forge American's future after he had spent so many years whipsawing it in the market. It was a doubly awkward position for California's S&L commissioner.

The 65-year-old white-haired Crawford looked like a stern grandfather. He acted like one too. He didn't believe the S&L industry in California should expand, and he said so. He said so a lot. He was going to put a stop to the industry's excessive growth.

As a result, Crawford was quickly becoming an enemy of the entrepreneurs who wanted to charter, and in some cases defraud, new thrifts. The criticism started shortly after Crawford took office in early 1985.

Some of his critics considered him a hypocrite since Crawford had made a fortune by starting and then selling S&Ls. In 1957, he founded Belmont Savings and Loan Association in Long Beach. Twelve years later, he sold it to Great Western. Five years after that, he founded Saddleback Savings and Loan Association of Laguna Hills, selling it in 1980 to Coast Federal. After those two deals, Crawford was a wealthy man. He could afford to work for the government.

Although he had profited from the ability to enter the industry, Crawford was now suspicious of new operators, some of whom looked at S&Ls the way a child views a carnival, as a whirling arena of endless excitement. He was particularly concerned about the new investment powers granted thrifts by the California legislature. He thought the growing demand for thrift charters had nothing to do with the need to provide financial services to California communities. Instead, he said, some entrepreneurs merely wanted to turn S&Ls into "money machines."

By June 1985, Crawford had virtually stopped the industry's expansion by denying applications for new charters, and he would approve only one charter in the next three years. Ed Gray shared Crawford's concern about the health of the industry, and the Bank Board was slowing growth by delaying or turning down applications for FSLIC insurance. Without the insurance, new associations could not open.

You could say what you wanted to about Bill Crawford, but he was nobody's fool. While at Saddleback Savings, he had seen his competitors at Charlie Knapp's State Savings make loans he had turned down because they were too risky. He had seen how the company neglected its foreclosed property, in some cases not even bothering to board it up, leaving it the unprotected prey of vandals and graffiti artists.

Crawford thought that after the big run in the summer of 1984, American Savings was dead before Bill Popejoy took command. The biggest mistake the company made was to place more than $1 billion in goodwill on its books. Writing off the goodwill alone would have destroyed the company. As the bad loans mounted, survival became increasingly doubtful. But, like Popejoy, Crawford believed that shrinking the company would only kill it.

Popejoy called in the spring of 1985 to ask for Crawford's help. The FCA chairman said he wanted to acquire retail branches for American Savings, that obtaining stable retail deposits was essential for the company's long-term health.

Crawford weighed the request. He certainly agreed that American needed a more conservative source of funding. Buying new branches would also improve the company's efficiency and give it access to new loan customers. In addition, American was buying branches that already existed, not starting new ones.

Since American was a state-chartered institution, the thrift could not expand without Crawford's approval, even though Jim Cirona in San Francisco and the Bank Board in Washington had backed Popejoy's move. Crawford decided to go along. As American's applications arrived, Crawford's department quickly processed them.

FCA announced in July 1985 that it had agreed to buy thirteen southern California branches and $436 million in deposits from Pacific Savings Bank, bringing its total network to 135 offices. The company would add a total of fifty-one branches and $1.7 billion in deposits by March 1987 under the expansion program and would continue adding branches gradually after that.

The additional branches made American Savings a tougher competitor, much to the dismay of executives at other S&Ls. Ironically, some of the S&Ls that sold branches to FCA would feel the heat as Popejoy kept trying to grow his way out of his problems.

Popejoy's search for $1 billion in capital began to take shape a short time later at a meeting in a Marina Del Rey hotel.

Outside, the sun bounced off the ocean in bright shafts of light as seagulls hovered over the enormous docks. Large expensive yachts sat in their slips, awaiting attention from their well-to-do owners. Inside conference room 204G of the Marina City Club, a casually dressed group of shrewd financiers groped for the answers to American's most pressing problems.

Bill Popejoy liked to appoint committees. It was a convenient and methodical way of addressing important issues. The more bright minds you could throw at big questions, the greater the chances for successful solutions. This group would focus on the future.

Vic Indiek had suggested that just in case FCA managed to survive the debacle over bad loans, the company would need to develop a cohesive strategy for long-term solvency. The first priority, he told Popejoy, was to harness a group of financial and real-estate experts to help FCA decide what direction to take.

From that conversation in the spring of 1985 evolved what Indiek called the global task force. Popejoy gave it a less formal title, calling the group the off-the-wall committee because the members were to consider all ideas, no matter how off-the-wall, that might guide FCA back to prosperity. The group held its inaugural meeting in mid-August, and members were cloistered throughout the weekend, discussing possible strategies for salvation.

Indiek, the chief financial officer, was quickly emerging as Popejoy's de facto second in command. He was involved in management matters that went beyond the typical role of a financial officer. The global task force was a good example. Clearly, the experts Indiek wanted on the committee would stumble across ideas that reached outside the realm of money matters. No one knew exactly what answers they would offer, and that was the point.

Indiek liked the sense of responsibility, and he enjoyed solving financial puzzles. A bright technically oriented manager, he was down to earth and easy to communicate with. Yet he often became fascinated by complex business questions. He could easily operate in the increasingly abstract world of modern banking, which required detailed knowledge of such esoteric matters as securities trading, hedges, swaps, futures contracts, reverse repurchase agreements, as well as a good instinct for impending changes in the direction of the economy.

As a finance man, he had rare qualities. Not only was he good with numbers and spreadsheets, but he could buy and sell bonds with the best of them, challenge even the sharpest real-estate developer, and be as ornery as a school-yard bully when the situation demanded. Later, some federal thrift regulators suggested that he did not always adhere to the rules, but no one questioned his loyalty to Bill Popejoy or FCA.

Joining Indiek on the off the wall committee were Dick Pratt, the former Bank Board chairman, and Dave Smith, cofounder and managing director of Kaplan Smith, a financial-services consulting firm in the Los Angeles suburb of Glendale. Stan Ross, co–managing partner of Kenneth Leventhal & Co., a Los Angeles–based accounting and consulting firm that specialized in real estate and financial services, also joined the group. So did Chip Schmidt, a partner at Peat Marwick and a savvy expert on taxes. Several FCA staffers served as well.

Much of the first day's agenda revolved around a review of the company's status, the size of its present and potential losses, the current economic environment, as well as predictions on the direction of interest rates and their impact on the company.

On Sunday, the group discussed several ways of recapitalizing and restructuring the company. Two key ideas emerged. One was a suggestion that American should segregate its bad assets from those still earning money. Stan Ross was generally credited with the idea, although others had been thinking along the same lines for several months. This later became known as a "good bank–bad bank" split.

The idea was to take all the nonearning assets and some of the riskier loans, and place them in a separate workout subsidiary. That way, American Savings could concentrate on rebuilding its business rather than remain preoccupied with collecting bad debts and managing real-estate projects.

Dividing the institution into two parts might make it easier to raise new capital. Real-estate investors might be interested in the problem loans, which they could purchase with the idea of collecting on the bad debts or completing the underlying project. Standard investors possibly would view FCA as a healthier institution once the bad loans were shed, and that could increase the company's stock price. Issuing additional shares of stock might become a realistic option.

In addition, having an S&L with nothing but earning assets could lower the company's cost of funds. Still tainted with a negative image, American was then paying a premium of half a percentage point or more than its competitors in the thrift industry. Once the bad assets were gone, American would be a much stronger, though smaller, institution and probably could lower interest rates on deposits. Lower interest payments would in turn reduce overhead.

The good bank–bad bank split had considerable merit but also raised some intriguing questions. Exactly how large should the bad bank be? How much capital could it attract? Who would manage the institution? What were the tax implications of the division?

Dave Smith, the consultant, favored the division, as did Dick Pratt, the former finance professor who frequently scribbled calculations and diagrams on a chalkboard in the conference room. Ron Struck, FCA's strategic planner, had his doubts. He had worked for several years in Washington and thought it would take too long for the regulators to approve any kind of dramatic move that entailed a total overhaul of the company, and he believed FCA couldn't get beyond its current malaise unless it acted decisively.

The other crucial idea to emerge that Sunday was a suggestion to grow the company, using mortgage-backed securities. Clark Coleman argued in favor of using mortgage-backed securities as an efficient way of adding new assets that could produce quick profits.

Of course, such a strategy left the company vulnerable to the vagaries of interest rates. When interest rates rose, the value of the bonds would fall, but if interest rates fell, the bond prices would rise, and FCA could earn a profit. However, interest rates were clearly unpredictable, and although a bond portfolio could be hedged, there was always the risk that the market would go soft at the very time the company would need to sell the securities. Depending on how the strategy was implemented, it might be little more than a huge bet on interest rates, which had been part of Charlie Knapp's strategy.

But these instruments were extremely well known to those on the committee. Popejoy, Indiek, and Struck had all worked at Freddie Mac, which helped develop the secondary market for mortgage securities. Stan Ross, the accountant, had won an award eighteen months earlier from *Professional Builder* magazine for work in developing the multibuilder mortgage-backed bond.

Building a portfolio of mortgage-backed securities might lead the company away from the path of high deposit costs. FCA could borrow directly from Wall Street at interest rates lower than those it paid on retail and wholesale accounts. However, this might prove risky as well. When interest rates fell and the securities declined in value, FCA would have to post additional collateral for the Wall Street loans.

As it had done during the deposit run, FCA could convert its loans to securities and then pledge those as collateral for Wall

Street borrowings under reverse repurchase agreements (it would agree to buy them back later). Obtaining additional securities would eventually give FCA enough income to cover the cost of its nonearning assets as well as profits that would shore up its sagging capital base.

Again, several essential questions quickly surfaced. What would be the correct size of FCA's assets? Did the company face a benign or a hostile interest-rate environment for the next few years? How would the portfolio be hedged against loss? Would the regulators approve the growth considered necessary to sustain the company?

When the meeting adjourned Sunday afternoon, no clear consensus had emerged on FCA's future business plans. At this stage, Indiek's committee needed too much information to reach a recommendation. But the group had identified two key ingredients for FCA's recovery: dividing the company into two parts and bulking-up with mortgage-backed bonds. Vic Indiek's committee had gotten off to a strong start.

By the fall of 1985, Bill Popejoy was in danger of losing his staunchest ally in Washington. Published reports suggested Ed Gray would soon resign because he was on the losing end of a bitter feud with Don Regan. Regan had recently switched jobs with James Baker and now served as the White House Chief of Staff.

Gray had never liked Regan, whom he found arrogant. For his part, Regan seems to have had little respect for Gray. The only thing the two men apparently had in common was a growing mutual dislike.

Regan had the upper hand in the relationship. While Gray had received a four-year appointment to the board, he served as chairman at the president's discretion, and Gray now lived in fear that Regan would engineer his demotion to the status of a regular board member.

In some ways, Gray would have been glad to leave Washington. The job was not only a difficult one that attracted criticism from many quarters, but it was tough on his personal life as well. He was trying to maintain a long-distance marriage. Although his wife traveled with him frequently on business, an arrangement that later would add to his embarrassment, that wasn't the same as having her home at night.

Loneliness wasn't the only problem. The cost of maintaining two households and two daughters in college was killing him. It was hard to live in Washington and pay for a house in San Diego on $73,000 a year. He began borrowing from banks to cover his expenses and even borrowed from his mother.

But for Ed Gray, money was one thing, and respect was something else. He worried that he might become the victim of a political smear job. He didn't want it to look as though he had been forced from office. Rightly or wrongly, he figured Don Regan or someone on his staff was behind the reports that he would soon resign, most likely after the U.S. League convention at Dallas in November. At one point, Gray tried to engineer a graceful exit. He wanted peace with honor. But the more he thought about it, the more determined he was to tough it out. If Don Regan wanted his scalp, he was going to have to come and take it. Ed Gray wasn't going without a fight.

Other battles needed his attention. Gray was wrestling with the White House over increased funding for his agency. He wanted to hire additional examiners and offer higher salaries. The Office of Management and Budget balked, offering to provide forty more regulators, according to Gray. In July, he started hiring several hundred. He did this by placing the examiners within the district banks, which were owned by member thrifts and were not subject to civil-service requirements.

Gray wanted a tougher police force because he was convinced that a few fast-buck operators and some bad investments at other companies were ruining the industry.

This allowed Gray to make hiring and salary decisions without the approval of the Office of Management and Budget. By the end of 1986, the supervisory staff had doubled to more than fifteen hundred. Under Gray, the Bank Board also increased the net-worth level thrifts were required to maintain, limited an S&L's direct investment in real-estate and other ventures, and clamped down on excessive growth. But many industry experts consider Gray's decision to put more examiners in the field as a check against fraud and unsound business practices one of his greatest accomplishments as chairman of the Bank Board.

Meanwhile, he was still warning anyone who would listen that the federal insurance fund would go bankrupt, repeating the message so often that many paid it no mind. Since the federal courts had struck down his rule on brokered deposits, Gray felt there was little he could do to limit them. So he kept jawboning, trying to convince S&L managers that a conservative company was a virtuous one.

The annual U.S. League convention is one of the industry's most important forums. Several thousand thrift members attended each year, and it gave Gray a chance to get his message across to them directly.

"I am not enamored of imprudent and excessive risktaking engaged in by high fliers and daredevils in the industry," Ed Gray declared at the industry convention in Dallas. Knowing that if an opinion poll was taken at the convention, he would not rank as a popular regulator, he went on to say: "Regulators are not picked to win, and should not be expected to win, popularity contests. Regulators are in no sense extensions of industry trade associations. Regulators are traffic cops who take a solemn oath to uphold the spirit and the letter of the law, and carry out their duties accordingly. . . .

"There must be, there simply must be, a renewed sense of discipline, self-discipline, in this industry. Safety and soundness and prudence may sound old fashioned. I assure you, these are not trite concepts. They spell the difference between survival and failure. They are as close to eternal verities as we can ever know in the savings institutions business."

Chapter 16

The Junk King and the Crawdaddy Man

Bill Popejoy's drive to rebuild American's substandard capital base soon led him in several different directions at once, including secret negotiations to sell the company. And his efforts received an unexpected boost when he heard an enticing offer from the king of junk bonds, Michael Milken.

In early 1986, Milken phoned Popejoy at the FCA chairman's office in Irvine and told him that Drexel was doing some "creative things" in the financial-services arena. "I have an idea to raise the capital you need."

"I'd certainly like to hear more about it," Popejoy said. "We've talked with a few investors, but so far, nothing's materialized. Right now, one of our biggest problems is being undercapitalized."

"I think I have a plan that will work. I think we could raise one billion dollars or more."

Milken had Popejoy's full attention. At the time, the junk-bond star of Drexel Burnham Lambert was at the height of his power and popularity, and was revered as a financial genius.* Popejoy thought it just might take someone with Milken's business acumen and leverage among investors to find the money FCA needed.

Indeed, even for the king, $1 billion was a lot more than mere pocket change. Mike Milken could raise that kind of money for power-hungry corporate raiders, but recapitalizing FCA might

*In the ensuing federal crackdown on insider trading, Drexel would plead guilty to six federal felonies and pay a record $650 million in fines and penalties. After plea bargaining with the government, Milken pled guilty in 1990. Drexel's parent company filed for bankruptcy protection in February of that year.

prove a tough sell, a very tough sell indeed. Unlike many of the companies for which Milken obtained financing, usually through high-yield junk bonds, FCA didn't have a lot of undervalued assets that could be sold to service the debt. Nor did it have that one key element that promised a smooth sale to investors: a strong and consistent cash flow.

Yet FCA fit nicely into Drexel Burnham Lambert's plans for the financial-services industry and underscored Milken's personal philosophy of dealing aggressively with bad loans. Milken thought America's large banks were weak and losing power to the Japanese in no small part because of bad debts to Latin countries and the lack of zeal with which bank managers attacked the bad credits.

Drexel had risen from the ranks of a second-rate Wall Street house to the front line of American finance, largely through Milken's network of junk-bond customers.* By the middle 1980s, the firm was one of the most powerful on the Street, providing money for a host of hostile takeovers that turned Drexel traders into multimillionaires and transformed some corporate chairmen from roaring lions into frightened kittens. Such was Milken's power within the firm that in 1978 he could move his entire junk-bond department from New York to Los Angeles, in part so that he could be near his family.

Thus, when Milken called, Popejoy was eager to talk.

"I've never seen a company that had too much capital," Milken said.

"We've been thinking about taking our problem real estate and spinning it off into a separate company."

"I think it is a good idea to identify your bad loans and work on them," Milken said. "You should bring in some experts, some people who really know the business. Give them an incentive, a share of any profits. That's the problem with a lot of the money-center banks today. They don't want to deal with their problem loans."

As Milken saw it, FCA would solve its loan-loss problem and

---

*One of Milken's ties to the thrift industry was his relationship with Thomas Spiegel, a former Drexel executive who ran Columbia Savings and Loan, another fast-growth thrift. Spiegel's strategy was to sell longer-term certificates of deposit and then load up on junk bonds, many of them sold by Drexel.

increase its capital at the same time. Milken envisioned raising capital through a package of securities that included a rights offering (an offer to buy stock at a specific price in the future), selling warrants (securities that are convertible into common stock at a specified price), and issuing some common stock.

Popejoy agreed to weigh a Drexel financing plan carefully. The men went on to discuss a capital infusion twice in person, and their staffs held several meetings over many months, with Indiek leading the FCA team. The financing plan would remain fluid for months with figures changing, but Milken emphasized the need to raise equity capital as opposed to selling debt. The more equity capital a company had, the stronger it was financially since debt had to be serviced and repaid someday. Equity was as good as cash in the bank.

The timing was good, for thrift stocks had come back into vogue. Reflecting the overall optimism about the industry in early 1986, FCA's stock had climbed back to more than $15 a share by March. Implicit in the discussions, however, was a belief that Drexel could raise the money only so long as FCA's stock remained buoyant.

As Popejoy was studying Milken's proposal for raising capital, Vic Indiek was busy talking with another large investor. He was trying to sell the company to General Motors.

The potential buyout began February 4 with a chance meeting in the first-class section of a jetliner bound for Dallas, where Indiek was to lay over on his way to Miami to give a deposition in one of the many lawsuits that arose around problem real estate. The seat next to Indiek was empty, and as it got closer to departure time, FCA's chief financial officer spread his work in front of him.

Minutes before the plane was to depart, a gray-haired man in a conservative business suit boarded, panting for breath, and took the seat next to Indiek's. After he was settled in, the man kept looking at Indiek's papers.

"Excuse me," the man said, "but I couldn't help but notice that you're with FCA."

The man introduced himself as Jim Duckels, who was in sales for Electronic Data Systems (EDS) in Dallas, founded in 1962 for $1,000 by H. Ross Perot. EDS had been purchased by General Motors in 1984 for $2.5 billion as part of the giant automaker's diversification drive into high technology.

For Duckels, meeting Indiek was the stuff of every salesman's dreams. He had been in Orange County during his weekly sales calls to California S&Ls. He had barely made the plane and decided to use some of his frequent-flier mileage to upgrade to first class. And now he was sitting next to the chief financial officer of the largest S&L in the world. You couldn't beg for better timing than that.

Naturally enough, the two men got to talking about the thrift business, whereupon Indiek mentioned the need to recapitalize American Savings and find a large investor. Duckels observed that GM had been throwing a lot of money around lately, having purchased not only EDS but Hughes Aircraft as well.

Indiek told Duckels he would appreciate any help he could get. After he returned to Los Angeles, he received a message from Duckels, who had set up a meeting with General Motors officers in New York. Indiek had other business in New York and went to see the GM people late the week of March 17, 1986.

Ron Struck, who was FCA's strategic planner and reported to Indiek, had prepared a briefing book that contained an overview of FCA and American Savings, and showed the impact of $1 billion in new capital. The investment could include a stock sale, issuing subordinated debt, or a combination of the two. A $1-billion investment by General Motors would mean a complete buyout of FCA.

Indiek thought the sale held great potential for General Motors. After suffering losses in the early 1980s because of the recession and heightened competition by Japanese automakers, General Motors had bounced back. By 1985, the company had record sales of $96 billion, in the process returning to the top spot on the *Fortune*-500 list. Judging by its purchase of EDS, the world's largest car company wanted to expand far beyond its core business.

By acquiring American Savings, GM would not only expand into financial services but could offset some of its earning with the thrift's accrued losses, lowering the automaker's tax bite. And there was always that old sense of competition in the auto industry as a further inducement. As part of its diversification drive, GM's old nemesis, Ford Motor, had purchased First Nationwide Bank, one of the country's biggest thrifts, in December 1985.

Nevertheless, a two-hour meeting in New York with Paul Stern, who worked on mergers and acquisitions for GM, and some members of the company's finance staff brought no results. Stern said a purchase of FCA was really more a matter for General Motors Acceptance Corp. (GMAC), a GM finance subsidiary. Stern suggested that Indiek and Struck meet with GMAC officials in Detroit.

However, GMAC executives had studied the possibility of investing in the S&L industry and in 1984 had decided against doing so. Not only was the industry heavily regulated despite all the new laws, but there was simply too much risk that rising interest rates would create large losses. Even in good times, it was difficult to make money at a thrift.

The industry exhibited an asymmetrical risk curve. When interest rates rose and the company lost money, you couldn't call the loans. But as interest rates fell and you had the chance to reap a bonanza, customers could pay off their loans early. It was like shooting craps and letting the dealer roll the dice. Rather than sink capital in a low-profit industry, GMAC had decided to embark on mortgage banking and later acquired two companies as it continued to expand beyond its core business of automobile lending.

As a consequence, an April 1 meeting in Detroit between Indiek and John Finnegan, GMAC's director of strategic planning, ended with Finnegan saying, "I don't want to discourage you, but I am not extremely optimistic about this undertaking."

A few days later, Finnegan followed up with a letter that said General Motors wasn't interested in FCA. Well, Indiek thought, it had been a long shot at best. But it was worth a try. Now Milken's financing plan was more important than ever.

Clark Coleman was discovering that trading complicated mortgage-backed securities differed little from buying and selling crawdaddies.

While his counterparts on Wall Street might devote hours to computer-based research of market trends, Coleman, a silver-haired former pilot from Miami, Florida, often operated on instinct. Trusting his judgment was a lesson learned back in the mid-1970s, when he had been a pilot hoping to land a job with a major airline. Instead, he found a way to exploit the boycott of U.S. fishing in the territorial waters of the Bahamas.

Crawfish, which look like miniature lobsters and are called crawdaddies in the South where they are considered a delicacy, sold in the Bahamas for $2 a pound. In Miami, the price was $4. Clark Coleman started swapping crawdaddies. He would fly to the Bahamas to buy a load of the fresh-water crustaceans and double his money back in Miami.

In April 1986, Coleman was preparing a trade that involved more than $4 billion in mortgage bonds and would incur the wrath of Wall Street.

At this point, FCA had more than $7 billion in mortgage-backed securities. Later, the company would add billions more. Some of these were loans the company had converted to mortgage bonds; others were purchased as investments.

The sheer size of the securities portfolio made FCA unique among all thrift holding companies in the country and also made Coleman's activities crucial for American's solvency. Not only did Coleman have to react quickly to changes in market conditions that would allow fast profits or avoid losses, but his bond trades became an essential part of offsetting American's nonperforming assets and real-estate losses.

Popejoy thought he had found the bulk of the bad loans back in the spring of 1985. Since then, however, the number of bad loans at American had risen every quarter. Real-estate losses would continue to increase, a situation that American could ill afford, given its depleted capital base.* Additional bad loans surfaced, in part because of the soft real-estate market and the adverse impact of the 1986 Tax Reform Act on property built as tax shelters, and because it took longer than expected to find all the bad assets put on the books during the Knapp years.

The mounting number of bad loans put pressure on the company to generate profits wherever possible. It fell to Coleman

*Actually, the capital situation was much worse than it appeared because of the $1 billion in goodwill. If FCA had been forced to remove the goodwill from its books, as commercial banks would have been required to do, the company would have been insolvent.

to execute the bond trades that would help keep American alive long enough for Popejoy's restructuring to take hold.

The continuing increase in problem loans was costing Popejoy some credibility. He was chairman of the largest S&L in the country, and yet he seemed to be surprised with new losses every quarter. Later, Cirona's staff at the San Francisco Home Loan Bank would come to believe that FCA was deliberately understating real-estate losses until profits rolled in from trading mortgage-backed bonds.

Ironically, Coleman had come to Popejoy's attention because the trader had been in danger of being bounced. Coleman had tangled with Ron Struck, the man who hired him as a trader. Ninety days after Coleman joined the firm in 1984, Struck threatened him with termination because Coleman had a $10-million line and had not executed any trades.

The easygoing Coleman, on the other hand, found Struck extremely demanding and difficult to work with. Struck was in fact a candid executive whom some found abrasive, though few doubted that this West Texas native was brilliant. Shortly after Popejoy took over the company, Coleman went to him and offered to resign because, he said, he could not work for Struck. Popejoy promoted Coleman out of Struck's line of authority. For a time, it was in serious doubt whether the acerbic Struck would be asked to continue with FCA. Although they were rivals, the two men had to work together. Coleman was in charge of the trades, but Struck, who had a staff of thirty reporting to him, monitored the value of the securities.

The bond portfolio required constant attention because small changes in interest rates could have a dramatic impact on the value of securities, so Coleman was constantly buying and selling bonds. In fact, a large bond sale was not at all inconsistent with a strategy of amassing securities. For instance, it might be necessary to sell a substantial amount of bonds to take profits out of the portfolio and then replace the securities later.

In fact, the ease with which the bonds could be purchased and sold was one of their most attractive features. The securities provided a high degree of liquidity because they were traded in bulk in financial markets every day. Unlike these guaranteed bonds, loans always carried the danger of default and would take more time to sell if the company needed to raise cash.

Mortgage bonds, however, had their own form of risk, and plenty of it. Increases in interest rates lowered the value of the securities, but falling rates also posed a hazard.

As a hedge to protect the company against rising interest rates, American had purchased nearly $4.5 billion in securities that had high yields (high "coupons"). The idea behind the purchases was that if rates rose, these bonds would earn enough interest to cover the higher cost of money American borrowed from depositors or securities dealers.

Indiek had noticed that with the cost of funds dropping in late 1985 and early 1986, borrowers could get fixed-rate mortgages of 10 percent, and adjustable rate mortgages, sold with cheap introductory rates, were even lower.

Many homeowners who had older mortgages costing 12 percent or more wanted to refinance their homes with cheaper mortgages. When they refinanced, the borrowers would pay off the old loan prematurely. Thus, they were "prepaying" their loans.

While cheaper rates would stimulate demand for mortgages and bring new revenue to savings and loans, it was bad news for bonds. If prepayments accelerated, the value of the high-yield mortgage bonds would plummet, almost certainly guaranteeing a loss for FCA. Prepayments could lower the yield on the securities by one-half; the interest earned on the investment would not cover the cost of American's funds.

Indiek, Coleman, and Struck had talked with officers of several Wall Street firms about prepayments. The Wall Street investors thought prepayments would not rise, but the FCA team harbored strong doubts. In late March, Coleman told Indiek he wanted to sell the high-coupon securities. He and Struck differed on who made the call first. Struck said he had already argued in favor of selling high-coupon bonds because he had heard that Freddie Mac, the quasi-federal agency that purchased mortgages from thrifts, was telling S&Ls that they could push refinancings. If refinancings rose, so would prepayments.

A little more than a year later, Struck would become disenchanted with the bond-trading operation and Popejoy's performance. He was subsequently hired as a consultant to a rival firm interested in buying American, and in a stinging memo, criticized the work of three senior members of the finance committee: Popejoy, Indiek, and Coleman.

Popejoy "has an obvious discomfort with the high tech aspects of this unit and as a result he has largely abdicated (not just delegated) his responsibility," Struck wrote. "This is strange considering the importance he places on MBS growth in turning around FCA, the current highly volatile market conditions which exist, and how easy adverse changes could occur in the MBS portfolio that could wipe out the firm overnight."

Indiek was portrayed as uncomfortable with technical aspects of portfolio management and relying heavily on outside consultants. Coleman, the old rival, was criticized as well. Struck said Indiek was aware of Coleman's "innate limitations" and that he placed little confidence in him. "However, Coleman appears to have the ear of Popejoy which creates a 'blind leading the blind' problem which has the potential for serious substantial mistakes and/or unnecessary risks in the ongoing management of the MBS portfolio." Struck warned that First Nationwide should remove Coleman as head of the bond-trading department if an acquisition of American was completed.

At a finance-committee meeting in early April, Coleman proposed selling the $4.5 billion in high-yield securities. The matter came up for a vote of the committee, which included Popejoy, Indiek, Coleman, Ron Struck, and two other FCA executives. Despite the risk of large losses if the mammoth trade proved unsuccessful, the committee approved the plan.

By the third week of April, Coleman was ready to strike. In the meantime, he worried about leaks. If Wall Street found out about the coming sale, the price of the securities would fall, bringing about the very crisis he sought to avoid by unloading the securities. Coleman kept his own counsel up to the last minute.

One afternoon, without warning, Coleman told FCA's traders he wanted their attention.

"Tell everyone you will call them back," he said. "I have an important meeting I want you to attend."

The traders complied and assembled around Coleman.

"I am going to hand each of you a piece of paper," he said

as he handed instruction sheets to the traders. "Call these dealers and ask them for a bid on the product. When they give you a price, hit the bid."

Once the trading began, Coleman resembled a caricature of a capitalist, standing in the middle of the room, barking, "Sell, sell, sell."

"One-oh-six bid," one trader yelled.

"Sell," said Coleman.

"One-oh-five and one-half," said another.

"Sell," Coleman commanded.

"One-oh-seven," someone shouted.

"Sell."

When the feeding frenzy ended a short time later, Clark Coleman had just sold tons of $2 crawdaddies for $4. FCA had paid about $103 for high-coupon bonds that it sold for between $105 and $107, netting more than $90 million and hitting close to twenty dealers.

With such an enormous trade clearing the market, the price of high-rate mortgage-backed securities fell. In response, so did low-interest mortgage bonds. FCA had just sold high-coupon bonds at a premium and would soon start replacing them with low-coupon bonds, buying these at a discount. It was now paying $1.75 for $2.00 crawdaddies.

But Coleman, who was quickly becoming highly revered on Wall Street for his swift execution and uncanny ability to spot market trends, had some explaining to do. Several Wall Street firms complained directly to Popejoy. Not only had the company dumped billions in securities, but it had sold to investment firms that were loaning FCA money, part of which had been used to buy the bonds that Coleman had just unloaded. Popejoy was surprised at the speed with which Coleman moved, and he wanted to make sure his chief trader had not overreacted.

"Clark, tell me what you did," Popejoy said. "Explain how it happened."

"When they gave us a price, we sold. We never quarreled with them.

"I didn't think you would be moving quite so fast, Clark."

"Well, they wanted to buy them," Coleman said. "It's as simple as that. It's kind of hard for me to say that I shoved five-hundred million dollars down some trader's throat."

Coleman explained that the sales had moved quickly because he had found willing buyers, and Popejoy agreed with the strategy. Gut instinct and raw nerve had paid off handsomely for FCA, giving American Savings additional money to cover its mounting real-estate losses. And as the bond trading took on ever greater importance at FCA, an obvious question arose: How long could the company outsmart the market?

"You don't have to look any longer," Popejoy told Merrill Butler. "I've found our man."

"That's great, Bill. Who is he?"

"You."

"Oh hell, Bill. I can't do it. Let me find you somebody else."

Popejoy wanted Butler to become American's top real-estate recovery man, for no matter how big and exciting they became, bond trades alone would never save his company. If Popejoy was to ensure American's survival, he would have to recover some of the nonperforming assets and put a stop to the real-estate losses once and for all.

What was needed was a new approach to the problem, nothing short of a separate division that would tackle the company's largest shortcoming head-on. Once again, Popejoy turned to his friend for help.

Butler had served a short stint on Indiek's real-estate task force, which had disbanded in early 1985 after issuing its report on problem loans. Indiek's task force was followed later that year with an asset-disposition group headed by Butler, who was in charge of selling problem loans for American Savings.

During a meeting in December 1985, Butler happened to mention to Popejoy that FCA essentially had two companies within American Savings. Of course, there was the normal S&L, writing mortgages and taking deposits, but there also was what amounted to a full-fledged real-estate operation. What American needed was to pull the various real-estate activities into one group that could manage problem loans and construction projects. The company should simply create a new division that would serve as an umbrella group for the various real-estate activities and keep it separate from the S&L.

Butler left the meeting after telling Popejoy that he would try to think of some candidates to head the new division. He had just returned to his office when the telephone rang. Popejoy was on the line, selling him on the idea of coming to work for FCA full-time.

"We could really use you, Merrill. You're the best. And you already know our operation."

"I've got other things I want to do."

"Will you do me this one favor? Will you at least think about it? Just give it some serious thought."

"I'll think about it," Butler said.

Think about it he did. Butler wrestled with his decision for nearly two months. He had been on his own since 1958 and liked being his own boss. He had begun winding down his real-estate business in the early 1980s, fed up with the turbulence in the industry and all the codes and restrictions adopted by various municipal governments. Since then, he had been doing fine as a consultant. A wealthy man who did not need to work, Butler was considering full-time church work, perhaps going overseas to help underdeveloped countries build water and sewage plants, and develop other basic infrastructure projects.

Yet, American Savings needed his help. There was no question about that. The real-estate portfolio was about as sturdy as a village of mud huts. Foreclosed real estate and partially completed projects were scattered around the country. The depression in the Energy Belt, by lowering land prices, had only aggravated the prospect of a flood at FCA. Torn between his desire for independence and his sense of duty, Butler decided to help.

On April 21, 1986, FCA announced the formation of the American Real Estate Group (AREG), which would oversee the S&L's joint ventures and construction loans as well as major troubled loans and real estate acquired through foreclosure. The announcement came just three weeks after FCA had once again announced that problem loans had increased. This time, the financial statements showed that problem loans stood at $1.98 billion at the end of February, a 13 percent increase in just two months.

While still serving as a director of FCA, Butler was also named AREG's president and was given a staff of four hundred, which would eventually grow to more than five hundred. The group took a builder-developer approach to real-estate workouts, in many cases completing projects that were idled when American foreclosed on unpaid loans. At one point, AREG had 9,000 pieces of property, including single-family homes, apartment buildings, condominiums, and hotels.

AREG had a staff of 100 working on loan management, another 100 assigned to marketing, 80 managing property, and still others helping to put together a network of real-estate brokers that eventually totaled 2,000, spanning 37 states. Other AREG employees concentrated on property development and construction inspection.

Besides the troubled real estate, there were companies to run. For a while, AREG managed a car wash in San Antonio until the company could find a buyer. Then there was a northern California company that made kitty litter. AREG ran that for a while, too, before selling it.

By recovering some of the money American had loaned on projects that went bust, Butler's operation played a crucial role in keeping American Savings alive a little longer. However, Butler was being asked to do the impossible. AREG kept recovering money for American, but every quarter, the amount of problem loans would rise. Butler and his team of experts kept trying to scale the mountain of problem credits but never succeeded because the distance to the top kept rising. But under Butler, AREG had become such a smooth-running operation that it attracted the attention of a mysterious Texas billionaire who was always on the lookout for a shrewd investment.

Bill Popejoy had another seasoned veteran trying to find a solution to the loan-loss drain at FCA. This time he tapped cautious, deliberate Dave Smith, who with his doctorate in economics, knew how to put the finishing touches on an important study.

What started as an idea to segregate American's loans into a bad bank had turned into a full-blown research project for Smith's company, the consulting firm of Kaplan Smith. The figures in Smith's study changed many times because of the complexity of the proposal, but his research showed that the best way to separate the bad loans was to divide American Savings into two distinct companies.

This was separate from AREG because the problem loans

under the real-estate division's management still showed up on the S&L's books. If two separate banks were created, the problem assets could be removed from the balance sheet, ridding American of a virulent infection. Under this scenario, proposed by Smith, the "good bank" would have about $22 billion in assets, while the "bad bank" would have about $6 billion in assets, including problem loans and bad real-estate projects.

The bad bank faced formidable challenges. Not only would this real-estate bank need around $500 million in capital, but it would also need a note from the good association. That note, or obligation, from the clean S&L would in turn have to be guaranteed by the FSLIC. In other words, the bad bank would have up to $6 billion in assets but would have no deposits as liabilities. Instead, it would have a $6-billion note from the good bank as its liability, which was to be underwritten by the federal government.

That was asking a lot, for by 1986, the FSLIC was rapidly going bankrupt and could not take on a $6-billion obligation. Other constraints required attention as well. FCA wanted to determine how dividing the company would affect the tax benefits built up from the accrued losses; a profitable firm might want to invest in FCA simply to use some of its tax losses to offset income.

Another major challenge was determining the exact size of the bad bank. With real-estate losses rising each month, calculating the correct amount of bad assets to put in the subsidiary wasn't easy. In late 1985, published reports indicated Popejoy wanted to spin off roughly $2.5 billion. Indiek recalled discussions revolving around $4.5 billion, while Smith said his study ultimately suggested that $6 billion was the correct figure.

Finally, the bad bank would require financing, and that would not be easy to find. Indiek's finance team talked with a variety of potential investors interested in participating in the bad bank, with the idea that they would put up some of their own money, manage the bad bank, and take a share of whatever profits might appear.

Meanwhile, on June 25, 1986, FCA began a three-day due-diligence effort in preparation for issuing additional shares of common stock. Drexel would be the lead underwriter in the offering. FCA started with $200 million, which could always be increased, possibly through other types of securities, to reflect FCA's much larger cash needs.

Dave Smith had just finished another important research project. This one would prove to be far more controversial and would make Popejoy the focus of intense criticism.

Popejoy had already decided that FCA had to expand or it would go out of business. The key question now was how big did the company have to become to generate enough earnings to stay in business and rebuild its capital? This question had surfaced months earlier in the off-the-wall-gang sessions that Smith had attended.

Although American Savings was back in the lending market and had written approximately 26,000 high-quality loans by this time, Popejoy thought he could not possibly grow quickly enough with mortgages. For this reason, American had eschewed adjustable-rate mortgages and marketed loans with fixed interest rates.

More than other southern California lenders, American needed to book immediate income in large amounts, and adjustables sold at a large discount from fixed-rate loans, sometimes as much as two percentage points lower. These "teaser" rates would rise at the end of six months or a year, but American would have to wait at least a year before the loans got up to the market rate of interest and the company could start earning interest income, although it would be able to book loan fees much sooner.*

Since Popejoy also had decided against junk bonds because

---

*Jonathan Gray considered the aversion to adjustables one of Popejoy's biggest mistakes. The fixed-rate loans exposed American to increases in interest rates, the very reason that thrifts had fought for the power to make adjustable-rate loans, a struggle in which, morever, Popejoy had been involved. The adjustables moved up with interest rates, protecting thrifts from being squeezed by the higher cost of funds.

Gray argued that Popejoy should have written adjustable mortgages and later sold them, acting as a servicer. In this manner, the company could have put its attractive branch network to use finding borrowers and selling the paper to other investors, earning servicing and fee income. Other large S&Ls operating within just a few miles of FCA's headquarters managed to make money with just this strategy, Gray noted.

he considered them too risky, he was left with mortgage-backed securities, a liquid investment with which he was familiar.

According to Dave Smith's research, FCA needed to expand to $38 billion in assets. At that size, the company could cover its nonearning assets, generate profits to restore capital, and reduce its interest-rate risk. Smith's study looked at wide fluctuations in interest rates and their impact on the portfolio and FCA's operations. The idea was that even if interest rates rose to the point that the securities would be worth less than the company paid for them, the investments would still generate enough positive cash flow to keep American Savings in business. And the company would use a variety of sophisticated hedges to guard against economic disturbances.

The growth could come quickly because FCA would not have to raise new deposits to fund the securities purchases. Instead, FCA would borrow from Wall Street firms and other broker-dealers in "reverse-repurchase" agreements, in which the company pledged to buy back securities sold to the brokers. The difference between the price dealers paid for the investments and the amount at which the company bought them back represented the interest cost of borrowing. The spread between the cost of borrowing to pay for the securities and the interest earned on the portfolio represented gross profits.

Popejoy forwarded Smith's study to Indiek, whose staff members reviewed it and conducted their own research. Indiek's analysis agreed with Smith's: $38 billion was the proper size (a one-third increase for a company that was originally supposed to strip itself of assets).

Dick Pratt, though, questioned the wisdom of amassing securities. True, S&Ls did not have to mark securities to their market value when bond prices fell, but Pratt feared that if interest rates rose too far, FCA could end up with sizable portfolio losses.

Pratt considered the growth plan sheer speculation on interest rates. Any thrift in the country could work its way out of its problem if it grew large enough while declining rates brought terrific new profits. He didn't think the government should up the ante at the roulette wheel. He thought Ed Gray and the Bank Board would never approve such a risky strategy.

Of course, he could understand why Popejoy would want to

grow his way out of his problem and use the bonds to do so. Popejoy had few other tools at his disposal. Popejoy's strategy embraced the age-old problem afflicting the thrift industry: borrowing short-term to obtain long-term assets. If interest rates fell, Popejoy would be a hero. If rates rose, FCA would be in deeper trouble.

Chapter 17

The End of the Road

Despite the advances he had made and his hope of progress yet to come, Bill Popejoy's reign as head of an independent FCA was drawing to a close. By the summer of 1986, Ed Gray had become convinced that the only way to rescue American Savings was to sell it.

Gray had two other options, but they seemed impractical. He could let American Savings limp along as a crippled company, low on capital and subject to sudden insolvency. Or he could withdraw the support of the Bank Board and watch American Savings become insolvent, an unpromising future in which the federal insurance fund might have to pay off a substantial number of depositors. At the moment, that was impossible because the federal insurance fund was essentially broke, and any infusion of capital would require congressional action upon which Gray could not depend. So Gray made up his mind to find a buyer for American.

Although FCA operated under strict supervision of the Bank Board, the company was still technically an independent institution. But Gray had begun to see American Savings as a member of the Management Consignment Program in everything but name.

Under the plan, instituted in 1985 as a way to salvage some insolvent thrifts, healthy S&Ls would temporarily loan seasoned managers to the defunct companies. The new managers would correct the weaknesses, and the government would find buyers. As with much of the federal government's involvement with the S&L industry in the 1980s, the program was largely a failure. Like Popejoy, the managers found deeper problems than they had expected and were gone much longer than their bosses had anticipated. Buyers were scarce. Few companies wanted anything to do with a derelict S&L laden with hidden losses.

With its capital position continuing to deteriorate as problem loans mounted, American was the paradigm of foundering S&Ls. At its present size, American would never generate enough earnings to rebuild its net worth, and it was far from certain that FCA could issue new securities. Dividing the thrift into a good bank–bad bank seemed unlikely.

In its current condition, American made an unattractive acquisition. The company's low earnings depended largely on its elaborate bond trades as its real-estate portfolio worsened each month. If American could report some hefty profits for a change, Gray reasoned, the government might find a buyer. Without some extra income, American would stay on the disabled list for the indefinite future, or even worse, go out of business.

Therefore, selling the company meant first letting it grow. After receiving some important assurances from Popejoy about the growth plan, the Bank Board chairman gave verbal approval to let American increase to $38 billion in assets.

Gray based much of his decision on personal trust. He thought Popejoy was doing a great job with American, as well as any one could expect, and he knew the FCA chairman would not depart from an agenda approved by the Bank Board. Over the last two years, Gray and Popejoy had developed a close working relationship, and Gray had almost complete faith in FCA's chairman. Popejoy always kept him informed of his intentions and seemed to have logical explanations and supporting evidence for his proposals.

Besides, the company was already expanding its presence in California by buying retail branches, a program that had accelerated in 1986. He also took solace from Popejoy's pledge to safeguard the portfolio of mortgage-backed securities against risk by using sophisticated financial hedges and interest-rate swaps.

Here, Gray made a serious miscalculation, compounding his previous error of allowing the merger in the first place. Simply put, Gray did not understand the risk inherent in building such a huge portfolio of mortgage-backed securities. FCA intended to buy these bonds on credit from Wall Street under reverse-repurchase agreements. True, no matter what happened with interest rates, the bonds would generate cash. But if rates rose, the value of the securities would fall, and FCA would have to post additional cash or securities to the Wall Street dealers. If rates went high enough, the company might run out of money posting collateral. And there was also the danger that the hedges FCA was using to support the securities might come apart in a volatile market.

Beyond the technical nature of the plan was the symbolic gesture it embodied. Gray was establishing a double standard in the S&L industry. He was allowing the largest S&L to grow rapidly and increase the risk to the federal insurance fund when he was on record as an ardent opponent of fast growth. Later, his critics would say American was growing at the expense of its competitors, increasing their cost of doing business and thereby weakening the system. Indeed, the erratic nature of the bond market meant that Gray was imperiling the S&L industry to save one company.

On August 15, 1986, in a conference call linking Washington with regulators in San Francisco, the Bank Board considered Popejoy's plan. Cirona didn't like it. He opposed any growth and wanted the government to cut its potential losses with American. Like Dick Pratt, Cirona considered the growth in securities a pure interest-rate bet. FCA was a sick patient that should be nursed along until the government could afford to let it die.

FCA obviously needed some earnings, but adding $8 billion in assets to such a weak company in such a short period of time posed its own perils. Board member Hovde also thought it was wise to err on the side of caution. As Gray and Hovde discussed the merits of the plan, it was clear that the two Bank Board members were willing to compromise on a growth figure.

They decided to let Popejoy take the company to $34 billion in assets. However, FCA had to reduce its one-year negative gap (the difference between the amount of liabilities and the amount of assets that reprice through increases in interest rates) to 40 percent, down from 69.4 percent in mid-1985. In other words, the total liabilities that could reprice within one year could not exceed 40 percent of assets, or $40 in deposits for every $100 in assets. A lower negative gap means a safer S&L because profits are protected against an increase in interest rates.

When Popejoy received word of the decision to hold the line to $34 billion, he was confused. He was certain that Gray had already given verbal approval to go to $38 billion, a belief seconded by Dave Smith, who was at the same meeting. Thus, the call in August, although listed by the regulators as the official approval, was really a decision to reign in Popejoy.*

Clark Coleman had already begun buying bonds at blinding speed. In just a few weeks, FCA had purchased $5 billion in new mortgage-backed securities. By September 30, total corporate assets reached $34.1 billion. These were highly leveraged transactions because FCA was borrowing much of the money from broker-dealers under reverse-repurchase agreements.

The hedges FCA used to offset the risk of rising interest rates were financial futures and options. Financial futures had developed in the early 1970s and quickly became one of the most actively traded of all futures contracts. Futures are literally an agreement to conduct a transaction in the future—to buy or sell a security at a specific price on a certain date. It's stud poker played for hundreds of millions of dollars, since one investor is betting the price will go down while another is certain it will rise.

FCA also used ninety-day Eurodollar time deposits to help protect the interest-rate spread on the portfolio. FCA would sell futures contracts short, agreeing to sell futures it did not own. If market rates moved up, the company would buy the contracts back at a profit. If rates declined, the contracts would be bought back at a loss. The loss was offset by the lower cost of borrowing to pay for the mortgage-backed securities. However, the portfolio might become so large that it could not be fully hedged.

Although he lobbied hard and often for additional growth, Popejoy said he was never completely comfortable with the plan, mainly because he did not like borrowing short-term at variable rates to buy long-term assets at fixed rates. He had been around the industry long enough to see S&Ls fail after

---

*Gray, however, disputed this account. He acknowledged that he or a staff member might have said the idea "sounds all right" but insisted he would not have given the company a definitive answer at that meeting. He wouldn't have approved an $8-billion purchase of securities based on a snap judgment. But a top Gray staffer said he had in fact given verbal approval, overriding Cirona's objection. Cirona in turn lobbied to limit the growth.

following that kind of strategy. And he thought financial futures were as complex and volatile as rocket science. As a backup to his own staff, Popejoy hired as a consultant Mark J. Powers, coauthor of *Inside The Financial Futures Market*. A leader in the field, Powers had developed the first foreign-currency and U.S. Treasury futures contracts. Popejoy gave a copy of Powers's book to all FCA directors to help them understand what the company hoped to accomplish.

If Mark Taper had walked into American's trading room three years after selling the company, he would have shaken his head in disbelief. The jargon alone would have gone over his head, and the strategy was foreign to his kind of thinking. Taper may have been tightfisted to a fault in running an S&L, but he believed in keeping a business simple. He thought an S&L should do two things: make loans and accept savings deposits.

In the deregulatory world of the 1980s, though, S&Ls had become complex institutions, not only lending money for tricky real-estate deals but becoming shrewd and important players in the financial markets. Now that it was buying so many mortgage-backed securities, none would become as complicated or controversial as FCA.

Still searching for additional capital, Vic Indiek and his FCA team met once again with Mike Milken and his Drexel crew on October 7. By now, it was clear that the good bank–bad bank structure was going nowhere. The FSLIC couldn't provide the necessary guarantee, and FCA had been unable to find investors willing to put up enough money. Even if the money had been forthcoming from private sources or Washington, there were many unresolved issues, not the least of which was the exact size of the bad bank and the proper legal structure. With so many roadblocks still left, the good bank–bad bank option was finished.

Milken, however, had an alternative. He proposed seeking $1 billion through a rights offering and recapitalizing American as a single entity rather than spinning off the troubled assets.

After the meeting, Indiek discussed the proposal with other FCA officials, particularly strategic planner Ron Struck, who warned that while the plan would help FCA raise cash, it might also provide Drexel with a means to acquire a large block of the thrift's stock at discount prices. When informed of the proposal a short time later, FCA's directors were also unenthusiastic. The board members feared that the value of current shares would be diluted if additional securities were issued.

As time passed, the debate became pointless because thrift stocks were dropping quickly in price, reflecting the industry's sagging fortunes, and making a public offering difficult if not impossible. At FCA's quarterly meeting with the regulators in early November, the company's senior managers informed the Bank Board that an equity offering was no longer feasible because of the soft market for thrift stocks. As a result, FCA had no choice but to shelve its financing plan. The search for $1 billion in new capital had failed. Now what?

Popejoy had been devastated by that November quarterly meeting with the Bank Board in San Diego. The company could not raise additional capital, and without that money, it was like a wobbly punch-drunk prize fighter trying to make a comeback while wearing a blindfold. On a personal level, Popejoy had had about all the jabs he could take from the regulators, especially the new hotshots Gray was recruiting.

As Popejoy drove home from San Diego with his wife, Nancy, he thought about that meeting and became angrier by the minute. He had tried to remain upbeat in the face of constant turmoil and to spread enthusiasm throughout the company, but there didn't seem to be any use.

The Bank Board officials had suggested it might be time to find a buyer for American Savings. Popejoy was already on record as supporting a sale of the company if an acquirer could contribute $1 billion, but he had still hoped to pull off the S&L industry's largest restructuring on his own. Now he was being told that in all likelihood, he would not get the chance, that Gray wanted to sell the company after all.

In addition, Popejoy had gotten off to a poor start with Michael Patriarca, Cirona's new second in command. Patriarca was head of the San Francisco Bank's "agency functions"; he ran the supervisory staff. Before joining the bank, Patriarca had been a star at the Office of the Comptroller of the Currency where he was the deputy director of multinational banking, directly responsible for regulating some of the country's largest banks. Patriarca had been personally recruited by Ed Gray, who liked the young lawyer's high standards and uncompromising attitude.*

Patriarca had learned as a young regulator at the comptroller's office to stand up to corporate executives and not to accept attempts to explain problems away. If the thrift industry had had more examiners like Patriarca, the crisis would still have occurred but would have been much less severe and thus less expensive for the nation's taxpayers. But his outlook troubled Popejoy, who felt Patriarca was treating him as though he had caused the problems, not been hired to solve them.

"I've never seen a balance sheet look as bad as this one," Patriarca said.

"Well, you should have seen it before we got here," Popejoy shot back.

If Patriarca, the new supervisory agent in San Francisco, was speaking for Ed Gray, that was a bad omen. Popejoy felt he was giving his whole life to American Savings, and though he drew a good salary, he now felt as though he were getting little but rebukes as rewards. "Why am I doing this?" he wondered. "For what? I'm fighting with the regulators all the goddamn time, and it's their problem."

A few days after the meeting, Popejoy phoned Ann Fairbanks to tell her he wanted to resign, that he had an opportunity to join a real-estate investment group in Orange County.

"What?" said Ann Fairbanks.

"I think it's time I did something else," he said. "I want you to put someone else in my place because I want out."

"I don't think Ed will like that," Fairbanks said. "He doesn't want to lose you. Why don't we discuss this with Ed? Don't make a decision until we talk to Ed."

---

*Indeed, he would later take center stage in the controversy over Lincoln Savings. Patriarca was with Cirona in April 1987 for the meeting with the five U.S. senators who said they were concerned that the regulators in San Francisco might be treating Lincoln unfairly. All five had received campaign contributions from the thrift's owner, Charles Keating, Jr. Patriacha spoke his mind. He told Senator John Glenn that if Lincoln were a bank instead of a thrift, it would be closed and that the regulators were making a criminal referral about Lincoln to the Justice Department.

Popejoy agreed to confer with Gray, and Fairbanks arranged a meeting between the two men a couple of days later when Gray was in San Francisco on business. Popejoy made his frustration with the San Francisco regulators clear.

Gray understood his feelings, for he often found himself disagreeing with Cirona over the proper course for American Savings. He believed that Cirona and his senior staff had been subjected to undue influence from industry interests. Cirona answered to a board of directors dominated by the heads of large California S&Ls, and Gray had been told the directors spent an inordinate time discussing American's affairs. He thought the powerful California directors wanted to see American Savings fail or be shut down by the government. If American closed, the company's competitors could carve up the corpse and grab market share.*

In fact, Gray had become so disenchanted with Cirona that he once asked him to resign but later phoned and said he had changed his mind. He told Popejoy that he would intercede on the company's behalf with the San Francisco regulators.

"You've got to stay," Gray told Popejoy.

"I've had some opportunities in the past that I have turned down," Popejoy said. "I really feel I'm doing this more as a public service. I can do better elsewhere."

"You know I think you've been doing a great job. Really an excellent job."

"Well, this is hard work. It's hard on my family. The company still has a lot of problems. Maybe it's time to step aside and let someone else take over."

"It would be very destabilizing and frankly irresponsible if you left," Gray continued. "We need you to hold this thing together. You've got to hold on. We're going to sell the company. It'll only be a matter of a few more months."

* * *

---

*Cirona and several directors denied this allegation, adding that they took a number of steps to ensure that American was not discussed at board meetings. Indeed, Cirona's supporters had believed that Gray wanted to force Cirona out of San Francisco so that Gray could get the better-paying job that was closer to his California home. One of Gray's closest friends, powerful S&L attorney Bill McKenna, had led the 1985 attempt to keep Cirona and make sure that Gray didn't get the job.

Vic Indiek's troops were ready for another assault on Wall Street. In early December, Indiek told Popejoy it was essential to take profits out of the portfolio. The bonds were trading at substantial premiums. The finance committee surveyed American's balance sheet and decided it was time for another massive securities trade.

During the first week of December, Coleman began to arrange the sale and repurchase of more than $4 billion in bonds. A few days later, Indiek came to him with orders for additional sales. Coleman figured that American would once again report huge loan write-offs and that the trades would be needed to cover those expenses. With Struck in New York, helping to arrange the movement of securities, FCA arranged to sell about $9 billion in mortgage securities and to buy back $8 billion by mid-December, garnering $304 million in trading profits.

Without those trades and the ones American executed earlier in the year, the company would almost certainly have become insolvent. Regulatory capital stood at $552 million by the end of the year. But American needed $463.8 million just to cover its provision for loan losses and discounts. Combined with other expenses, the loan losses would have wiped out its capital. Even after gains on sales of securities and real estate totaling $568 million for the year, FCA finished the year with a scant $95-million profit.

Although the trades saved the company, they aroused mistrust among regulators at the San Francisco Home Loan Bank, who were even more convinced that Popejoy's staff was intentionally underreporting real-estate losses until Indiek and his team made money trading bonds.

Under securities laws, the company was supposed to disclose losses as soon as they became apparent, not wait until profits emerged from an investment portfolio. Indeed, the regulators in San Francisco said they found a clear pattern of reporting loan losses after profits from securities trades were announced. In Popejoy's defense, some industry experts, however, argued that while the company had an incentive to take a light touch with loan losses, American was operating in a gray area. The regulators could easily insist on a higher loss reserve at many banks and thrifts.

Coleman and Indiek both said they never waited until they made profits on the trades to report loan losses. Instead, the trades were based on market timing. Some members of FCA's board of directors said Popejoy informed them of the regulators' concern but discounted the allegations. They said Indiek and Coleman had only done what was necessary to keep American Savings alive.

Within weeks of the huge trade, Popejoy faced criticism from outside the company and a serious challenge from his staff. Two weeks after the huge securities trade, in an article that seemed to reflect the S&L industry's dissatisfaction with Popejoy's leadership, *Forbes* lambasted him and Ed Gray, saying the growth plan was a grave error.

Under the headline "Shades of Charlie Knapp," the article said, "Some folks will never learn: Financial Corp. of America is betting the bank on interest rates . . . again." *Forbes* said in the December 29 issue that by borrowing short and buying mortgage-backed securities, Popejoy left the company vulnerable to increases in the cost of money. If long-term rates rise, the article said, the securities "drop in value and he's dead."

The magazine pointed out that at least $6 billion of the portfolio was unprotected by hedges that were designed to offset the risk, adding that a one-point increase in rates would blow the capital-short company away. *Forbes* went on to say that Gray was more than a little responsible for the potential fiasco, having first approved the FCA–First Charter merger back in 1983 and then approving Popejoy's growth plan in the summer of 1986.

Strangely enough, though, this criticism from outside the company coincided with a serious challenge from Popejoy's inner circle. Clark Coleman had also become gravely concerned about the direction of interest rates and their impact on FCA's securities portfolio. In a four-page memo dated December 29 (the date of the *Forbes* article) distributed to the members of FCA's finance committee, Coleman called for a sharp reversal in strategy. At a time when Popejoy was still asking the regulators for permission to grow to $38 billion, Coleman argued that now was the time to shrink.

In a bull market, FCA's strategy was well advised, Coleman

said, but he predicted a run-up in rates within three to six months and said the company should be ready to change course abruptly:

> Once we are faced with a rising rate scenario, we must understand that no matter how complete or precise a futures hedge is, it will not offset a rise in rates on a one-to-one ratio. The only solution that I know of will be to Shrink or Sink.
>
> I think it is of utmost importance that we develop a sale strategy in the amount of at least $5 billion. A sale of this size will, of course, have initially a dramatic and negative impact on our General and Administrative accountability [overhead costs]. If timed properly, however, it should not affect the targeted growth of the company by the end of the year.

Coleman also warned that higher rates would reduce or eliminate the marketability of the securities, since they would decline in price and the company then would have to hold the securities or sell them at a loss. He also warned of the inevitable negative press that would ensue if the company got stuck with securities that fell in value.

"I'm not one to base a trade on the acceptability in the eyes of others, and yet," Coleman added, "I do believe we will be held accountable for inaction, and rightfully so."

Coleman said his suggestion was considered at the finance-committee meetings in January, February, and March 1987, and was finally turned down. Headed by Popejoy, the committee's members decided the federal government might not let FCA replace the securities once they were sold. If FCA shrank, then the company wouldn't have enough earnings to sustain it. Shrinking was out of the question. At least for now.

FCA would stick with the original game plan. If interest rates rose and the value of the securities fell, the bonds would still generate cash flow. However, the portfolio was not fully hedged against higher rates. And the company faced another substantial risk. As rates rose, the value of the securities would fall, and the securities would be worth less than what FCA owed on them. When the value declined, Wall Street dealers would ask the company to post cash or additional securities as collateral. If these collateral calls reached a high enough volume, they would bring a liquidity crunch similar to that of a depositor run.

Ron Struck, the strategic planner, also argued in favor of selling securities. In a private meeting with his old friend Vic Indiek, Struck said that he didn't feel he could remain the strategic planner if the company refused to follow his advice and sell off a substantial portion of the portfolio. Indiek told Struck to follow his conscience. A few weeks later, Struck resigned, just as interest rates were heading up once again.

Mindful of Ed Gray's desire to sell the company and unable to stop the real-estate losses, Popejoy had begun looking for a buyer. As part of his search for new capital, Popejoy had already contacted investment bankers at Salomon Brothers about a potential sale.

Acting on his own, though, he also arranged a meeting with William French Smith, the former U.S. attorney general in the Reagan administration. A partner at the Los Angeles law firm of Gibson, Dunn & Crutcher, Smith also served as a director of San Francisco–based Pacific Telesis Group, one of the "Baby Bells" that had been formed after the breakup of AT&T.

Like S&Ls, utilities also had been given broader investment powers and were diversifying their balance sheets. Pacific Telesis served more than 20 million telephone customers, many of whom were potential clients for credit cards, savings accounts, and home loans. With more than $9 billion in revenues, Pacific Telesis was one of the largest companies in the country.

On March 25, Popejoy met Smith for lunch at the California Club, an exclusive enclave in downtown Los Angeles. As Popejoy envisioned the buyout, Pacific Telesis would invest nearly $2 billion to bring American Savings up to a 6 percent capital level, would be protected against real-estate losses by the FSLIC, and would own the entire holding company. FCA's shareholders would obtain a subordinated stock position in the acquiring firm. A few days later, though, Smith told Popejoy that Pacific Telesis wasn't interested.

The prospect that FCA could conduct its own sale of the company or find new capital on its own now looked extremely doubtful. Two top staff members had suggested shrinking. The Drexel deal had fallen through, Indiek's pitch to General

Book Three

The Fire Sale

Chapter 18

The New Man in Town

Washington had become an unfriendly town for Ed Gray. When Don Hovde left the Bank Board in late October 1986, Gray temporarily served as the sole person on the board—Mary Grigsby had left the previous summer—delaying important decisions on regulatory matters as well as action on the rapidly mounting caseload of problem institutions. In fact, the industry was spiraling out of control, and Gray was ill prepared to cope with the overwhelming task that faced him as he was bogged down in one conflict after another.

By the summer of 1987, Gray felt more alone than ever, and some aides worried about his emotional stability. He was hobbled by debts and financial scandals, the loss of close friends in the Reagan administration, pressure from politicians, and frequent absences from his wife on the West Coast. He had recently quit smoking, which increased his anxiety.

Larry White, a distinguished economics professor and a Democrat who had served the Carter White House, had recently been placed on the Bank Board.* White and Gray were at odds over the Bank Board's largest problem institution, American Savings. Gray was moving at breakneck speed to sell the company before leaving office, but White wanted to proceed cautiously.

Other difficult issues haunted Gray as the end of his adminis-

*The White House chose Atlanta attorney Lee H. Henkel to fill Hovde's seat, but that nomination was doomed by Henkel's embarrassing ties to industry maverick Charles Keating, who owned Lincoln Savings. George Bentson, of the University of Rochester, was denied a seat on the board because of industry opposition.

tration quickly approached. The most embarrassing episode had begun back in December 1986 when Gray had once again found himself the target of a government probe. His expense accounts triggered an investigation by the Office of Government Ethics, and the Justice Department was asked to delve into the matter.

The Bank Board chairman came under scrutiny for billing thousands of dollars in travel costs to the twelve regional Home Loan Banks, which are owned by S&Ls. In essence, Gray had accepted industry money for travel expenses, a practice he quickly repudiated.

The disclosures included $3,800 the Dallas Home Loan Bank spent in 1985 to chauffeur Bank Board officials in limousines during an industry convention, the one where Ed Gray had extolled the virtues of fiscal restraint, and more than $5,000 spent in August 1986 to pay for a dinner in Gray's honor.

Following the investigation, the chairman also reimbursed the regional banks for some $26,000 in personal costs. Of that, $14,000 went to pay the tab on a chartered Learjet Gray had used for an emergency flight to California to visit his sick father. Gray paid $12,000 in expenses for his wife, his frequent travel companion, then wrote a letter to Congress, apologizing for his "flawed judgment," and adopted reforms. Henceforth, using regional-bank money for Bank Board expenses could result in criminal charges.

Although the ensuing scandal involved small sums of money, the timing was particularly bad. Here was Ed Gray, warning thrift executives and Congress about waste and risky investments at the companies he regulated, financing what appeared to be a lavish lifestyle from funds that ultimately derived from the industry.

Even worse for Gray's administration, Congress had ended its 1986 term without adopting legislation that would have recapitalized the FSLIC. Jim Wright, who was scheduled to become the next Speaker of the House in 1987, had undercut passage of the recap bill. Wright stalled action until he received assurances from the regulators that they would ease the pressure on troubled thrifts in Texas, which had become the plague of the

S&L system because of the energy depression and rampant fraud.*

In March 1987, government investigators determined that the FSLIC had a $6-billion deficit; the insurance fund was bankrupt and had no money to dispose of problem associations. Nevertheless, Speaker Wright favored a $5-billion recap bill, as did many industry representatives, but Gray was pushing for a $15-billion package. Finally, Wright came out in favor of the larger package after the FSLIC filed suit against fellow Texan Donald Dixon, and Congress ultimately compromised at $10.8 billion, a fraction of what was needed.

Even Gray had been much too optimistic in his assessment of what it would take to rebuild a moribund industry that rested on a weak foundation and was ill prepared for the competitive pressures of the modern financial age. Some observers had even begun to question the need for a separate thrift industry. Now, with the steady rise of the secondary market, more heavily capitalized commercial banks could afford to make home loans they quickly sold to investors, turning the S&L industry on its ear. Some reformers even suggested curtailing deposit insurance or scrapping it altogether.

Reflecting the insurance fund's bankruptcy, insolvent thrifts littered the corporate landscape. One-third of the industry (about 1,000 firms) was bleeding to death. More than 250 were technically dead but remained in business because the federal regulators couldn't afford to bury them. These zombie institutions exacted a heavy toll on the rest of the industry, and ultimately on the taxpayers. In a failed bid to fend off death, they often hiked interest rates, increasing the costs of business for

---

*Wright kept meddling in the Bank Board's affairs. He personally pressured Gray to aid some Texas constituents, beginning in 1986. The most controversial was Donald Dixon, the owner of Vernon Savings and Loan Association of Vernon, Texas. Wright called Gray and asked him to delay a federal takeover of Vernon. A spokesman for the former Speaker said the Congressman only wanted FSLIC to wait a week. But the agency did not move until March 1987. By then, 96 percent of all loans at Vernon, which had $1.4 billion in assets, were delinquent.

The FSLIC later sued Dixon and six associates for allegedly defrauding Vernon. The agency said Dixon took nearly $9 million in salaries and bonuses from the thrift in four years and the company had $5 million in paintings, five airplanes, a $2-million beach house, and a large motor yacht.

other thrifts, and then plowed insured deposits into highly risky ventures in the vain hope that the last-ditch efforts might pay off and save the firms.

Despite his other concerns, Gray paid particular attention to American Savings, which he hoped to sell before leaving Washington in June. He had made disposing of American one of his top priorities, but selling American was proving difficult because of the company's declining fortunes.

In April, rising rates had prompted Wall Street dealers to ask FCA to cover the withering value of the mortgage securities. The company promptly posted $900 million in cash and additional collateral. Popejoy said the company met the collateral calls easily and could have done so for another week, with cash to spare. But Cirona's team in San Francisco once again worried about the company's liquidity, wondering if it would have enough cash to meet business needs, and transmitted those fears to Washington.

A week after the collateral calls, FCA reported another earnings reversal. Net income for the first three months of the year dropped 81 percent, to $9.2 million, and the company actually lost money on an operating basis. Continuing its practice of posting additional reserves for loan losses every quarter, FCA placed another $79.8 million in the loan-loss reserve, bringing the total to $854 million.

Shortly before the earnings announcement, the Bank Board had hired Salomon Brothers as its investment bankers, and the firm had talked with several investors interested in acquiring American. By mid-June, one of those investors, Ford Motor, was the clear front-runner. In fact, Gray was convinced that an agreement was in hand and that he would resolve the American problem before leaving office in a few days. That, however, would require Larry White's cooperation.

Larry White's doubts about arranging a sale were strengthening. The professor didn't think Salomon Brothers could conclude such a complicated deal before Ed Gray left for the private sector.

Those concerns crystallized just after noon on Tuesday, June 16, when White was on a twenty-five-seat puddle jumper flying back from a conference in White Sulphur Springs, West Virginia, to the international airport at Dulles. There he was to grab a ride downtown from a Salomon investment banker before flying to the West Coast later that night for another S&L conference.

Seated beside him on the plane was a junior member of the Salomon team, who had brought along a briefing book for White to read. White liked the broad framework of an offer by Ford, which wanted to buy American Savings and fold it into its First Nationwide subsidiary, but found that too many details still needed to be addressed. An old phrase popped into his head: "The devil's in the details." With so many unanswered questions in the proposal, White felt it could take months to conclude the negotiations.

His suspicion grew when he arrived at Dulles where he was met at the airport by a senior member of the Salomon team. Gerard Smith was a former army intelligence officer and Vietnam veteran. A blunt and aggressive investment banker who collected artworks of birds because he loved to hunt them, Smith was himself convinced almost from the beginning of his involvement with American that finding a buyer would be difficult.

As it happened, Popejoy had contacted Salomon Brothers about finding an acquirer in late 1986. On January 6, 1987, Smith went to FCA's offices in Irvine to meet with a group of top FCA officials to collect information for a sales brochure. What would normally have been a relatively routine task took several weeks because FCA didn't seem to have reliable financial information.

Of far greater concern to the Salomon team were American's enormous unrealized losses. The company was essentially insolvent. However, under the magic of regulatory accounting, it still had a positive net worth. Smith spotted losses estimated at $7 billion and filed a memorandum to that effect with Lew Ranieri, Salomon's vice chairman. FCA had more than $1 billion in goodwill (that alone would have destroyed its stockholders' equity); approximately $4 billion in losses in the loan portfolio; and unrealized losses on mortgage securities and new fixed-rate loans whose value was dropping in the current higher-interest-rate environment.

Informally among themselves, the Salomon team started calling FCA Chernobyl because the institution was moving toward a meltdown. The only reason the company was in business, it seemed to Smith and many others on Wall Street, was the "comfort letter"—the letter to the company saying the Bank Board would take no action against American Savings solely because of its capital shortage. Absent that single piece of paper, Wall Street dealers would not provide repo lending, and the company would in turn lose scores of depositors, and its stock price would plummet.

On the ride downtown, White peppered Smith with questions about the negotiations. White made up his mind that he would tell Gray that the chairman could not count on his support. An agreement with Ford, even a tentative one, was premature.

Gray did not take the news kindly. He thought White was thwarting the sale because he did not want to act until Gray's replacement took office. Years later, he would still personally blame White, not lack of time, for killing the deal. Two weeks later, on June 30, after four stormy years at the helm, his life in disarray, Ed Gray left the Bank Board, turning over his job to a man who was about to make him look heroic in comparison. Now his successor could tackle American Savings.

Bearded, balding, bespectacled M. Danny Wall, a man who liked to wear the vest of his three-piece suit, was a lifelong public servant with no use for hobbies. Politics was his life and had been for as long as he could remember. He liked to think of himself as Mr. Clean. Near the top of his official résumé, Wall listed his rank of Eagle Scout.

The new Bank Board chairman hailed from a small town in South Dakota where his parents impressed upon him the importance of political involvement. His father held several local political jobs, and his mother was active in the Republican party. After college, Wall entered government service on the local level. From 1964 to 1971, he was an urban planner, directing urban renewal efforts in Fargo, North Dakota. He moved to Salt Lake City to do virtually the same thing from 1971 to 1975, becoming the executive director of the city's redevelopment agency.

Danny Wall's political fortunes brightened considerably in

1975 when he was plucked from this obscure position and given a shot at big-time national politics. U.S. Senator Jake Garn, a Utah Republican who had earlier served as mayor of Salt Lake City, asked Wall to run his legislative staff in Washington. Wall jumped at the chance.

His thirteen-year employment for the conservative Republican senator taught Wall the inner workings of Washington that few regulators had ever witnessed firsthand. Many banking regulators were career bureaucrats or were rotating through the government on their way to better-paying jobs.

As a key Garn staff member, Wall helped shaped the landmark Garn-St. Germain legislation deregulating financial services, which many blamed for the current crisis that Danny Wall would now have to resolve. Wall considered his congressional experience a strong asset at the Bank Board because he would need to unite Capitol Hill and the diverse elements of the fractured S&L industry.

Despite this vast government experience, Wall's personality worked against him. There was a tenacious, almost stiff-necked aspect to Wall's personality that made him seem cold and austere. Where the garrulous Gray was only too glad to talk someone's head off, Wall was private and aloof. He liked secrecy and found it an important element of his leadership at the Bank Board, but this left him with few allies in the agency or other branches of government. Staffers joked that Danny Wall played his cards so close to his vest that not even he could see what hand he had been dealt.

Ironically, despite his many years working on Capitol Hill, Wall was at the very least politically naive. He saw nothing wrong in meeting with the heads of companies against whom his agency was taking tough action. This lack of judgment hastened his eventual demise, for it soon would be made public that he had met personally with none other than Charles Keating, Jr., shortly before the Bank Board rejected a recommendation from Cirona's regional bank that Lincoln Savings be seized. In fact, Wall met two more times with Keating and said there was nothing improper about those conversations. Keating's companies had donated more than $25,000 to the Garn Institute of Finance at the University of Utah. Wall denied a charge by Congressman Gonzalez that he had personally solicited donations from Keating while still an aide to Senator Garn.

Keating was the central figure in one of the worst of the many scandals that shook the S&L industry in the 1980s. Besides American Savings, the case that would cause Wall the most controversy and a crucial issue upon which his administration would be judged, there was Lincoln Savings, another of the high-risk, fast-growth thrifts damaging the federal insurance system. An ardent crusader against pornography, Keating plundered Lincoln's assets and used the money for a variety of political contributions, most notably to five U.S. senators who had been pressuring Gray to get off Keating's back.*

After Wall joined the Bank Board, Keating's institution was allowed to remain open for an extra two years beyond the time that Jim Cirona and his staff wanted to take action. Indeed, the Bank Board transferred supervision of Lincoln Savings away from Cirona in San Francisco, in a move that stunned regulators throughout the country. Delays in closing Lincoln increased the eventual cost to the taxpayers, a price tag that approached $2 billion, and allowed Keating to sell worthless bonds to unsuspecting customers who thought they were getting federally insured accounts.

Wall's handling of Lincoln was not his only, and may not have been even his most serious, mistake. Whereas Gray constantly warned of an eventual taxpayer bailout, Wall consistently downplayed the scope of the industry's mounting losses. His gross miscalculations eventually had him at odds with his fellow board members, who were predicting much higher cleanup bills. In addition, Washington insiders accused Wall, who was becoming a scapegoat for years of problem S&Ls, of intentionally misleading Congress and the American public about the size of the impending disaster until after

*In October 1989, Common Cause, the political reform group, called for an investigation by the Senate Ethics Committee of Senator Alan Cranston, D-California, and four colleagues for their role in the Lincoln affair. The reform group had earlier demanded a similar investigation of Jim Wright. After a damaging probe by the House Ethics Committee of his personal affairs, the Speaker resigned.

the 1988 presidential elections, presumably to help George Bush's election efforts.*

Under Wall, the Bank Board adopted the Southwest Plan of consolidating insolvent oil-patch thrifts, primarily in Texas, with an eye toward selling them. The Bank Board granted generous terms to investors, including covering some legal fees, guaranteeing a return on bad assets, and requiring little initial capital from the buyer.

The new chairman got off to a shaky start with American Savings, for despite its weak financial condition, he was in no rush to rescue the company. In fact, he thought the Bank Board had no business contracting with an investment banking firm in the first place. As he saw it, the S&L was neither insolvent nor under the control of the FSLIC. Thus, the Bank Board lacked the legal authority to sell American.

On Wednesday, July 1, his first day on the job, Wall received a staff briefing on American's deteriorating condition and the prospects for finding an acquirer. The two investors mentioned were Ford/First Nationwide and a joint venture of Investment Limited Partners and Equitable Life. Ford seemed like the stronger of the two.**

That very day, FCA announced an expected loss of between $150 million and $200 million for the second quarter of 1987. "It's certainly a setback for us because we have been making a great deal of progress toward rebuilding our capital," Popejoy said. He ended on a positive note, though, concluding, "We've been through setbacks before and we've weathered them."

One of Cirona's examiners went to FCA's mortgage-backed-securities trading facility to monitor the reaction of Wall Street dealers to the impending loss. If Wall Street saw the loss as a serious setback, the dealers might decline to extend credit, bringing about another substantial cash drain. The examiner would remain there for weeks, keeping a careful eye on FCA's trading operation.

---

*Angered at first by Wall's embarrassingly bad accounting and later by his involvement with Lincoln, Henry Gonzalez, chairman of the House Banking Committee, led the 1989 drive for Wall's dismissal.

**HF Holdings, an investment group headed by former Treasury Secretary Bill Simon that included former Fed vice chairman Preston Martin, wanted out of the bidding.

Despite his ambivalence, Wall decided the Bank Board should search for a buyer after all. He made it clear, however, that there was no urgency. Although the company was the largest troubled thrift in the country, Wall did not personally tackle the case of American Savings, as Ed Gray had. No, he had just the right man in mind for that job.

Chapter 19

The Switchblade and the Taurus

Day in and day out, the bureaucracy in Washington tested the limits of Roger Martin's patience. He had little appreciation for the exigencies of government forms, and the unnecessary delays in getting simple items for his office made his nostrils flare with frustration. It took five weeks to obtain a telephone credit card, even longer for a simple in-basket. But the broken phone in his official car proved too much.

After five weeks of waiting for the government to fix it, Martin borrowed a switchblade from his chauffeur, cut the cord, and dropped the phone in front of the Bank Board's chief of staff. That sure got his attention—and a $16 bill for destruction of government property.

The portly, balding Martin, who impressed his allies and adversaries as gruff and unpretentious, was the only member of the Bank Board from private industry. At Milwaukee's Mortgage Guarantee Insurance Co., he had earned a reputation as an ace troubleshooter. In one example of his tenacity, he once tracked down eight thousand mobile homes whose owners had defaulted on mortgages insured by his company so that he could get the deadbeats to pay. Martin had also served on the board of directors of the Chicago Federal Home Loan Bank and worked in Washington from 1969 to 1974 as the general manager of the Airline Pilots Association International.

The unfriendly skies of the S&L industry taxed his abilities as an administrator. Facing the enormous volume of federally assisted acquisitions that required his attention, Martin relied heavily on Elise Paylan, his attractive, ambitious executive assistant, to keep him on track.

Shortly after joining the Bank Board, Martin went to visit

Popejoy at FCA's headquarters in Irvine. Though he was concerned about the company's mortgage-backed securities, its real-estate losses, and the value of the new loans written under Popejoy's administration, the two men hit it off despite the innate adversarial relationship. Martin found himself stepping into a white 1962 Buick Skylark convertible. Popejoy had the top down. A fellow classic-car buff, Martin loved riding in the car.

Popejoy and his staff gave Martin a long overview of the company, its history, current condition, past and projected real-estate losses, the way the mortgage-securities trading desk worked, and the company's plans for the future. Martin was impressed most of all with the quality of the mortgages the company had made since Popejoy took over. Out of more than 30,000 real estate loans worth roughly $8 billion, the portfolio sustained only a handful of losses. An incredibly strong performance, Martin thought. In fact, by the end of Popejoy's tenure, American would write 44,000 mortgages, of which only 36 would default. Even old Uncle Mark Taper could be jealous of that performance.

Shortly after returning from his fact-finding mission, Martin assumed responsibility for overseeing American in addition to attending to more than one hundred insolvent thrifts in Texas, which made him the overseer of some of the most deeply troubled financial institutions in the country. He faced a confining set of constraints.

American alone would eat up a large portion of the $10.8 billion that Congress had authorized the FSLIC to borrow. Indeed, American would likely require $2 billion or more in federal assistance and $1 billion in new capital from an acquirer. Actually, the Salomon team believed American would easily devour more than twice that amount since the investment bankers thought there were about $7 billion in losses embedded in the institution. Although he thought the new loans at American exhibited excellent underwriting standards, Martin worried about their value in the market because the bulk of them were fixed-rate loans.

As an alternative to the Ford proposal, Martin studied a plan offered by Popejoy to divide the company four ways. On Friday, September 18, Martin announced that the Popejoy proposal "looks awfully good" on the surface but that "there's a lot we have to do to get the rabbit over the fence." For his part, Popejoy said the plan, which had developed from FCA's continued search for capital, was a "long shot."

Under the proposal, the four new entities would remain wholly owned subsidiaries of FCA, which would receive the same kind of assistance from the FSLIC as an investor acquiring the company would. The question was, would the proposal by Ford (still considered the strongest suitor) or FCA's plan be cheaper for the insurance agency?

Popejoy's team envisioned dividing the company so that a healthy retail S&L would emerge after all the changes. FCA's chairman wanted to split the company along these lines:

- "Old American"—with approximately $1 billion in assets and savings deposits, and the lucrative tax benefits that resulted from the company's accumulated losses—which would be sold to investors.
- "New American," a retail S&L with about 170 branches and $20 billion in assets that would retain the existing net worth of American Savings. FCA would use the proceeds from the sale of Old American to bolster the capital of New American.
- The "Mortgage-Backed Securities Thrift," with a portfolio of approximately $14 billion in mortgage-backed securities, financed primarily by the reverse-repurchase agreements and a secured note to New American.
- The "Real Estate Thrift," which would have a portfolio of about $5 billion in troubled loans and real estate, financed by a secured note to New American. The MBS and real-estate thrifts would require FSLIC assistance to guarantee the notes to New American and to cover the operating losses at both subsidiaries.

Shortly after disclosing the breakup plan, Martin said he preferred it over the Ford proposal because the FCA restructuring would cost the insurance fund less money. Martin placed the restructuring cost to the FSLIC at between $1.2 billion and $2 billion, and said a Ford acquisition would total between $3 billion and $4.5 billion.

Martin seemed to be playing to the press, using the media as a tool in the negotiations. Obviously, he wanted the Ford negotiators to accept less favorable terms. But if he thought they would cut their bid in half, Roger Martin had another think coming.

Three days later, on September 21, the investigation by the SEC that had dogged the company for years finally came to a close. FCA, in settling charges that it had illegally inflated profits in quarterly and annual income statements dating back to 1980, stipulated to a permanent injunction barring it from further violations of the Securities and Exchange Act of 1934 but neither admitted wrongdoing nor restated any earnings.

Although some of the business practices that FCA agreed to reform occurred while Popejoy was chairman, the bulk of the twenty-five-page settlement centered on the Knapp years.

SEC investigators found that under Knapp, FCA had overstated its earnings in part by improperly accounting for land-sale and loan transactions in a series of deals designed to allow the company to book nonexistent but anticipated future profits. The extra profits stemmed from the "buy-sell" transactions in which the thrift subsidiary, then State Savings, appeared to purchase property from a third party and then resell it to a real-estate developer in an arm's-length transaction.

Actually, FCA would purchase land from a developer who had it under option and would then add to the sales price 50 percent of the profit anticipated upon completion of the project. FCA would then resell the land to the developer at the higher price, extending land-acquisition and development financing to the buyer to cover the increased cost. Then the profit on the sale and the loan-origination fee were booked as immediate income. For instance, the company would buy land for $700,000 that was estimated to be worth $1.1 million when developed. Then FCA's executives would add $200,000 to the price of the land, reselling it for $900,000, taking the profit and booking-fee income on the inflated loan amount. FCA cooked its earnings by $13.3 million in 1980 and $7 million in 1981 as a result of these improper transactions.

The agency's complaint censured FCA for failing to maintain adequate loan-loss reserves, which also served to pump up the profits when Charlie Knapp ran the holding company and Foster Fluetsch was in charge of the S&L. Failing to maintain the proper level of reserves to cover the costs of loans that turned sour, the SEC said, led FCA to file materially false and misleading income statements. The SEC did not directly address the issue, but clearly some investors purchased stock in the firm as a result of the false financial filings, which appeared to back up the grandiose comments Knapp made to stock analysts and the media.

Noting that as a result of Popejoy's real-estate task force, FCA had hiked its loan-loss reserve by $422 million for 1984, the agency said that new management filed accurate year-end earnings reports for 1985 and 1986. But under Popejoy, FCA filed potentially misleading quarterly reports for both years. Inadequacies in the accounting system meant that FCA could not identify loan losses, except on a task-force basis, at the end of each year. The company failed to provide an accurate depiction of bad loans with the quarterly reports publicly held companies are required to file and make available to investors. FCA placed $182 million in 1985, and $464 million in 1986, in its loan-loss reserve.

Thus, some investors may have purchased stock earlier in each of those years without access to the damaging information obtained with the full-scale annual audit. As part of the settlement with the SEC, FCA agreed (1) to hire Peat Marwick, its outside accounting firm, to audit the quarterly financial statements to ensure that investors received accurate information and (2) to review internal controls on accounting for loans and real estate.

Although he had not received a blanket statement of support, Popejoy was pleased with the settlement, telling the press he was glad to put the inherited problems behind him. But FCA was like a river raft surviving a perilous course through whitewater rapids, only to round the next bend and face a steep waterfall. Left unresolved were hundreds of class-action claims filed after the SEC forced the company to restate its earnings two weeks before Knapp's ouster in 1984. These complicated and time-consuming suits, alleging violations of federal securities laws, reckless business practices, and a waste of corporate assets, threatened to capsize the company.

FCA had reached an agreement in principle to settle the shareholder claims and another class-action case in January 1986, and later that year agreed to issue common stock to investors who purchased the company's securities between April 1, 1980, and April 8, 1985. The settlements were valued at a minimum of $32 million. The settlement agent received claims of more than $400 million. Trouble was, FCA had placed only $35 million in reserve to pay the claims. As a result, the company was attempting to restructure the settlements.

But as October approached, and the bulls in the stock market were being spooked into a stampede, the SEC's permanent injunction and the enormous legal challenges would be the least of FCA's worries.

Turning Tony Frank loose on the federal government was like giving Mario Andretti five free laps at Indianapolis. That Frank was brilliant was not in doubt. He could quickly shift gears from one subject to the next, and he drove his Ford-owned company with the pedal pressed to the floorboard. But by the fall of 1987, some members of the Bank Board staff in Washington thought Frank was just a tad too smart.

Tall, trim, and articulate, with the sharp angular features and command presence of a Prussian military officer, Anthony M. Frank was chairman of First Nationwide Financial Corp., the holding company for First Nationwide Bank, the nation's sixth-largest thrift. An avowed bookworm who claimed not to own a television set, Frank was also FCA's leading suitor.

The son of Ph.D. economists who fled Nazi Germany in 1937, Frank was a naturalized U.S. citizen who grew up in southern California. After getting his undergraduate and graduate degrees in business from Dartmouth, Frank joined Mark Taper's American Savings. He left in the mid-1960s, trying his hand at a variety of businesses, running a hospital chain and a sheet-metal factory, before becoming in 1970 the chairman of the San Francisco Federal Home Loan Bank. The next year, he landed a job as president of First Nationwide, then called Citizens Savings. Citizens was just another small S&L association with a comfortable niche in northern California when Frank arrived. But Frank aspired to become the leader of the largest S&L in the land.

In 1980, Citizens was sold to National Steel, which took the renamed company public two years later. After the prolonged recession in the steel industry weakened National Steel, Frank offered to sell the subsidiary. He called on each of Detroit's Big Three automakers, offering them the chance to diversify into deregulated S&Ls to become less dependent on cyclical car sales.

Ford already operated Ford Motor Credit Co., the world's second-largest finance company. Ford itself was emerging from the ravages of recession with a host of new products intended to compete with the onslaught of popular Japanese and European cars. First Nationwide would further strengthen Ford's balance sheet, and the automaker completed its purchase of First Nationwide in late 1985.

Frank saw a way to leverage Ford's investment as he strived to live up to the First Nationwide name. First Nationwide had been the first thrift in the country to operate offices on both coasts. Shortly after the Ford acquisition was complete, Frank and Paul Weinberg, the thrift's senior vice president for corporate planning and development, drafted a plan to make First Nationwide a thrift of dramatic proportions.

The expansion plan called for a series of acquisitions that would build First Nationwide into an S&L holding company earning $500 million a year by the early 1990s. To accomplish that objective, First Nationwide would need total assets in the neighborhood of $60 billion, a sixfold increase from 1985 assets of $11.6 billion.

American Savings fit nicely into First Nationwide's objectives. Dreaming, like Popejoy, of returning to his alma mater, Frank wanted to bolster First Nationwide's presence in the lucrative southern California market, where American's branches were heavily concentrated.* First Nationwide also needed some streamlining to improve efficiencies and lower overhead. By acquiring American, which was twice the size of First Nationwide,

*He had long been concerned about American's health. In fact, when Frank, who liked to speak in parables, tried to explain to people the incredible risk Charlie Knapp was taking at Financial Corp. in the late 1970s, he said it was like walking into a casino in Las Vegas and finding your minister gambling with church funds. You have two choices. You can say, "You're under arrest," or ask, "Are we winning?"

Frank could consolidate operations and drive down his costs as he shot past his competitors.

Wells Fargo had already proved the enormous advantages of buying a competitor in your home market. Wells purchased Crocker Bank in 1985 for roughly $1 billion, then the largest banking acquisition, and began slashing the work force as it removed redundant jobs and branch locations. Like American, Crocker had a strong presence in the southern section of the state.

Frank had similar designs on American Savings. He planned to fire dozens of senior executives, starting with Popejoy and all the executive vice presidents, sell or consolidate more than forty branches, and furlough thousands of workers as entire departments were eliminated.*

That is, if he could reach an agreement with the Bank Board, which was proving to be an exceptionally difficult endeavor. Frank thought he could have come to terms with Ed Gray, but once Gray left office, the talks lost momentum. After Roger Martin was placed in charge of negotiating the sale, the pace quickened once again. But Frank and James Ford, who was president of Ford Motor Credit and conducting the negotiations along with Frank and the First Nationwide team, couldn't seem to break through.

The proposed deal had plenty of positive attributes. Unlike the dubious merger of Knapp's State Savings with American, which ultimately destroyed both companies, a combination of American and First Nationwide seemed ideal. With so many banks and S&Ls in serious trouble, with hundreds of thrifts still insolvent and others no better than marginal performers, a linkup of the two giant thrifts would greatly enhance the economic efficiency of the system. The Bank Board would be replacing a huge brain-dead company with one admired for strong management.

Moreover, Ford, having rebounded from the recession with new plants and products, including the highly popular Sable and Taurus, had registered record earnings in 1985 and 1986. The

---

*Frank had hired Ron Struck, FCA's former strategic planner, as a consultant. In a long memo, Struck was highly critical of the mortgage-backed securities and attributed certain deficiencies to Popejoy, Indiek, and Coleman.

company was awash in cash, with $9.4 billion in cash and marketable securities on hand, and by the end of 1987, the cash cushion was expected to reach $11 billion. To cinch the deal, Ford was offering to put up $1 billion in new capital and to absorb 20-25 percent of all future losses, which could cost hundreds of millions.

The enormous losses were part of the downside, however, for FCA's shareholders would likely be wiped out in the deal. The Ford–First Nationwide team refused to discuss the prospect of giving compensation to the shareholders, citing the Bank Board's own policy against funneling FSLIC money to the investors in an insolvent thrift. Ford wanted FSLIC assistance worth up to $3 billion and did not want to share any of FCA's tax benefits with the emaciated agency. Instead, Ford wanted less assistance from the federal agency, evidenced by its willingness to absorb a substantial portion of American's losses.

Under the Ford proposal, First Nationwide would liquidate American's mortgage bonds and would receive FSLIC assistance on three pools of assets. The pools covered bad loans and foreclosed real estate, the mortgage-backed securities, and a "phantom" pool. The phantom pool had $600 million in nonexistent mortgage securities on which the FSLIC would pay a subsidy to First Nationwide. The phantom pool was created to safeguard Ford's return. Ford wanted a 14 percent return on equity, or $140 million for every $1 billion invested. Without the phantom pool, the numbers wouldn't come out correctly.

The Bank Board and FSLIC officials were wary of Ford for another reason. Ford had run what amounted to a credit check on FSLIC, and like a car dealer that requires a cosigner for a risky customer, wanted some strong reassurances. This had been one of the biggest obstacles in the negotiations. Ford did not trust the value of FSLIC notes or the ongoing ability of the agency to fund its commitments. When disposing of an insolvent institution, FSLIC issued notes to the acquiring company and agreed to cover certain future costs, depending on the agreement in question.

But because the FSLIC was by now insolvent by several billion dollars, Ford had severe reservations about the value of those notes and whether assistance payments could really be guaranteed. Congress had earlier said that all insured deposits at S&Ls were backed by the full faith and credit of the U.S. government. Since Congress had not made the same statement about the FSLIC notes, it was conceivable that Ford would end up an unsecured creditor, holding worthless FSLIC paper.

Without the full faith and credit of the Treasury behind the deal, Ford would have to put a footnote on its financial statements, saying billions in receivables covering the American acquisition might have no value. Not even the nation's second-largest automaker wanted that kind of exposure.

Then there was the issue of Tony Frank's credibility. Whether it's a real-estate deal, a labor pact, or the sale of a company, negotiations often hinge on personal trust. In this realm, Tony Frank's reputation as a shrewd negotiator worked against him. Some Bank Board staffers believed he wanted to take advantage of the FSLIC. The doubts stemmed from the incredible deal Frank had negotiated with the agency back in 1981 when he pulled off two federally assisted acquisitions, one in Florida, the other in New York. In exchange for his providing $75 million in new capital, Frank got the FSLIC to guarantee payment and cover expenses on bad loans for ten years. The government had already paid First Nationwide $500 million on the deals. Now he was back, asking for $3 billion in assistance to take care of American, a figure that some Bank Board staffers found too rich.

Frank had learned one crucial lesson from the 1981 talks. He did not want to see the books of the insolvent companies he was acquiring, an examination process referred to as due diligence. If the company performed the standard due-diligence inspection, it still might not see all the bad loans but then would have difficulty going to the government and asking for compensation when loans went into default. He had also declined to see American's books because it was a useless exercise. Popejoy was the chairman of the company, and every single quarter, the loan portfolio gave him new surprises. If the chairman of the company couldn't get an accurate accounting of bad assets, how could an outsider?

Ford submitted its latest proposal to the Bank Board on October 5, and the talks progressed. By the following week, Roger Martin was anxious to strike an accord. He had been worried about the value of American's mortgage securities since visiting

Popejoy the previous month. As interest rates ticked up again, the value of the portfolio was falling fast, leading to another liquidity crisis because FCA had to post additional collateral to cover the weakening bond prices. The Salomon team referred to changes in the value of the portfolio as "mood swings," which were measuring $500 million. With such violent mood swings, FCA was headed for a nervous breakdown. It could happen any moment, unless of course interest rates started falling by some strange fluke.

Chapter 20

Full Faith and Credit

By Saturday, October 17, Roger Martin feared the worst. Not only did he think American Savings was on the verge of collapse, but he realized that the company's failure could disrupt financial markets around the globe. Wall Street already had the shakes.

On the nineteenth floor of a glass-and-steel high rise in lower Manhattan, Martin was meeting with the federal government's potential rescue team. The investment bankers and lawyers representing the Bank Board hoped for a speedy sale of American Savings to Ford.

Throughout the week of October 12, the stock market behaved erratically. On Friday, the Dow Jones Industrial Average plummeted 108 points. The highly watched bellwether index of the stock market is the pulse of the Street and reflects the outlook of the investing public. Although no one could forecast if a falling market meant a major correction or just the temporary madness of crowds, the outlook for American Savings and the rest of the financial-services industry was poor. As stocks dipped, interest rates rose. With every slight upward adjustment, the value of American's mortgage securities fell again.

In Irvine, Vic Indiek's frenzied finance staff rushed to meet a wave of collateral calls from Wall Street dealers. The company had nearly run out of bonds to post as collateral but still had cash and Treasury securities in reserve. However, Coleman worried that if he began using cash, the Street would know he was out of collateral, and that might further inflame the situation.

Based on information from Wall Street and from estimates of the Bank Board's staff, Martin calculated the loss in American's bond portfolio at more than $2.6 billion. He also suspected that Wall Street was so busy that week that the broker-dealers had failed to catch up with all the paperwork. He felt that once all the orders were processed, American could well miss its collateral calls.

If American couldn't post additional cash or securities to cover the losses in its portfolio, the dealers might start liquidating the securities in an already jittery market, creating a sinister chain reaction. Once the selling started, who could tell where it might end? Jerry Smith at Salomon Brothers and Rodgin Cohen, a prominent banking attorney and partner at the law firm of Sullivan and Cromwell, recently hired to advise the Bank Board, thought that some of Wall Street's strongest firms might go under.

Dumping billions of securities on the market would drive prices down further and cause another wave of panic selling that would drive prices down again. Collateral calls would strike other financial institutions. And that was no small matter. American had pledged nearly $13 billion as part of its repo lines, and U.S. banks and thrifts had a total of $200 billion serving as collateral for loans from Wall Street. A disaster on Wall Street, the pinnacle of the capitalist system and a symbol of a smoothly running American economy, would almost certainly affect financial markets in other industrialized nations.

Although disposing of American was in the national interest, it didn't make fashioning an agreement any easier. By now, mutual suspicions had crept into the talks between Ford and the Bank Board. David Hilder, an aggressive reporter for the *Wall Street Journal,* had stayed on top of the developing story at FCA. His reports on the negotiations were considered accurate, so much so that Tony Frank and Roger Martin now teased each other about being Hilder's "leak." They were only half joking. Rodgin Cohen, one of the best deal makers advising the banking industry, felt the leaks alone could destroy the talks.

Press leaks were only part of the gulf separating the two sides. There was dissension in the ranks. Despite his own concerns about American's perilous condition, Roger Martin thought that Cohen was in too big a hurry to strike a bargain with Ford and that he was willing to grant generous terms to the rich automaker. Actually, Cohen had been ignoring some of his best clients to work on the sale of American. He liked to say that every deal has its own dynamics. And Cohen should know. He had been involved in some of the largest takeovers in the banking industry and had a high success rate. Cohen thought it was time for a settlement.

Tony Frank and James Ford sensed they were on the verge of a breakthrough. They had been frustrated for weeks because they thought the Bank Board staff didn't understand the deal they proposed, especially the crucial nature of the full-faith-and-credit issue.

Indeed, at one point, Ford had even asked the government to post collateral from other S&Ls to cover the American agreement. But this raised several complex and far-reaching questions. How much collateral should the Bank Board post? Would the government have to provide collateral in other deals? And if the collateral was posted, wouldn't that be tantamount to saying FSLIC notes had no real value?

The Salomon team had warned the regulators that the creditworthiness of the FSLIC would make American a tough sale. But the investment bankers had recently been told that if all other aspects of a deal could be resolved, the full-faith-and-credit issue would no longer be an obstacle. With that in mind, the two sides moved closer to a deal at this Saturday bargaining session.

Tony Frank and his boss, James Ford, thought they could compromise with Roger Martin. Ford Motor was now willing to provide an additional $100 million in capital, bringing the total to $1.1 billion. At the same time, the company would conduct a due-diligence inspection of the portfolio of single-family mortgages and would assume the risk of bad assets after an initial round of tossing out any delinquent loans. This was in sharp contrast to Tony Frank's normal negotiating demand of not knowing the full extent of troubled loans in a federally assisted deal and not accepting responsibility for those that later defaulted. The Ford team also agreed to provide the FSLIC with a share of any operating earnings that American might generate. But the government would remain responsible for the bulk of American's bad loans, especially the highly questionable commercial credits.

After meeting for several hours in a Salomon Brothers conference room, the negotiators prepared to retire. Perceptions on what happened at the conclusion of the discussions varied widely. Tony Frank still maintains that he had reached a tentative agreement with Roger Martin and shaken hands on it, adding that he remembers it clearly because he places great stock in handshakes in business deals.

Roger Martin and his assistant, Elise Paylan, said there was no deal, only that Martin agreed to certain parameters for additional negotiations and that he had to check with the other members of the Bank Board before continuing. Besides, Martin doubted whether Jim Ford had the authority to agree to a deal.

Rodgin Cohen thought that important progress had been made but that no deal had been struck. In fact, Cohen's instincts told him to keep talking because the two sides would lose important momentum by recessing. If they stayed longer, working through the night if necessary, they could reach a general agreement and later negotiate the unresolved items. Once they had a general agreement, he believed, the two sides would be committed to resolving their disputes.

The two sides agreed to meet again in Washington on Tuesday. When Roger Martin left and stepped into the brisk fall air, some of the negotiators thought he was flying home to Milwaukee to spend the weekend with his wife. Instead, Martin was headed back to Washington for a secret meeting of top economic officials concerned with finding a way to keep American Savings from collapsing and pulling other financial institutions down with it.

On Sunday, October 18, while most of the country's citizens were attending church, watching football games, or reading the Sunday paper, ranking members of the Reagan administration were studying plans to avert a national financial disaster.

Beginning at 3:00 P.M., they met at the Bank Board's squat sand-colored building across from the old Executive Office Building. To avoid attracting attention, the participants drove their own cars rather than government vehicles.

Danny Wall and Roger Martin represented the Bank Board, and Jim Cirona flew in from San Francisco. The San Francisco Federal Home Loan Bank was producing daily summaries of American's cash position. Manuel Johnson, the Federal Reserve's vice chairman, and George Gould, under secretary of the Treasury, were there as well. Top staff members from all three agencies attended.

Martin, who believed the company could go under as early as Monday morning, began by asking for access to a $4-billion line of credit at the Treasury, available under the National Housing Act. Gould declined to make the money available.

Federal Reserve officials in Washington wanted American to exhaust its credit with the San Francisco Federal Home Loan Bank and other district banks before lending directly to the thrift. For his part, Cirona was reluctant to lend American additional money. If he did and American failed, his bank would find itself in financial difficulty.

When the meeting broke up at around 6:00 P.M., the Federal Reserve had agreed to act in its capacity as lender of last resort, but only after American had exhausted all hope of borrowing within the thrift system. Martin didn't think that was much of a contingency plan, considering how quickly American could be wiped out.

On Monday, October 19, the stock market crashed. The 508-point decline in the Dow was the steepest numerical descent in the market's history, larger than the great crash of October 1929. In a single day, nearly $500 billion of investment value was destroyed.

Roger Martin spent much of Monday glued to the color TV in his fifth-floor office as news reporters and television commentators provided updates on the unfolding drama. Driven by panic, investors issued a wave of sell orders that overwhelmed the market, but when scenes of the crash flickered on the television screen, Martin cheered. Upon taking the job with the Bank Board less than three months ago, he had sold all his common stock. And American's bonds were gaining in value.

Meanwhile, in New York, Gerard Smith and Paul Wetzel of Salomon Brothers were meeting with FSLIC officials to explore ways of hedging American's mortgage-securities portfolio. Later that day, Smith and Wetzel flew to Washington to confer with Roger Martin to prepare for the next-day meeting with Ford. American Savings was emerging from the crash. As stocks plummeted, the bond market rallied. The stock-market crash was rescuing American Savings.

On Tuesday, when stock markets were being pummeled in Europe and Asia, the rally in the U.S. bond market continued. Interest rates had begun a sharp decline, in no small measure the result of the Federal Reserve's decision to fight the financial bonfires by opening the spigot on the nation's money supply. (An increase in the money supply drives down interest rates and improves the prices of bonds.)

Martin and the Salomon team met with the Ford negotiators that Tuesday at Sullivan and Cromwell's offices in Washington. Rodgin Cohen's hunch had been right. The decisive moment of action had evaporated. Tony Frank thought Roger Martin was distracted. He was often interrupted during the talks by aides handing him slips of paper, which were messages regarding the bond market and American's liquidity position. Finally, Martin left the room and seemed to take forever in some other meeting. When he came back, he sounded as though the two sides had never come close to an agreement just four days earlier.

Now that the bond rally had restored value to American's securities portfolio, there was no crisis. Martin seemed to be taking his sweet time so he could drive a harder bargain. Ford and Frank decided it was useless to keep negotiating with Martin and left.

Ten days later, the government came calling once again when the FSLIC asked Ford to revive the talks. A flurry of papers traded hands, starting on November 9. Now more than ever Ford looked like the most logical suitor. FCA's breakup plan would take too long to implement, and Citicorp, the nation's largest bank, had recently dropped out of the bidding after an extensive analysis of American's health.

After leaving Ford's headquarters in Dearborn, Michigan, on the afternoon of Monday, November 23, Frank and two top aides flew to Chicago for a meeting with Martin scheduled for the next day at the Home Loan Bank of Chicago. The talks progressed smoothly, even though one Ford negotiator suffered from chest pains and was in fact having a heart attack.

Here all the major economic items were resolved. The framework of the deal was similar to that discussed in New York in October, dividing American into a healthy thrift and three pools that would receive payments from the FSLIC. Ford had decided to reduce its profit on the acquisition to close the deal and would eventually lower its demand to a return on equity of 12 percent.

Still in dispute, however, was the FSLIC credit issue. By the time the two sides met again on December 19, Martin had asked the U.S. attorney general's office for a statement that FSLIC notes had the full faith and credit of the government behind them, a request that was denied.

On Saturday, December 27, at his home in Milwaukee, Martin took a phone call from Stuart Root, the FSLIC's new director, who expressed concern over additional demands Ford was now making. When Martin returned to Washington, he had lunch with Root, who told him that every time the two sides come close to an agreement, the Ford negotiators would make additional demands. Based on Root's assessment, Martin decided it was time to tell the Bank Board's lawyers to go home. No deal could be reached with Ford.

Frank, on the other hand, was all set to announce the merger, believing that only a few minor items remained unresolved. Indeed, First Nationwide had already filmed television commercials to commemorate the acquisition, reserved air time at television stations in major media markets in California, and bought 300,000 fortune cookies as part of the marketing campaign. Frank had done a training film for American's employees.

Then, on January 7, the *Wall Street Journal* reported that the two sides had resolved all the major issues except the one regarding FSLIC credit. But that day, the Bank Board issued a statement saying it had broken off talks with Ford. What the Bank Board's statement didn't reveal, however, is that Martin had recently learned that a shy Texas billionaire just might be willing to take American Savings off his hands.

Chapter 21

The Texan

Elise Paylan gunned the blue Mercury Cougar she had borrowed from Roger Martin and shot out of the parking lot. Something entered her peripheral vision, but she wasn't sure what because of the car's big blind spot. Suddenly, an oncoming car bore down upon Paylan and her passengers. She was botching her undercover assignment. She was supposed to smuggle an ultra-secretive Texas billionaire and his two top aides through the back entrance of the Bank Board without attracting attention, not get them all killed in a car crash. Paylan pulled away from the other car just in time to avoid a collision.

That was a close call. If Bob Bass had been injured in an auto accident in the nation's capital, you can bet the *Washington Post* would pick up the story. Not a good development for a man who is shy to the point of being paranoid about his privacy, especially anything to do with his business deals. And crashing your boss's new car isn't exactly the path to a brilliant career.

When Paylan arrived at the Bank Board, she directed the three takeover artists to an elevator that would bypass the reception desk. Bass was joined by Bernie Carl, a financial whiz and former amateur race-car driver, and David Bonderman, an attorney who liked to wear bright yellow or vivid pink socks. Paylan wanted them to avoid signing the official visitors' log, which Jim McTague, of the *American Banker*, was in the habit of checking to see who was talking with the Bank Board about American Savings.*

---

*In fact, that's how McTague got on to the story that Citicorp was interested in buying American's branch network, and some angry officials of the nation's largest bank complained about the ensuing publicity when pulling out of the talks. The Salomon Brothers investment bankers figured Citicorp was a long shot anyway because the company would have to write down American's goodwill, destroying a chunk of Citi's capital with a couple of computer entries.

Bob Bass and the Bank Board weren't taking any chances with McTague or the rest of the media. Although Bass was not a recluse like Howard Hughes, the wealthy Fort Worth native, a former underachiever turned shrewd corporate raider, was far too shy to handle the pressure of the national press corps.

Even as a youngster, Bob Bass had been bashful, standing in the shadow of his older and more outgoing brother Sid. Bob Bass didn't really come into his own until well into his thirties. In that regard, he took after his late great-uncle Sid Richardson, who had laid the foundation for the family fortune.

Sid Richardson was a Texas wildcatter known for the longest time for his propensity to drill dry wells. He borrowed money from people on the streets of Fort Worth, wore rumpled old suits, and used a pay phone at a local lunch counter for an office.

Finally, in 1930, at the age of 39, Richardson's luck changed, and he became the wildcatter of folklore. He struck oil in East Texas and went on to discover the rich Keystone Field in the western part of the state. Out of 385 wells he drilled in Keystone, only a handful came up dry. Within thirteen years, he had made some $800 million and shared the wealth with his friends by handing out gold money clips studded with diamonds. He spread the wealth among family members as well.

A lifelong bachelor, Richardson died in 1959, leaving $12 million to his only nephew, Perry Bass, Bob's father. Each of Perry Bass's four sons inherited $2.8 million—not a small sum, to be sure, but not enough to make any one of them into the next J. P. Morgan. The next year, the sons combined their assets to form Bass Brothers Enterprises as an investment vehicle.

Although the Bass clan was one of the wealthiest families in Fort Worth, the sons were expected to make something of themselves, not just act like indolent rich kids. Indeed, Perry Bass kept detailed files at his offices on all of his children, including their receipts for clothing expenses.

Like his brother Sid, the smooth-talking extrovert of the family, Bob Bass attended Phillips Andover Academy in Massachusetts, went on to Yale (also Sid's alma mater), and then enrolled in the graduate business-administration program at Stanford, where Sid had gone. When Bob returned to Fort Worth in 1974,

Sid and his wife, Anne, were the celebrity couple of Fort Worth. Bob Bass seemed content to let Sid take the lead.

Along with Richard Rainwater, a Stanford classmate, Sid transformed Bass Brothers Enterprises from a $50-million investment fund into a colossus worth more than $4 billion. The group held investments in oil, real estate, and finance. Their investment in Texaco and Walt Disney Co. alone netted more than $1 billion.

While he remained in the background, Bob Bass occasionally brought in some deals on his own. In 1981, he bought stock in Marathon Oil and recommended it to Sid and Rainwater. After the Bass brothers accumulated a 5.1 percent position in Marathon, the company was courted by Mobil Corp. and U.S. Steel. An initial investment of $165 million yielded a profit of $160 million, proving that brother Bob had good instincts.

What seems to have been the turning point for Bass had little to do with business. Instead, in the early 1980s, he became involved in the fight to stop a Fort Worth freeway expansion that threatened the downtown historic district. Political activism thrust him into the limelight, and Bass later became well known for his civic, political, and charitable work. He served as chairman of the National Trust for Historic Preservation, and his $2-million purchase of Ulysses S. Grant's mansion in Georgetown fueled speculation that he had national political ambitions, which would seem to make sneaking in and out the back doors of government buildings a bit more difficult.

In 1983, Bob Bass struck out on his own, forming the Robert M. Bass Group with offices one floor below his big brother's in the family-owned skyscraper. David Bonderman, who had just won an insider-trading case argued before the U.S. Supreme Court and shared Bass's concern for historic preservation, became his first employee. Bernie Carl followed soon afterward.

Bass had a flair for finding talent. By recruiting several sharp legal and financially oriented managers to work for him and harnessing his own investment instincts, he soon set about creating a takeover empire that made him the center of attention in financial circles. The boyish-looking conservatively dressed Bass became a master of the leveraged buyout.

A little of the luster later faded from his star when his hostile bid for publishing giant Macmillan failed, but in the spring of

1988, Bass was known for an impressive string of highly profitable victories. *Forbes* estimated his net worth at $1 billion. In October 1987, Bass and a Japanese partner bought the chain of Westin hotels from Allegis Corp. for $1.5 billion. Two months later, Bass helped take Bell and Howell Co. private with a group of company managers in a deal valued at $702 million. In March 1988, he sold the Plaza Hotel in New York to real-estate magnate Donald Trump.

Now, just one month after the Plaza sale, Bass was embarking on the biggest deal of his life, the purchase of American Savings. Not only would he make an entry into the banking world in a big way, but under his plan, he would operate a takeover fund with billions at his disposal. But before he could consummate the transaction, he had to pass the personal inspection of a government official who earned in one year what Bob Bass could make in an hour.

As he sat in his office awaiting the arrival of Bob Bass and his two key negotiators, Danny Wall reflected on similar misgivings he had felt years ago as a young urban planner in Fargo, North Dakota. Back then, he had been spooked by a deal in which he didn't meet one of the key financial backers until the negotiations were well under way. Wall didn't like that up-in-the air feeling that he was negotiating with someone whose intentions weren't completely clear.

Bob Bass made him feel just as uneasy. There was so much secrecy surrounding the man that it was impossible to know exactly what he wanted to do with American unless Wall talked with the billionaire face-to-face. He wanted to "take the measure of the man." The Bass group was proposing to buy American for $550 million in capital and an operating agreement in which the S&L would be divided along lines similar to those proposed several months earlier by Popejoy's team in Irvine. In exchange, the Bass group would share future earnings and some of the tax benefits with the FSLIC.

All that was spelled out in a ten-page term sheet the investment group had given the Bank Board. What concerned Wall was the group's demand for an exclusive negotiating agreement. Wall understood that Bass wouldn't want to spend millions in legal and due-diligence fees, only to have the Bank Board talk with other potential acquirers or, worse, slip the term sheet to other bidders. While Bass wanted protection against possible duplicity at the Bank Board, Wall needed his own reassurances. He did not want to suffer the professional embarrassment and thrust the Bank Board into additional controversy by selling American Savings on extremely favorable terms to a rich takeover artist, only to have him sell it six months later at a fabulous profit. Wall needed insurance against a quick flip by Bob Bass.

Beyond that, other doubts nagged Danny Wall. He thought the Bank Board had come close to a tentative agreement with Ford three separate times. He did not want to be bogged down for months, effectively taking the company off the market, only to have a deal disappear. In addition, because of its size and complexity, the sale of American Savings would set a precedent for other thrift disposals.

Wall had confidence in the professionalism of the Bank Board staff members, but they lacked experience in this kind of transaction. The agency had not successfully negotiated such a large sale before, and Bass was known as an astute bargain hunter. With so much money at stake, the sale of American Savings would invite, and eventually receive, intense scrutiny from the media and Congress.

And yet Wall had to sell American Savings. The company had become a symbol for the thrift industry's many ills and the inability of the Bank Board to dispose of problem institutions. The previous year, the industry had lost $13.4 billion, twice the $6.6 billion earned at healthy firms. Some 500 insolvent S&Ls awaited action, and another 300 to 500 were operating with negligible net worth. Federal regulators were liquidating or arranging the sale of one thrift a week. Nevertheless, even if the government could liquidate the companies in a day, it could not take fast action to recover money by selling assets. The zombie S&Ls had so many real-estate loans in their portfolios that selling it all in a hurry would only drive down real-estate prices, further weakening the system.

On top of it all was the delicate matter of a huge outpouring of deposits at American. In late January, Bill Popejoy announced that another round of losses had rendered FCA insolvent and that he had asked the federal government for a $1.5-billion package of aid, $300 million more than the Chrysler bailout. Popejoy called it a long-term "earnout" in which the government would inject capital into the company and then participate in future earnings.

FCA lost $467 million for all of 1987, bringing its negative net worth to $163.4 million. Although the holding company was insolvent, American Savings still had a positive net worth, thereby avoiding a government takeover. But plenty of other problems at American required his attention.

A few days later, on February 11, FCA said it was complying with a Bank Board directive to sell some $2.5 billion of mortgage-backed securities. That same month, the Bank Board had faced a revolt from Wall Street. Wall had been warned many times about the importance of renewing American's comfort letter to securities dealers but had remained gun-shy of signing a document that said the regulators would take no action just because American failed to meet its net-worth requirement. Yet without that letter, the dealers were worried that the government could close American and freeze its assets, so that they could not sell the company's collateral to cover the debts on mortgage-backed securities. When the dealers started threatening not to roll over American's repo lines, the Bank Board was forced to go along. But this time, the agency provided a modified comfort letter that allowed the dealers to operate without any interruption if American had to be closed.

Then, on February 18, Popejoy had written to Roger Martin, warning that American might lose its water and power. Indeed, Southern California Edison was requiring American to post a $210,000 deposit or lose its electrical service, and the Department of Water and Power also wanted deposits, or it would turn off American's water in the Los Angeles area.

Highlighted by the announcement of the securities sale, adverse publicity was causing other headaches as well, Popejoy informed the Bank Board. Sears had been discussing a piece of property with American for a branch relocation but mysteriously stopped negotiations. Merrill Lynch had agreed to lease a piece of property to American only after the company paid the term of the lease in advance. Local newspapers wanted American to pay for space the week before advertisements appeared.

"Obviously, we are trying to handle these matters quietly," Popejoy wrote. "Events such as these, if known to the media, could only create additional concerns and deterioration of confidence."

The very next month, to stem an outflow of deposits at American, the Bank Board was forced to offer an unprecedented blanket guarantee to all depositors and general creditors. American was still too big to fail. Effectively, the federal government had insured all of American's deposits, regardless of size, against loss. American had lost some $476 million in deposits in January and February. However, despite the Bank Board's unprecedented assurances, money would continue flowing out of American that summer. American Savings was broke and under siege by its depositors.

Despite the dire circumstances, Bass had been interested in the company for months. Exactly how he became motivated to buy American Savings is subject to dispute. The official version is that Ann Fairbanks, Ed Gray's old chief of staff, also the godmother of Bernie Carl's daughter, told Carl about Merrill Butler and the job he was doing with American Real Estate Group. The Bass Group liked what it saw and in mid-November 1987 made a bid to buy AREG, which owned a lot of distressed real estate in Texas. Under the proposal, AREG would sign a management contract with American Savings. FCA turned down the leveraged buyout of AREG. But Bass's interest was piqued, and the investment group began to consider buying the whole company.

Afterward, Popejoy flew to New York and met with Bonderman and Carl. He then set up a meeting for them with Roger Martin in Washington. Popejoy also went to Fort Worth to talk with Bob Bass over lunch. The two men took an instant liking to each other. Like Popejoy, Bass liked automobiles and had married his high school sweetheart. Later, after the sale, Bass gave Popejoy a blue-and-white 1955 Chevrolet convertible with wide white-wall tires after Popejoy happened to mention he wanted to get a car that commemorated the year he married Nancy.

Some investment bankers, however, suggested a different explanation for the events that led to the talks. They said the Bass Group had received the Salomon Brothers briefing book long before Bass submitted his bid. By asserting that Bass came directly to the government, the Bank Board might avoid paying Salomon a finder's fee.

Regardless of which version is true, Danny Wall was well aware of the story of how Bass started with an interest in real estate and wound up wanting to buy the entire S&L. That was one of the puzzling factors. Was American Savings just another piece of real estate to be bought and sold?

The three takeover artists were ushered into Wall's spacious office, and after the formal introductions were concluded, Danny Wall gazed directly into Bob Bass's eyes, sizing up his adversary. The polite, shy man before him stood in stark contrast to the popular image of a Texas billionaire as a highflier with a shady streak.

Wall came straight to the point: He had asked for the meeting because he wanted to assess the plans Bass had for American Savings. Bass told him that although he had diverse interests, including real estate and cable television, he was essentially in the banking business.

Banking revolved around the efficient application of capital, and that was what Bob Bass did for a living. He said he saw bright prospects in a traditional S&L because financial institutions are by their very nature highly leveraged enterprises. A small spread on the company's total assets translated into a large return on equity. Financial services, said Bass, held promise for the long run, indicating he wouldn't just spruce up American Savings and sell at the first chance he got.

In turn, Bass had questions of his own. He wanted some sense of Wall's personal commitment to the deal and his views on where Congress was headed with the S&L industry. By now, there were predictions that the thrift industry was no longer viable and would be wiped out by its own profligacy or by tough new capital standards that few companies could meet. Wall said he didn't think Congress would adopt a punitive prescription that would cure the industry's ills by killing all the patients.

Wall also assured him that he wanted to strike an accord over American and was willing to grant exclusive negotiating rights. Bass asked for one more agreement. Although both sides were confident they could wrap up the Rubic's Cube of economic, legal, and regulatory issues in a little more than two months,

Bass wanted to be able to reach Wall directly in case of a breakdown. Wall considered himself an accessible leader and said he would talk with the billionaire directly if that's what it would take to resolve any snags.

On Monday, April 18, the Bank Board announced its intention to sell American to the Bass Group and its extension of a seventy-five-day exclusive negotiating agreement. Later, Larry White, the economist on the board, would say talking exclusively with the Bass Group was a bad decision because it weakened the Bank Board's bargaining position. The agency was committed to a sale without the benefit of healthy competition. As the talks dragged on well past the original deadline, Wall's commitment to talk directly with Bass would become one of the most important aspects of fashioning a pact.

Five weeks later, on Tuesday, May 24, Bill Popejoy presided over his last annual shareholders meeting at FCA, giving the anxious investors some grim news.

Speaking at the Irvine Marriott across the street from FCA's headquarters, Popejoy told the gathering that although he expected the Bank Board to reach an agreement to sell American Savings to the Bass Group by July, the shareholders had only a "remote" chance of salvaging any part of their investment. Despite this, he strongly defended his highly criticized tenure as chairman.

"Others could say we should have performed differently," Popejoy said. "With the benefit of hindsight, I don't see many things we could have done differently. So I make no apology; but I'm terribly sorry, when I talk to people and we talk about their retirement, that much of their life's work was being wiped out because they invested in this company and had confidence in this management.

"There is no way I can convey my sorrow and my regrets. But I don't know what we could have done differently. We worked as hard as possible. We made some very bright moves in retrospect, and even with the condition of the company today, I'd do it again. I may sound like I've taken leave of my senses. But not everyone finishes achieving their full victory. Not everyone does the amazing turnaround. But someone has to try and that is just what we've done. We've tried, and we've given it our best."

Not all the stockholders were impressed with Popejoy's honesty. One angry stockholder, John D. Turner, who owned 1 million FCA shares, accused Popejoy of breaching his fiduciary duties by not disclosing the full extent of the company's bad loans.

Citing the proof-of-loss statement the company had filed in its suits against the insurance companies, Turner said he would never have purchased stock in the company if he had known the full extent of American's unsafe lending practices. Later in the meeting, Turner called for the board to appoint an independent shareholder committee to investigate questionable loans. Although nonbinding, the resolution carried on a voice vote.

Three months later, just days before he expected the Bass deal to go through, Popejoy amplified on his comments to the shareholders in an interview with two reporters from *American Banker*. Popejoy said that overall he had to rate his own performance as "unsatisfactory," a rare admission for a top corporate executive, and said the company's continued deterioration had given him many sleepless nights.

"I did not achieve that which I desired—and that was a turnaround without government assistance. Maybe it was impossible. Maybe it couldn't be realized. But that was my goal. So, anything short of that, in my grading would be unsatisfactory."

Popejoy acknowledged that he should have steered the company more toward the adjustable-rate mortgages that had become popular with consumers and with his S&L competitors. And he said that if he had understood the full extent of problems in American's loan portfolio, he would have asked the government for a "quasi-bailout" in which the regulators disposed of some of the bad assets.

He lashed out at the regulators again, saying they sometimes treated him as though he had caused American's problems. "You feel like throwing them out the damn window when they start talking like that." Popejoy said he had not made up his mind about what he would do after leaving FCA. He intended to spend more time with his family, particularly his wife, who had been seriously injured in a bicycle accident in Europe and lost the use of one eye. And finally, if the merger went through as planned, he hoped the Bass Group and the Bank Board would "look back on my involvement as helpful, that I did as much as I could do."

Chapter 22

The $600,000 Question

When Larry White arrived at the airport in Nairobi, Kenya, a harried travel agent handed him a message. It was a slip of paper with a Washington telephone number. White was startled, for he recognized the number right away as the one for the phone in the Bank Board's official boardroom.

Making some quick calculations of time-zone changes between Africa and Washington, he thought there must be some mistake. His colleagues couldn't possibly be there this late, not even workaholic Danny Wall. He first phoned Wall's office, just in case the chairman was still attending to his heavy caseload. As he suspected, there was no answer. So White gave it a shot and called the boardroom. A Bank Board assistant came on the line. Something was up. Something Big.

What White didn't know was that while he was flying between London and Nairobi, Wall was anxiously trying to track him down to put the finishing touches on the negotiations with Bob Bass. And what a tough set of talks they had been.

Indeed, the two sides had twice extended their original deadline. Although the talks had dragged on for months, in early September, they took on new urgency. Just two weeks earlier, on August 19, the board of directors of the San Francisco Home Loan Bank had decided not to loan any more money to American until the FSLIC guaranteed repayment. That was a serious blow. The regional banks are supposed to help member institutions maintain their liquidity. Part of the safety net for American Savings was being sliced away. The San Francisco Bank also was refusing to renew a $200-million advance that came due on August 31 unless the FSLIC provided the guarantee.

Alarmed, Popejoy wrote to Stuart Root at the FSLIC on August 30, warning of American's low level of cash. The company could not meet its federally mandated liquidity standard; it had less cash on hand to meet business needs than the regulators required.

"I suspect our attorneys will indicate that this action by the San Francisco Bank must be publicly disclosed," Popejoy wrote. "Headlines emanating from this disclosure would be very negative."

FCA's board was scheduled to meet the following Wednesday, and the Bank Board staff heard that one item on the agenda was the possibility the company would file bankruptcy rather than spend most of its depleted cash reserve to cover an interest payment coming due September 15. Once again, the Bank Board feared a run on American Savings.

Despite the strong desire by both sides to complete the transaction, the Bass deal had nearly fallen apart just before Labor Day when federal regulators sharpened their pencils and made a last-minute demand that the Bank Board cut its contribution by $200 million. Stuart Root, the FSLIC director, informed the Bass negotiators that the exclusive agreement had expired and that Ford had made a more attractive offer for the company. Thus, Bass would have to muster more money.

On Friday, September 2, after a brief meeting with Danny Wall, a frustrated Bob Bass walked out of the talks, refusing to cave in to the Bank Board's demand. Bass had already agreed to concede some legal and technical points but drew the line at shelling out an extra $200 million. Members of his team were incredulous. They thought they were supposed to tie up some loose ends, not start what to them amounted to negotiations over a new agreement.

As they had so many times in the past, fickle bond prices figured in the future of American Saving. That same Friday, the bond market rallied, putting in its strongest performance in seven months. By the end of the day, the losses in American's securities portfolio had shrunk by $100 million. After additional recalculations, Bank Board staff members decided the extra value in the securities and other changes would cover the $200 million after all.

What the Bank Board members did not know was that if the deal didn't come together over the weekend, Bass was ready to sue Ford on Tuesday. Using as a precedent the successful suit

Pennzoil had filed against Texaco, which lost $3 billion, the Bass Group would have alleged wrongful interference by Ford in the exclusive negotiating agreement. That First Nationwide officials had said publicly they wanted the right to bid on American and that a Ford lobbyist had just been seen in the Bank Board building seemed to strengthen their case.

After one last meeting adjourned around 10:00 P.M., Bonderman and Carl left the Bank Board building, still not certain they had a deal. Although not legally bound to do so, Wall did not want the federally assisted acquisition of American to go through unless the vote of the three-member Bank Board was unanimous. There was too much at stake, and already some members of Congress were criticizing the Bank Board for sticking to its exclusivity agreement.

Wall and Martin favored the deal, but Larry White was out of the country and unable to vote. He had jetted off to Kenya, which, like the United States, had deregulated its S&L industry with disastrous results, to give a talk on thrifts. White had then gone to London on vacation to take in some plays and had frequently ducked into phone booths to keep abreast of developments in Washington.

On Friday, White was on a jetliner headed back to Kenya where he would visit a game preserve. Wall was trying to track him down through British Airways, which passed word on to the travel agent who found White. The connection on the satellite call was exceptionally clear. Wall brought him up to date on the latest developments. White liked the deal. He signed on, then headed for the game preserve.

On the evening of Monday, September 5, Labor Day, the Bank Board announced the sale of American to Bass. Under the terms, the Bass Group would provide $550 million in new capital, and the FSLIC would post some $2 billion in assistance. A new holding company would have four operating subsidiaries. The so-called good bank, New American Savings, would have good real assets of $9.3 billion and deposits of $14 billion. The good bank also would have a note to the bad bank worth nearly $7 billion.

The bad bank would have about $5 billion in bad loans and foreclosed property, and more than $15 billion in mortgage securities. The collecting bank would also receive the $2 billion in FSLIC assistance to cover losses for loans and securities. The association would also count as a liability the note received from the good bank. In other words, the FSLIC-guaranteed note was an asset for the good bank and a liability for the bad bank, so the accounts would equal out. The FSLIC would receive 75 percent of the bad bank's tax benefits and 30 percent of the good bank's profits.

The other two subsidiaries were the American Real Estate Group and the merchant bank, called Robert M. Bass Investors, Inc. Operating under contract from the S&L, AREG would manage problem real estate and sell the properties as well. The merchant bank, though, differed substantially from a traditional thrift. If a standard S&L was a steady sailboat with a full balanced keel, the merchant bank was a nuclear-powered attack boat.

Besides making commercial loans, the merchant bank could invest in stocks, bonds, and other securities; make acquisitions, and conduct leveraged buyouts. The unit had a $1.5-billion line of credit from a service-corporation subsidiary of the good bank, which was making the money available at extremely favorable interest rates. In a concession that appeared to ease the concerns of some leading members of Congress, the merchant bank was forbidden from conducting hostile takeovers.

On Tuesday, the inevitable occurred. Pending final arrangements with the Bass Group, American Savings went into receivership. The FSLIC pumped in $200 million in capital to hold the company together.

Bill Popejoy had failed. He had been hired to rescue American Savings from insolvency, but he had learned that stopping a run and coming up with an action plan was not enough. He could not stop the hemorrhaging from loan losses. No, he had not proved Mark Taper wrong. He was not the savings industry's Lee Iacocca.

The next day, Popejoy resigned as chairman of FCA, and the company said it intended to seek protection from its creditors in federal bankruptcy court. And the Bank Board negotiators started work on the final arrangements with the Bass team.

The two biggest hurdles left were approval by the Internal

Revenue Service, which was almost a formality, and approval by Bill Crawford, California's outspoken S&L commissioner. The federal regulators weren't worried. They knew they could count on Crawford.

Three years as a state bureaucrat hadn't shaved the sharp edges from Bill Crawford's personality. Indeed, he was famous for telling a 1987 congressional committee investigating fraud in the S&L industry that the "best way to rob a bank is to own one."

Now Crawford, the man who was suspicious of the new operators in the thrift game, would determine the fate of a deal worth billions of dollars. On October 4, just under a month after the Bank Board announced the sale of American to an investment group headed by the Texas billionaire, Bob Bass and his associates were in San Francisco for two key meetings with Crawford and Jim Cirona's staff at the Federal Home Loan Bank.

Their first stop was the California Department of Savings and Loan's northern California office in San Francisco's financial district. In a second-floor conference room of a nondescript building two blocks from the towering Transamerica Pyramid, Crawford assembled his staff to greet the painfully shy billionaire.

Because American was based in Stockton, a team from the department's northern office had been assigned the job of reviewing a draft application submitted by Bass. The whole transaction hinged on Crawford's approval. American was a state-chartered institution, and the Bass Group wanted the right to establish a controversial merchant bank that could invest in common stock and other risky ventures, powers that were not granted federally chartered S&Ls. If Crawford balked, the deal was off.

Bass wanted to meet personally with Crawford and Jim Cirona at the Federal Home Loan Bank of San Francisco. The takeover talks had been difficult enough, and Bob Bass didn't want anything else to go wrong.

More than any other aspect of the deal, the merchant bank made Crawford nervous. He didn't really understand it, and he doubted whether his staff could supervise such an exotic institution. Although other California S&Ls made direct investments, no company came close to the kind of clout that Bass would have in the takeover game. And no other company, he believed, could take such unbridled risks with federally insured money.

Crawford wanted every member of the team analyzing the Bass corporate structure to attend the meeting. In all likelihood, it would be the only chance these state employees, many of them poorly paid and unappreciated by the public they served, would have to meet a billionaire and ask him any question they considered important. And he would have to answer them.

For his part, Bass wanted this session to go smoothly. Not only would Crawford have to approve their application, but his department had principal supervisory controls over the S&L, and the Texan knew the importance of being earnest with government officials in a regulated industry.

His team had already received the cooperation of another state official whose performance on his behalf was an essential part of the acquisition. State Representative John Garamendi had earlier submitted a bill that would allow the Bass Group to receive the assistance payments from the FSLIC without paying state taxes. Garamendi sought and obtained legislation clarifying existing state law, which made paying taxes on the federal benefits a possibility. In exchange, Garamendi received a pledge from Bass that the Texan would keep American's headquarters in Stockton, in the representative's district. Once again, a state law was changed so that American could be sold.

Now Bass was in a drab conference room with ten state regulators. The billionaire introduced himself, talked about his background, and told the bureaucrats why he was attracted to the industry. Bonderman and Carl also addressed the group, going over the business structure that would emerge once the transaction went through. Also representing the Bass Group was Norm Raiden, a Los Angeles attorney with McKenna, Conner and Cuneo who had been the Bank Board chief counsel under Ed Gray.

The Bass team members, having braced themselves for some tough questions, were surprised when the state officials started throwing what they thought were a series of softballs, things like whether a subsidiary would have the word "corporation" or "company" in its title. The Bass associates were bewildered and a little disappointed. After all, these were some very bright guys used to intense mental challenges, and they were ending up in a cakewalk.

Actually, though they may have seemed like a group of lightweights, the state regulators had already picked the deal apart and didn't like it at all. Crawford had already made it clear that he would not overrule his staff, and at this meeting with Bass, he wasn't dropping any hints.

Bass and company got a more lively reception at the Federal Home Loan Bank of San Francisco, where the group headed after meeting with Crawford. Jim Cirona was polite and seemed genuinely to want to help as much as he could, though the staff had a number of reservations, asking if the deal could be improved from the government's standpoint. Bill Black in particular peppered them with questions.

A sharp, strong-willed attorney with red hair and a full beard, Black served as Cirona's chief counsel. A fiercely independent lawyer with an undergraduate degree in economics, Black was the FSLIC's former director of litigation and was used to seeing corporate executives in court. He could not be intimidated by powerful politicians or rich Texans. He had serious doubts about the propriety of the Bass acquisition overall and had an especially hard time accepting the merchant bank. The Bass team came under heavy fire from Black.

At the meeting's conclusion, Cirona told the Bass team to stay in touch, adding that he would be happy to meet with them later if they had any questions about management at American or other concerns. The Bass negotiators left the meeting thinking that Jim Cirona was a good guy, probably pretty easy to work with. But Bill Black was another story. He did not leave a favorable impression. The Texas billionaire and his shrewd negotiators just didn't know how much trouble Bill Black could cause.

Each weekday morning, Bill Crawford would leave his Orange County home at 6:00 to beat the traffic that choked the freeways around Los Angeles. Riding with him was his scrupulously groomed top deputy, Bill Davis. By October, Davis and Crawford spent much of the one-hour drive to and from work discussing the complexities of the Bass takeover and the potential pitfalls the department would encounter. American Savings had come to resemble a knot of crosstown traffic, and with the Bass acquisition, Crawford could see a traffic jam up ahead.

Crawford feared he might become the fall guy if he waited too late to render a decision, for many of the lucrative tax benefits would expire at the end of the year. If he waited until the last minute, he would be pressured into saying yes, or the federal regulators in Washington would accuse him of killing the deal.

Crawford had enjoyed a friendly relationship with the Bank Board when Ed Gray was there. Gray seemed to bend over backward to keep him informed, particularly regarding developments at American Savings, the largest association under his review. But after Wall took over, the relationship quickly soured. Crawford had served on an important advisory committee to the Bank Board but said he was dropped after Wall took over and no one even bothered to tell him. He did not learn of this development until his secretary phoned to ask why the department had not heard of any meetings.

Moreover, neither Roger Martin nor Danny Wall bothered to tell him that the Bank Board was ordering American to sell $2.5 billion in mortgage securities. Even worse, news stories about the impending sale, in which Martin was prominently quoted, telegraphed the sale to the market. Anyone with even a cursory knowledge of the bond market could tell you that once word of the impending sale hit the street, the price would drop pretty quickly; you wouldn't make nearly as much profit on the sale, maybe even lose money.

The bond flap had occurred the previous February. Shortly after the sale was ordered, Popejoy introduced Crawford to Martin at an S&L conference in Palm Springs. Crawford and Martin discussed a variety of subjects, including the federally ordered sale of mortgage securities. Martin recalled that Crawford was informed of the negotiations with Bass, that they presented what appeared to be the only reasonable treatment for the festering wound at American Savings. Martin also recalled that Crawford said he would help in any way he could. Based on that meeting, Martin thought Crawford had at least given his tacit approval.

But Crawford was on record as opposing the kind of direct investments that Bass would be able to undertake. He couldn't stomach the merchant bank. Bass had structured his new holding company so that in essence the merchant bank would take the $1.5-billion line of credit and funnel it into a takeover pool. The beauty of the arrangement, besides the cheap interest rate, was the extra leverage it entailed. Because you can buy stocks on a margin of only 50 percent down, the buyout fund was really worth some $3 billion—and possibly more, depending on the kind of investment.

And to Crawford, the really incredible thing was that the feds approved it, knowing that Bass was putting only $50 million in capital into the merchant bank. A fund with $3 billion in purchasing power on top of only $50 million in capital was leveraged at 60 to 1. Bill Crawford was no match for the brilliance of Bass, Bonderman, and Carl, but he figured a guy could get himself into big trouble pretty fast throwing around $3 billion with a shoestring capital budget.

The state team studying the Bass acquisition pored over the documents they received from the Bank Board and the Bass Group. In addition, they talked frequently with Bill Black of Jim Cirona's staff, who helped unlock some of the mysteries of the complex business arrangements. The more Crawford's staff dug, the less appealing the merchant bank became.

Beyond the inherent business risks, Crawford questioned whether his staff could even supervise the merchant bank, since it was a subsidiary of the holding company, not the S&L. As such, the investment outfit would be chartered in Delaware, and it was Crawford's understanding that it would operate out of New York. Thus, if he wanted to curb a practice that he felt was incorrect or violated regulations, he foresaw difficulty convincing a court that a California regulator had jurisdiction over a New York company incorporated in Delaware. In addition, the Bank Board had stipulated that the examiners couldn't march in until the merchant bank was insolvent by $300 million. He could order the nuclear attack boat to stand clear only after it had launched all its missiles and was sinking. By then, of course, it would be too late.

On October 11, in a meeting with Stuart Root of the FSLIC, two members of Crawford's staff said the department would require that the merchant bank be a subsidiary of the S&L, a restriction that would stifle much of the unit's investment opportunities. This set off a series of hectic phone calls between the state and federal regulators, beginning with a call from Root to Bill Davis later that same day, saying he was displeased with the department's position.

Three days later, Danny Wall telephoned Bill Crawford. The exchange was not pleasant for either man. Crawford recalled that Wall asked if Crawford didn't want the assessment from American Savings. The state's budget derived from assessments on S&Ls, and American represented $600,000 a year in revenue, out of a budget of $8 million. Crawford had worked hard to rebuild his department after severe budget cuts in the early 1980s decimated the staff. The resulting shortage of examiners had aggravated the thrift crisis in California. Crawford well understood the impact of losing $600,000 in revenue but was uncomfortable discussing the budget as it related to the takeover of American. A good regulator did not look at the financial impact of his decision on his own department. He looked at the merits of the case.

Wall later denied saying anything about the American assessment, but he was clearly frustrated with Crawford. He had several key points he wanted to make, not the least of which was that the state regulator was being more restrictive than necessary. A California charter clearly allowed the kind of investment activities Bass had in mind. But Crawford didn't appear to be listening. He was on a squawk box, and Wall could hear him talking to Bill Davis, who was sitting in the room. Chairman Wall's voice took on a chilly tone. The two men were not communicating. Finally, Crawford said that the department lacked enough information to make a decision on the Bass deal.

Crawford's staff, which had been holding daily meetings on the Bass proposal, unanimously opposed the takeover. On October 17, Crawford told Wall that if a decision had to be made that day, the department would reject the application, even though Bass had not officially filed one and couldn't have because his group was still working out the final terms with the Bank Board.

When on October 20 he rejected the request for a state charter, Crawford mentioned his misgivings about the merchant bank. "I don't know if I've got the expertise to tell who's got the expertise to run a merchant bank," he said. "I don't have any expertise to supervise a merchant bank. My job is to supervise savings and loans. That's why they call me the savings and loan commissioner. They didn't call me the merchant banking commissioner."

Chapter 23

The Air Bank

Danny Wall was becoming paranoid about press leaks. That old Shakespearean rag about how even the walls have ears just might be true. It was almost as though the Bank Board had been bugged.

After he got the upsetting news that Crawford intended to reject the Bass acquisition of American, which obviously could destroy the whole deal, Wall suggested an alternative to some staff members. Why not have Bass assume control of a defunct thrift in Texas, where there was no shortage of insolvent S&Ls, and use that company to run American's branch network in California?

The next thing he knew, Wall was reading about his suggestion—and it was just a suggestion, he reminded himself—in the newspaper. That only reinforced his belief that he had to keep the information flow to an absolute minimum, which was one of the reasons why Crawford was often kept in the dark.

Neither Wall nor Bass wanted to see the negotiations end in failure, so they began work on a way to get around the state charter. The two sides discussed developing a new federal charter that would permit merchant-banking activities. Bass would be given a thrift unique in the S&L system, one with a custom-made charter.

Despite this huge concession on the Bank Board's part, by mid-November, the talks were bogging down again. Stuart Root at the FSLIC didn't want to take any chances. In theory, Bass had every incentive to reach a final agreement by December 31, when nearly half of American's more than $1 billion in tax benefits would expire.

Root felt that if the only thing he did as FSLIC director was arrange the sale of American, that would be his most important contribution. He was worried that if interest rates rose again, the value of American's mortgage securities would plummet, threatening financial markets. In fact, the regulators were so worried about the securities, they had even obtained from the company a copy of the computer tape that showed the entire portfolio, down to the last dollar. The regulators then hired a Washington-area consultant to run the computer and provide a constant tracking of the portfolio's value.

As a contingency plan, Root decided he should once again take a run at Ford Motor Co. He brought his plan to Wall, who didn't give him formal approval but allowed that he was free to strike a bargain with Ford if he could do so.

On November 17, Root contacted the Ford–First Nationwide team and asked if they had any more interest in making a bid for American. The Ford negotiators knew the company was being used as a Trojan horse for Bass, yet they couldn't afford not to take a chance. Why pass up billions in assets and 185 branches just because the Bank Board had treated them shabbily a year earlier? Besides, James Ford and Tony Frank were no longer on the scene. Ford had retired, and Frank had gone to Washington to become the U.S. postmaster general. And they would be dealing primarily with Root, not Roger Martin.

As prudent businessmen, Ford officials wanted some protection. The negotiators knew that Bass was ready to sue Ford if the talks broke down, for that little nugget had appeared in David Hilder's page-1 story in the *Wall Street Journal.* Although the exclusivity agreement had expired because it depended on Crawford's approval, the Ford team telecopied a letter to Root asking for indemnification in case Bass threw a Pennzoil suit at them. No way, said Root. Ford and First Nationwide officials huddled. Since Root had come to them, they figured they were in the clear. Despite the risk of litigation, Ford moved ahead. Later, when Bass team members heard of the talks going on behind their backs, they contacted a litigator and prepared to sue but did not actually draw up a legal complaint.

The two sides devised a way to solve the FSLIC credit issue. They simply created an "Air Bank," an S&L with a separate charter that in case of a run had nothing but thin air for assets. It worked like this: The Bank Board would create a thrift with $3 billion in deposits from American. That thrift would have a note from First Nationwide as its asset covering the deposits. If depositors removed their money, First Nationwide would default on the note, and FSLIC would have to come to the rescue. *Poof*, the full-faith-and-credit issue was resolved. If Bass got cold feet, the Bank Board had a handsome suitor waiting at the altar.

While Root was lining up Ford as a fallback position, Bill Black was busy shooting down the Bass deal.

Throughout the fall of 1988, Black was instrumental in the long memos drafted at the San Francisco Federal Home Loan Bank and sent to the Bank Board, criticizing the Bass acquisition of American. Although the Bank Board could approve a federal charter without Cirona's approval in San Francisco, in practical effect, that would be difficult to achieve. Cirona was being asked to declare that he and his staff could supervise American with its unusual charter.

Black knew how to buck the bureaucracy. Before joining the San Francisco Bank in 1987, he had worked for Ed Gray in Washington as an acting deputy director at the FSLIC. Acting in that capacity, he had attended the five senators' meeting in which Cirona's team argued in favor of closing Lincoln Savings and had also clashed with House Speaker Jim Wright.*

Because of a number of long-standing disputes with the Bank Board in Washington, Jim Cirona's regional bank was viewed with some suspicion. Ill feelings still smoldered from the showdown over Lincoln Savings in which Wall removed the San Francisco Bank's jurisdiction over this loss-ridden company, an action that figured heavily in the two-year delay in closing Lincoln, at great expense to the taxpayers.

In the case of American Savings, no one in Washington made the accusation directly, but it was clear from some of the snide remarks that they thought the San Francisco staff wanted to

---

*At the five senators' meeting, Black was the only one in the room taking notes. Those notes formed the basis of a memorandum to Gray that was later reprinted in the book *Inside Job*, a look at fraud in the S&L industry. According to the Phelan report on Wright's activities, Black and Wright argued over Vernon Savings of Texas, and the Speaker subsequently tried to have Black fired. House Ethics Committee members probing Wright later said Black was one of the most impressive witnesses ever to appear before them.

kill the Bass deal so that Ford could emerge triumphant. After all, First Nationwide was one of the San Francisco Bank's largest members.

Well, the Washington regulators could think what they wanted, but Bill Black and the San Francisco team thought the acquisition had a number of fundamental flaws. Like Crawford, Black took special exception to the merchant bank. The team working with him had determined that the preferential interest rate the merchant bank would receive was worth as much as $1.5 billion and should be added to the total cost. If the preferential interest rate was factored in, the Bass deal would cost substantially more than Ford's offer. Thus, Bass would receive wider powers and more generous terms.

In addition, the deal was structured so that while the S&L shared its profit with the FSLIC, the company kept most of the money made at the merchant bank. Bass was supposed to be providing $550 billion in new capital, but all but $150 million of that amount would be borrowed from banks or through bond sales. Even worse, Bass was using the stock in American Savings as collateral for the debt.

The economics were bad enough, but as a litigator who had sued wayward S&L executives, Black found the preferential interest rate appalling. The merchant bank, which would be used to further Bass's investment goals, including takeovers, would pay a little over prime plus 2 percent in the beginning, and the rate would drop by a quarter of a percentage point. That was substantially less than Bass would have to pay in the open market, and he could line up the money at a moment's notice. It was like walking into a department store for takeovers and opening a revolving charge account.

From the standpoint of public policy, the arrangement showed poor judgment. The merchant bank was an affiliate of the holding company and as such would receive funds at favorable rates. This was precisely the kind of insider self-dealing that had destroyed far too many S&Ls and for which the Bank Board would sue a company's executives. The Bank Board would be inviting insider abuses on a grand scale. If Bass had a federal charter specifically allowing these kinds of transactions, then why couldn't every S&L in the land do the same thing?

In late November, Bill Black flew to Washington to represent the San Francisco Bank. He was originally supposed to be there for one day, but the series of meetings in which he pointed out the deal's shortcomings stretched into nearly a week. Black achieved his goal. As more of the deficiencies came to light, the Washington regulators had a change of heart. They felt there was no choice. They had to get rid of the merchant bank.

With so many roadblocks left in the negotiations, Danny Wall decided it was time for one of those little parleys with Bob Bass. He had to tell him that the merchant bank would never be approved. It was too risky and too controversial. Wall, the veteran of Capitol Hill, was only too aware that if the merchant bank was approved, the Bank Board would face strong criticism from Congress.

An arbitrary deadline to complete the sale of American expired at 2:00 P.M. Friday, December 2. The deadline came and passed. Still no agreement was in hand. Wall had other concerns as well. This wasn't the only set of negotiations under way, not by a long shot. In fact, the Bank Board hoped to close the books on some forty federally assisted acquisitions by the end of the month. The largest was a package in which FSLIC would provide $5.1 billion in assistance for five thrifts purchased by an investment group headed by Revlon chairman and corporate raider Ronald O. Perelman. But because of the symbolic nature of the deal, American was the high-profile case.

At 4:00 P.M., Danny Wall grabbed a staff member and headed for a law firm representing Bass. Outside, a brisk wind was blowing. Despite the chill air, Wall, the North Dakota native, did not put on an overcoat. He and his aide drove the few blocks to see Bob Bass.

On the way, Wall wondered if he was tough enough for the job. Congress undoubtedly would put this deal under a microscope. Could he stand eyeball-to-eyeball with a Texas billionaire and demand better terms for the U.S. government? And more important, could he get them? What if he had agreed to exclusive talks, only to have the negotiations end in failure? Ford was ready to rush in, but an agreement with the automaker had eluded the Bank Board three times. When he mentioned he was leaving to talk with Bass, one of the staff members yelled out,

"You're drawing to an inside straight," which any decent poker player knew was a sucker's bet.

Wall had a wild card he had not yet played. Dick Pratt had phoned Wall and said Bass wanted American badly enough to drop his demands for a merchant bank operated as a separate subsidiary. Despite some of the damaging disclosures about the deal, Wall still trusted Bass.

He took Bass's decision to hire Mario Antoci, the president of H. F. Ahmanson & Co., parent of Home Savings of America, as a show of good faith. Home Savings had passed American as the nation's largest thrift and had a reputation for profitable and conservative management. The Bass Group was interested in Popejoy, but he wanted to move on to something new. If Bass didn't really intend to run a traditional thrift, Wall wondered, then why hire Antoci, a man known as a cautious lender?

When he arrived at the Bass camp, Wall told the billionaire, who was joined by Bonderman and Carl, that if a vote was taken today, he would have to turn the deal down. Wall didn't think the board would go forward on a 2–1 vote. The chairman sensed that Pratt's prediction was true. When Bass said he was willing to compromise, Wall was relieved. He could still salvage the deal.

Bernie Carl played negotiating emcee. He would write out the remaining issues one by one on an easel, and the resulting agreement then was typed out. The last thing Carl wrote was "No More Changes." It was the end of the line for haggling over new points. Bass would give up the merchant bank subsidiary, but he wanted many of the same activities invested in American Savings. In return, he would drop his investment from $550 million to $350 million. He would be allowed to borrow much of the capital, but he would not use American's stock as collateral. He would post an additional $150 million later.

At the end of that two-hour meeting, Wall headed back to the Bank Board, told his staff to get ready for a long set of negotiations, and picked up his car. He then drove over to the Bass camp, arriving at about six. There, over the next six hours, the two sides went through the crucial last-minute details of a deal. Just to make sure the talks stayed on track, both Bass and Wall were there, talking to each other frequently as their harried negotiators plowed through the paperwork and key calculations.

When Wall left at about 12:30 A.M., the deal was essentially finished, although it would require mind-numbing hours of work to translate all the agreements into legal documents as thick as the Manhattan telephone directory. In all likelihood, no one could accurately predict the final price tag, but the revamped acquisition was estimated to cost the FSLIC about $1.7 billion based on optimistic assumptions and on a net-present-value basis. That meant the deal would cost far more by the time the last penny was paid, but all the money was worth $1.7 billion in 1988 dollars.

The agency estimated the value of the tax benefits at $650 million and its 30 percent share of American Savings at an additional $650 million. So an outlay of $3 billion would be cut by the $1.3 billion the FSLIC would receive from the Bass Group.

American's assets, which had dropped to $30.1 billion, were split into two concerns. The good bank would be called American Savings Bank. Headquartered in Stockton, it would have $15.1 billion in assets. An interest-bearing promissory note from the bad bank represented half the assets.

The bad bank would be called New West Federal Savings and Loan and would have $21.9 billion in assets to start. The troubled assets would be liquidated over time, with the FSLIC protecting Bass against any losses.

The Bass team handled the merchant bank beautifully. The Bank Board said the concept had been eliminated, but in reality the structure of the company changed while Bass got many of the powers he had been seeking.

The new subsidiary approved by the federal regulators, called Stockton Capital Corp., would invest in and acquire "profitable" businesses. Bass planned an initial infusion of $600 million. In exchange for the power to buy stocks, Stockton Capital would not invest in real estate or participate in hostile takeovers. Stockton Capital was allowed to open an office in New York.

Danny Wall stayed at the Bank Board's office until 1:30 A.M., talking with two key staff members about the deal they had just concluded. Flushed with success, he was keyed up. He drove seventeen miles to his home in suburban Virginia, woke his wife, and told her about the deal. He was proud of himself. He had finally done it. The five-year roller-coaster ride at American Savings was over. Finally.

Everything was set. The press release was written, and the news briefing was scheduled for later that day, December 28, 1988. After nine months of negotiations and weeks of completing all of the paperwork, it was time for a little celebration.

Bernie Carl joined Roger Martin and Elise Paylan, and over lunch at a bustling Connecticut Avenue restaurant, the trio relived the deal, making observations about the many twists and turns it had taken and some of the people involved in the momentous bailout.

All three were glad to have the negotiations behind them. They were finished and heading back to complete the deal when Carl climbed into Martin's staff car. The driver gave him a message. There was an emergency. Check in immediately.

Bill Black informed the Bass team that the San Francisco Home Loan Bank had the right to call a $1.2 billion loan to American. If that occurred, Bass would have to fork over the money as early as the next day.

Now, at the last possible moment, the deal was in grave jeopardy. As the Bass Group officials viewed this development, the company would be insolvent less than twenty-four hours after they owned it. If the San Francisco Bank did not yield, the deal would die.

The press conference was pushed back as Bank Board and FSLIC officials and their lawyers scrambled for a solution. After a flurry of phone calls, the San Francisco Bank agreed to extend the credit for at least six months. At least the company wouldn't be broke the next day.

But the Bass Group needed more protection against sudden insolvency. The Bank Board adopted a handwritten resolution on a scribbled-up piece of paper that allowed American to apply to other regional banks for loans if the company's credit was called in San Francisco.

Bernie Carl had a big decision to make, one of the biggest of his life. The former race-car driver felt an adrenaline rush. Should he commit his company to such an enormous deal with so much up in the air? Well, he had a show of good faith by the federal government, and the Bass Group trusted the government. Carl signed the closing documents. Now, Bob Bass, the shy billionaire who had done such a good job of sweet-talking Danny Wall, owned American Savings. This time, it really was the end.

Epilogue

On Wednesday, August 9, 1989, an oppressively hot day in the nation's capital, Danny Wall's job was abolished.

But Wall, who was by then embroiled in a great controversy regarding the propriety of his actions—or more precisely, his alleged inaction in the case of Lincoln Savings—was temporarily saved from unemployment. He was named to head the new Office of Thrift Supervision.

Wall's change in status occurred when President Bush signed into law sweeping new legislation that once again restructured the S&L industry in a hodge-podge fashion. The changes occurred as part of a $159-billion federal bailout, the largest in U.S. history. Within weeks, observers were already predicting the price tag would rise by a minimum of another $50 billion, and perhaps double that figure.

Sponsored by the president and dubbed the "Bush bill," the Financial Institutions Reform, Recovery and Enforcement Act radically changed the way S&Ls are supervised and hastened the demise of inefficient firms that had begun years ago.

Some observers said the new law would mark the savings industry's death. Ed Gray, now a prominent source for media accounts of the S&L crisis, said he doubted the term "savings and loan" would be a part of the national vocabulary by the turn of the century.

Others, however, said that hundreds of firms would perish because they could not meet tough new capital standards, but the industry would remain intact. Perhaps no more than five hundred to one thousand well-run, strongly capitalized companies would still be in operation, but there would always be demand for a business that specialized in home lending.

Although it will probably prove deficient for the task ahead, the act was the most complete and complex package of reforms adopted since the New Deal. It also was a full-employment bill for lawyers, real-estate appraisers, and problem-loan specialists. Some $400 billion in distressed real estate must be liquidated, the biggest fire sale in history.

Danny Wall's old agency, the Federal Home Loan Bank Board, ceased to exist once Bush signed the bill. The Bank Board was replaced with the Office of Thrift Supervision, with Wall serving as director. The FSLIC also was abolished. The agency's longtime rival, the FDIC, which insured banks, received greatly expanded authority. Among other things, the agency was placed in charge of the new Resolution Trust Coporation, which is responsible for reworking hundreds of failed firms and disposing of their assets.

Although his position was abolished, Wall remained as Bank Board chairman for sixty days after the law took effect to oversee the transfer of employees and property to other agencies. The law allowed him to get the new job without facing difficult Senate confirmation hearings. Wall's old boss, Senator Jake Garn, had gone to bat for the embattled former chairman. Finally, though, after being hounded for months by criticism of the way he handled Lincoln Savings, Wall announced his resignation in December 1989.

Meanwhile, the Bush plan also called for tougher action against fraud and insider abuses. Thrift managers faced stiffer civil and criminal penalties, including hefty fines. Federal prosecutors can now seek penalties against a wider circle of people employed at federally insured financial institutions. S&L lawyers, appraisers, accountants, consultants, joint-venture partners, and controlling stockholders face federal prosecution for letting violations go unchecked.

Whether all the reforms will work can hardly be determined at this early date, but given the federal government's poor track record with thrifts, it is highly doubtful that they will. In all likelihood, additional problems and economic distortions will have been created.

Indeed, by early 1990, the plan was already in disarray. L. William Seidman, the FDIC's chairman, was predicting that the Resolution Trust Corp. (RTC) would need extra money, probably between $50 billion and $100 billion. In February 1990, Seidman said that in the six months since Congress had authorized the industry's rescue, the RTC had seized 300 thrifts but had liquidated only a fraction of them, a mere 40 S&Ls in all. He predicted that the government would have to dispose of 600 thrifts, one-fifth of the industry.

In addition, the RTC itself was mired in controversy, regulatory snafus, and turf battles. Fed up with interference from the Treasury Department, Daniel P. Kearny resigned his job as president of the RTC oversight board on February 9, 1990, embarrassing the Bush administration.

Despite this difficult start, the new act did bring the expensive experiment with deregulation to a close. Many commentators have blamed deregulation as the root cause of the S&L crisis. Yet, as we have seen, the crisis began with years of economic mismanagement in this country, bloated federal budgets, high interest rates, and finally the ravages of inflation. But the inevitable decline of the thrift industry was greatly compounded at a substantially higher but incalculable expense to the taxpayers by the poorly conceived attempt to restructure federally insured financial institutions by applying free-market principles.

Ironically, deregulation had attempted to stop the natural efficiency of the marketplace. With computers and toll-free telephone lines, mutual funds were set to drive S&Ls to extinction—that is, if the fund managers were left to their own innovations. Fund managers were tied into the financial markets around the globe. They could make decisions in seconds. They did not have to invest their money in illiquid real-estate loans.

Rather than let the market rule, the state and federal officials attempted to prevent the inevitable consolidation of the financial services industry by giving S&Ls new powers. If anything, deregulation came too slowly. By the time thrifts won new powers, the market had already left them behind.

Theoretically, deregulation would increase competition and safeguard the industry. But allowing S&L executives to compete with the money funds by paying whatever interest rates they chose only guaranteed that more firms would die.

Like commercial banks, S&Ls were caught in a great Darwinian struggle for survival. As Dick Fredericks, the noted banking analyst at Montgomery Securities, Inc. in San Francisco, has pointed out, the struggle revolves around capital. Companies with solid capital levels will survive in the coming area of nationwide banking. Companies with a weak balance sheet will die.

Deregulation delayed the natural-selection process of Darwinian banking. By lowering capital standards, the Bank Board allowed weak S&Ls to appear strong enough for the struggle. Companies doomed to be swallowed by larger and more efficient enterprises or to quit the fight altogether remained in business. Taxpayers picked up much of the cost of their mistakes and fraudulent transactions.

The lax new attitude in Washington provided a gold mine for criminals as well. Fraud's full contribution to the crisis has not yet been tallied, but a relatively small fraction of a bailout that will total more than $200 billion would produce an alarmingly large number.

At every juncture in the road that led to the industry's bailout, government officials made enormous mistakes. And nowhere were those mistakes more obvious than in the case of American Savings.

Despite repeated attempts, the regulators were unable to crack down on the questionable lending practices at American's predecessor, State Savings, and were too slow in uncovering the mess in the first place. The merger of those two companies should never have been allowed. Had it been blocked, the ultimate and unavoidable cost of liquidating American would have been greatly reduced.

Dick Pratt was right. American Savings should not have been allowed to grow with mortgage-backed bonds. For Popejoy, the strategy seemed to be his best option. And for a while, it worked. Securities sales saved the firm in 1986 and continued to produce operating income to the end.

But the growth made for bad public policy. A federally insured institution fighting for its life took an unabashed bet on interest rates at a time when Ed Gray, the top regulator, had already decided that the company would have to be sold. When rising interest rates sharply diminished the portfolio's value around the time of the 1987 stock-market crash, the entire thrift system was threatened.

Whether the Bank Board got the best possible deal in its sale to Bob Bass cannot be determined because the exclusive negotiations with the Bass Group made that an impossibility.

The public, at whose expense the agreement was fashioned, will never know if another suitor could have countered with a better offer.

But from the simple standpoint of market efficiency, Ford was clearly better than Bass. Ford would have put $1 billion in capital into the thrift, closed or sold redundant branches, and eliminated thousands of jobs—all in line with the drive for greater efficiency in financial services, and all for a mere 12 percent return on equity.

Although the Bank Board estimated the cost of the Bass deal at $1.7 billion, the company had $7 billion in distressed real-estate and bad loans. Thus, in all likelihood, the bailout will cost much more than the government's official estimate. For his part, Roger Martin said he always figured it would require between $2 billion to $3 billion to take care of American, depending on what happened with interest rates and the market for loans in general.

Under Bass, American Savings Bank, the successor company, became a roaring success, largely because the bad assets were removed from the balance sheet as part of the government bail-out. In 1989, American Savings Bank earned a phenomenal $214.2 million, making it one of the most profitable savings and loans in the country. Based on the Bass group's initial investment of $350 million, much of it borrowed, American Savings Bank earned a startling 61 percent return on equity. Shortly before publication of this book, however, the Bass Group attempted to downplay its high earnings as an anti–savings and loan bias swept the nation in late 1990, amid disclosures that the cost of the S&L cleanup would continue to rise—to perhaps more than $500 billion.

To be sure, the government, through its 30 percent stake in American, will share in the company's success and its high earnings. But all in all, Bob Bass and his business associates profited handsomely from the industry's misfortunes and the horrendous failures of the federal government.

And what of the other men and women whose lives intersected at American Savings?

Ed Gray is now president of Chase Federal Savings and Loan in Miami. He frequently speaks on the S&L crisis. His former chief of staff, Shannon Fairbanks, is an executive vice president with the American Real Estate Group, now a part of the Bass operation.

Roger Martin and Larry White both left the government after the Bank Board was eliminated. Larry White went back to teaching at New York University, and Roger Martin returned to Milwaukee where he became a general partner in a mutual fund investing in stocks of financial institutions, including S&Ls. Martin's former assistant, Elise Paylan, went to Wall Street, working on S&L mergers and acquisitions for Kidder Peabody.

Jim Cirona's Home Loan Bank in San Francisco lost its S&L regulatory authority along with the eleven other regional banks in the old system. Cirona, however, remained president of the regional bank, which now answers to a five-member Federal Housing Finance Board in Washington. Mike Patriacha became the district director of supervision in San Francisco, and Bill Black was named the district counsel for the Office of Thrift Supervision.

Vic Indiek became the president of Far West Savings and recruited Ron Struck to be its chief financial officer. Both men were fired in February 1989 in a dispute with management and are suing the company for wrongful termination, according to Struck. Indiek was at work on his real-estate broker's license with an eye toward starting his own company. Struck was a financial consultant on portfolio management for financial institutions.

Clark Coleman returned to Miami to work as chief financial officer at American S&L of Florida, no relation to his previous employer, and later moved to Tokyo, where he is an official with Bear Stearns & Co., Inc.

Jonathan Gray is still an analyst with Sanford Bernstein in New York. Ernie Leff relocated his law firm to downtown Los Angeles and still represents S&Ls.

Jack Pullen retired from the Federal Home Loan Bank and was in failing health. Mark Taper was still living at the house on Alpine Drive in Beverly Hills. He was 88 in December 1989.

Tony Frank is still the U.S. postmaster general. His former corporate planner, Paul Weinberg, is an executive vice president with San Francisco Federal Savings & Loan.

Art Shingler started a real-estate company in San Diego. Foster Fluetsch formed his own real-estate and mortgage-brokerage operation in Stockton.

Bill Popejoy became the chairman emeritus of New West Savings, the "bad bank" with assets that formerly belonged to American Savings. The position was not a full-time job. Popejoy decided to take some time off from running companies. He underwent extensive and painful oral surgery and also took some time to spend with his wife and family. He had not yet determined what he would do in the next phase of his career but said he was in no hurry to wear a white shirt and necktie.

Charlie Knapp once again became the center of controversy. He was the subject of long and unflattering portraits in the *Wall Street Journal* and *Los Angeles Times*. The newspapers detailed troubles with his professional and personal finances.

His Trafalgar Holdings Ltd. was portrayed as a financial house of cards. A mortgage-brokerage operation had fallen far short of its goals, and an insurance business was in disarray. At one point, Knapp was nearly $200,000 behind in support payments mandated by his 1986 divorce from Brooke, who is now a political consultant.

Separately, one of Knapp's former business partners accused him of racketeering and sued him and Trafalgar interests, claiming he was bilked out of assets worth about $133 million. The litigation charges Knapp with willful violations of the Racketeer Influence Corrupt Organization Act (RICO) for investment activities in mid to late 1988.

Knapp's former partner accused him of fraudulent misrepresentations and employing false financial statements as part of an unlawful and intentional misappropriation of property. The lawsuit named former California S&L commissioner Lawrence Taggart as Knapp's coconspirator.

Meanwhile, FCA's shareholder lawsuits were settled out of court in 1989. As part of the settlement, the litigation about Knapp's severance pay also was resolved. Charlie Knapp got to keep the $2 million. Your tax dollars at work.

Sources

The bulk of the information in this book comes from interviews with the participants in the drama at American Savings. More than sixty-five people were interviewed, nearly all on tape. I employed the standard reporting technique of using information from earlier interviews to flesh out new details and cross-check information with other sources.

The tapes were transcribed by an assistant, who also proofed the manuscript after the third draft to ensure the accuracy of the narrative. After that, some sources were phoned back once again for additional verification of the facts.

Because I chose a narrative style, the book contains little direct attribution. The reader should not assume that those quoted in reconstructed dialogue actually spoke with the author. Some words and thoughts attributed to various individuals may not have come directly from those mentioned.

Many sources agreed to talk on a not-for-attribution basis. Some key officials refused to speak at all. In most cases, the reconstructed dialogue was verified by several sources. This proved problematic with Charlie Knapp, who declined to be interviewed until several months after the book was finished. However, several of his key associates did speak with me and verified the authenticity of his remarks; either he relayed the story to them, or it was consistent with his general attitude and actions at the time.

In some cases, it was better to deviate from a narrative style and attribute information to sources. Doing so, I felt, provided an added insight into the disagreement among those involved in the story. Sometimes, the disagreements were as important in explaining what went wrong at American Savings as sorting out the conflicting accounts.

I also obtained some official chronologies from regulators and some of the negotiators. A chronology of supervisory actions at State Savings and American Savings, provided by James M. Cirona to the House Banking Committee, proved invaluable.

The Freedom of Information Act (FOIA) was not particularly helpful for this book Because of the restraints imposed to protect financial institutions from public disclosure. However, under the FOIA, I did receive copies of the operating and merger agreements between the Bank Board and the Bass Group, and a few other important documents.

Some of the information in this book also comes from the minutes of directors' meetings, internal memoranda, and some confidential documents at FCA. I also received access to FCA's business plans submitted to the Bank Board. Although FCA faced hundreds of lawsuits, little information emerged from them because of the secrecy involved in the cases.

Several hundred newspaper and magazine articles were used as background for interviews as well as research for the book in general and will be cited accordingly.

Prologue. This chapter relies largely on interviews with those involved. However, an excellent piece on Ed Gray by Jim McTague of the *American Banker* (June 25, 1987) was helpful. Additional information on the Federal Reserve is contained in *Secrets of the Temple* by William Greider (Simon & Schuster, 1987). More details on the problems that led to the run at Continental Illinois are in *Belly Up* by Phillip Zweig (Ballantine Books, 1985).

Chapters 1–2. Information about the merger between State and American comes largely from a bound history of the transaction provided by Ernie Leff. An overview of the early years at both companies is contained in *American Spirit* (American Savings publication, 1985).

Articles regarding Mark Taper and the S&L industry in California included those in the *Los Angeles Times* by Henry Sutherland, May 16, 1965; John Lawrence, June 15, 1969; Robert Wood, April 18, 1971; Doris Byron Fuller, November 7, 1982. Insights on Taper's tightfisted tendencies are in a piece by John Merwin of *Forbes* (December 6, 1982).

Besides those cited in the text, additional information on Charlie Knapp included two excellent pieces by Gary Hector, *Fortune* (July 12, 1982, and April 18, 1983) and a piece by G. Christian Hill, the *Wall Street Journal* (April 6, 1981). The first mention of Knapp's fascination with Cash McCall was contained in *Newsweek*, September 5, 1983. The book *Cash McCall*, by Cameron (1955), also was used for extra insight on Knapp's attitudes.

Chapter 3. Several books were crucial for an overview of the S&L industry and the impact of deregulation. In addition, I attended some courses at the Pacific Coast Banking School in Seattle. The lectures by Steve Happel and the writings of George Kaufman were particularly helpful.

The books include *Thrifts Under Siege* by R. Dan Brumbaugh, Jr. (Ballinger, 1988); *A Guide to the Federal Home Loan Bank System* (FHLB System Publication Corp., 1987); *Inside Job* by Steve Pizzo, Mary Fricker, and Paul Muolo (McGraw-Hill, 1989); *The Bankers* by Martin Mayer (Ballantine Books, 1984); *Handbook of Savings Institutions* (The Institute of Financial Education, 1986); *Savings Institutions Today*, Chapter 2.

For a thorough look at the industry in the 1980s, more than 200 articles in *American Banker* covering 1980 through 1986 were used. Some specific ones were those written by Nina Easton (November 10 and December 15, 1986) and Richard T. Pratt (February 25, 1983). President Reagan's comments to the U.S. League of Savings Institutions are contained in a piece by Lisa J. McCue (November 17, 1982). Other articles are those by David B. Hilder, *Wall Street Journal* (June 20, 1988), Nathaniel C. Nash, *New York Times* (June 12, 1988); Tom Furlong, *Los Angeles Times* (March 5, 1989); "Going for Broke," *Newsweek* (June 20, 1988); "Sinking in a Sea of Bad Loans," *Time* (November 8, 1986); "The S&L Mess and How to Fix It," *Business Week* (October 31, 1988); "Who's Killing the Thrifts," *Newsweek* (November 10, 1986); Seymour Freedgood, *Fortune* (May 1958).

Chapters 4–8. Most of the information about the merger comes from the history of the transaction. Direct quotations from Ed Gray's speeches were compiled by the former regulator. Additional information about Gray came from the following articles: McTague, *American Banker* (June 25, 1987); Monica Langley, the *Wall Street Journal* (March 22, 1985); John Liscio, *Barron's* (February 27, 1989); Michael Binstein, *Regardie's* (October 1988); *Business Week* (May 27, 1987).

Information on American's problem loans and other troubles was contained in a proxy statement May 16, 1983, in Jonathan Gray's lengthy research report, and in the chronology by the San Francisco Federal Home Loan Bank.

Some articles also used to document American's demise include *Business Week* (February 13, 1984); Gregory Miller, *Institutional Investor* (April 1984); *Forbes* (July 30, 1984). Reports on Knapp's ouster and the run at American Savings include those by Katherine Macdonald, *Washington Post* (August 28, 1984); Robert Luke, *American Banker* (August 28, 1984). Several pieces in the *Wall Street Journal*, particularly the stories by Frederick Muir, were essential for reporting this section of the book.

The rise of the secondary market and its importance in the financial services industry is traced from a variety of sources. Particularly helpful was a publication by Freddie Mac, *A Citizen's Guide to the Secondary Mortgage Market.*

Chapters 9–13. These chapters rely mostly on interviews. Some stories were needed for additional information. Details of Knapp's return to business and his offer to buy some of American's bad loans are contained in articles by Stephen J. Sansweet, *Wall Street Journal* (May 30, 1989), which document that Knapp began dating his third wife before his divorce from Brooke, and two more from 1985. Other articles that were helpful include *Business Week* (November 11, 1985); Tom Furlong, *Los Angeles Times* (February 22, 1987); and several pieces in the *Los Angeles Times* for 1986.

Tom Furlong of the *Los Angeles Times* documents the increase in loan losses at American Savings. Other stories include *Business Week* (March 25, 1985); Jennifer Bingham Hull, *Wall Street Journal* (April 2, 1985); Kathleen A. Hughes, *Wall Street Journal* (June 24, 1985 and December 17, 1985).

Information about Popejoy's early career and the obstacles he faced at FCA are detailed by Teresa Carson, *Business Week*

(December 24, 1984). Details of the "Peat Marwick" board meeting in Chapter 15 come from minutes to the meeting and supporting documents, besides conversations with the directors. The same is true for the meeting at which the directors decided to sue Knapp.

Ed Gray's frequent absences from the Bank Board and his need for security is documented by Monica Langley, the *Wall Street Journal* (March 22, 1985). Other important stories include John Liscio, *Barron's* (February 27, 1989); Michael Binstein, *Regardie's* (October 1988); *Business Week* (May 27, 1987).

The Ohio run received extensive coverage by the *Wall Street Journal*, including a chronology of the disaster that ran March 18, 1985, and a piece about the spillover effects by G. Christian Hill on April 8, 1985. *Business Week* also examined the ensuing run in Maryland as part of the worsening thrift crisis in this country in a piece that ran on May 27, 1985.

Chapters 14–17. These chapters on the Popejoy years also rely heavily on taped interviews. Stories covering Popejoy and his strategy for FCA and American Savings include David B. Hilder, *Wall Street Journal* (March 30, 1987); Howard Rudnitsky and Allan Sloan, *Forbes* (December 29, 1986); *Business Week* (October 5, 1987); Mark Basch, *American Banker* (September 22, 1986); *Savings Institutions* (June 1987); Pamela Levin, *American Banker* (May 25, 1988); Nina Easton, *American Banker* (December 1987). Popejoy's comments about his tenure and his frustration with the regulators are detailed by Michael A. Robinson and Robert Luke, *American Banker* (August 1988) and Tom Furlong, *Los Angeles Times* (February 22, 1987).

Information about Mike Milken, the early years of his career, and early involvement in FCA are detailed in *The Predators' Ball* by Connie Bruck (Penguin Books, 1988, 1989). Milken's views about the financial-services industry and his attempt to put together a financing package come from other sources, including those close to Drexel Burnham Lambert.

The documentation of Knapp's questionable business practices relies largely on the Proof of Loss that FCA filed with its insurance companies. Supporting interviews were also conducted with a number of executives who formerly worked at

American Savings and FCA. One story that was particularly helpful was written by Jaye Scholl, *Barron's* (September 26, 1988).

The information concerning the congressional report on fraud in the industry and the criticism of the Justice Department for failure to act in the case of American Savings was obtained from a piece by Tom Furlong and Bill Sing, *Los Angeles Times* (October 20, 1988).

The increasingly important role of mortgage-backed securities is highlighted in several articles and academic studies. They include a piece tracing a home loan's movement through the national market written by George Anders, *Wall Street Journal* (August 17, 1988); a look at hard times in the market by Evelyn Wall, which ran in *American Banker* (February 9, 1988); and a piece that assesses the impact of the Tax Reform Act on the MBS market that appeared in the *ABA Banking Journal* (February 1989).

Chapters 18–23. Details of the negotiations to sell American Savings are contained in two excellent pieces by David B. Hilder, *Wall Street Journal* (September 7 and December 30, 1988). Specifics of the first Bass agreement and the group's strategy in running an S&L are in an article by Nathaniel C. Nash, *New York Times* (September 8, 1988). Additional information on Pennzoil suit can be found in *Oil & Honor—The Texaco-Pennzoil Wars* by Thomas Petzinger, Jr. (Berkley Books, 1987).

Stories about Bob Bass, his early years, and business strategy include those by Peter Applebome, *New York Times* (June 5, 1988); "The Bashful Billionaire," *Business Week* (October 3, 1988); William Meyers, *Institutional Investor* (August 1988); William P. Barrett, *Forbes* (February 22, 1988).

Dozens of articles in *American Banker* from 1987 through mid-1989 document problems at the Bank Board, controversy over the agency's "Southwest Plan," and the negotiations with Bass. Jim McTague's profiles of Danny Wall and Roger Martin were especially good. Another piece on Roger Martin was in *Business Week* (January 18, 1988).

Details on Larry White's nomination to the Bank Board were contained in an article by Nina Easton, *American Banker* (October 21, 1986). Information about Ed Gray's career and his last months at the Bank Board come from the McTague piece in *American Banker* as well as *Inside Job,* which also documents the time Wall was surreptitiously recorded by the FBI.

Two articles by Jonathan Lansner of the *Orange County Register* provided excellent background on the impact of the Bank Board's decision to have American liquidate part of its MBS portfolio. The mood of Stockton during the summer of 1988 before the Bass deal was completed comes from a piece by Michael A. Robinson in *American Banker.*

Observations about Tony Frank and First Nationwide come from the author's writings about the company and its chief executive for *American Banker.* Tony Frank was profiled by Tom Furlong, *Los Angeles Times* (August 2, 1985) and Jonathan B. Levine, *Business Week* (October 26, 1987). A story detailing Ford's cash cushion was written by Amal Kumar Naj, *Wall Street Journal* (June 6, 1983).

Bill Crawford's early career and some criticism of the S&L commissioner is recounted by Nina Easton, *American Banker* (July 21, 1987). His views on the influx of new thrifts in California appeared in a piece by Tom Furlong, *Los Angeles Times* (February 5, 1985). Criticism of Crawford also appeared in a piece by John O'Dell, *Los Angeles Times* (June 19, 1985).

Lincoln Savings became big news in 1989. The transcript of the "Five Senators' Meeting" is contained in *Inside Job.* Dozens of stories about Lincoln, Danny Wall, and the San Francisco Federal Home Loan Bank ran in *American Banker* in 1988 and 1989.

American Banker's reporting on the Bush bill was invaluable for the Epilogue of this book. *American Banker* published a special section on August 10, the day after the president signed the law, and followed the changes in the industry with countless other stories.

Author's Note

In late May, this author wrote Charlie Knapp a letter advising him that I would come to Los Angeles for an interview to get more of his side of the story. The letter, transmitted by fax machine, was a follow-up to two telephone conversations a few days earlier in which Knapp had first claimed that I had made no attempt to contact him while researching the material for *Overdrawn*, but then acknowledged that he had not been available for interviews. Knapp went on to discuss with me some of the matters in this book.

One of Knapp's assistants confirmed receiving the fax transmittal, but Knapp did not respond to the request. However, some of the information from the two telephone interviews was incorporated into the book and Knapp was advised in writing.

On October 10, 1990, just days before the printed book was to be bound into hard cover, Knapp's attorney wrote to this author's attorneys. The five-page letter followed a front-page article in the *Stockton Record* about the contents of this book.

Among other things, Knapp's attorney, Arthur N. Greenberg of Los Angeles, disputed the conclusions in the proof of loss discussed in Chapter 14 of this book. He said FCA had not provided any evidence to support the claims of wrongdoing or misconduct made in the proof of loss, a document which was filed in a lawsuit brought by FCA against its insurance company on a fidelity bond. Greenberg said FCA was sanctioned $30,000 the previous January for failing to produce information in that lawsuit to support its allegations in the proof of loss.

In addition, Greenberg pointed out that on February 6, 1990, FCA filed an amended complaint in the fidelity-bond case that eliminated any reference to Knapp. Further, Greenberg noted that Knapp has consistently said that the dealings referred to in the original proof of loss, as well as those forming the basis for allegations of misconduct printed in the media, were disclosed to a wide variety of key officials before the transactions occurred. These officials include FCA's auditors at the time, Arthur Andersen & Co., the SEC, the Federal Home Bank Board, and the company's attorneys.

As early as 1982, Greenberg said, Knapp advised the Federal Home Bank, in writing, of FCA's corporate plan including the fact that 5 percent of all loans might end in foreclosure and made specific proposals to deal with anticipated loan problems.

Finally, Greenberg said, unlike situations widely reported at other savings and loan institutions, there has never been any suggestion that Knapp engaged in self-dealing of any type or that he misappropriated any money or assets.